God is the Umbrella of Women in the Bible

Florence Mutambanengwe
MAY 2009

authorHOUSE®

AuthorHouse™ UK Ltd.
500 Avebury Boulevard
Central Milton Keynes, MK9 2BE
www.authorhouse.co.uk
Phone: 08001974150

© 2012 Florence Mutambanengwe. All rights reserved.

No part of this book may be reproduced, stored in
a retrieval system, or transmitted by any means
without the written permission of the author.

Published by AuthorHouse 08/13/2012

ISBN: 978-1-4772-2185-3 (sc)
ISBN: 978-1-4772-2186-0 (e)

This book is printed on acid-free paper.

Because of the dynamic nature of the Internet, any web addresses or
links contained in this book may have changed since publication and
may no longer be valid. The views expressed in this work are solely those
of the author and do not necessarily reflect the views of the publisher,
and the publisher hereby disclaims any responsibility for them.

Contents

1.	A Crippled Woman Healed on the Sabbath:	1
2.	A Levite Concubine:	4
3.	A Wise Woman – In Abel Beth Maacah:	7
4.	Abigail – (1 Samuel 25:1 – 42)	9
5.	Abihail the Wife of Abishur the son of Shammai:	18
6.	Abijah the Wife of Hezron.	19
7.	Abishag – Warmth for King David	20
8.	Adah – Lamech's wife	23
9.	Adah/Judith – the Wife of Esau:	26
10.	Aiah – Who bore Rizpah – Saul's Daughter:	29
11.	Anna – the Prophetess:	31
12.	Asenath – Joseph's Wife	34
13.	Atarah - the Wife of Jerahmeel the son of Hezron:	38
14.	Athaliah – the Mother of Ahaziah:	39
15.	Basemath – the Wife of Esau	45
16.	Bathsheba – the Mother of King Solomon:	48
17.	Bilhah – the Mother of Dan and Naphtali:	56
18.	Candace, queen of the Ethiopians: (Acts 8:26 – 32	59
19.	Deborah – the Prophetess:	60
20.	Dinah – the Daughter of Leah:	65
21.	Elizabeth – the Mother of John the Baptist:	71
22.	Eve –the Mother of Cain and Abel:	78
23.	Hagar – the Mother of Ishmael:	84
24.	Hamutal the Daughter of Jeremiah:	88
25.	Hannah – the Mother of Samuel:	89
26.	Hazzelelponi – The daughter of Etam:	98

27.	Herodias – the wife of Philip:	99
28.	Huldah – the Prophetess:	102
29.	Jael - the Killer of Sisera	107
30.	Jochebed – The Mother of Moses	110
31.	Jehosheba – the Wife of Jehoiada the Priest:	114
32.	Jezebel –the Wife of Ahab:	116
33.	Ketura – The Wife Abraham Married after Sarah Died:	121
34.	Leah – the First Wife of Jacob:	124
35.	Loice and Eunice – the Grandmother and Mother of Timothy:	131
36.	Lot's Wife:	134
37.	Lydia – the First Convert of the Apostle Paul:	139
38.	Mahalath: the Daughter of Ishmael:	143
39.	Martha the Sister of Lazarus:	146
40.	Mary the Sister of Lazarus:	154
41.	Mary Mother of Jesus	162
42.	Mary Magdalene	173
43.	Matred – The Mother of Mehetabel, The Wife of Hadad:	178
44.	Mehetabel – The Wife of Hadad:	179
45.	Merab – Saul's Daughter: (See Aiah)	180
46.	Michal – the Wife of David:	181
47.	Milcah – the Wife of Nahor:	185
48.	Miriam – The Older Sister of Aaron and Moses	188
49.	Naomi –Elimelech's Wife	193
50.	Noah's Wife:	208
51.	Orpah – the Wife of Mahlon:	211
52.	Peninnah – The Second Wife of Elkanah	215

53.	Peter's Mother-in-Law	220
54.	Phoebe and the Other Women:	222
55.	Priscilla – the Wife of Aquila:	225
56.	Puah – the Hebrew Midwife:	228
57.	Queen Esther	231
58.	Queen Maacah	239
59.	Queen of Sheba	243
60.	Queen Vashti	247
61.	Rachel – the Wife of Jacob:	254
62.	Rahab – the Prostitute:	264
63.	Rebekah – the Wife of Isaac	272
64.	Reumah – Nahor's Concubine:	284
65.	Rizpah – the Daughter of Aiah: (See Aiah)	285
66.	Ruth – the Wife of Boaz:	286
67.	Saffira – The Wife of Ananias	301
68.	Samson's Wife –	303
69.	Samson's Mother:	309
70.	Sarai – Sarah – Mother of all Nations	314
71.	Serah – The daughter of Asher the son of Zilpah:	320
72.	Shelomith – the Daughter of Zerubbabel:	322
73.	Shiprah – The Hebrew Midwife	323
74.	Shua's Daughter – the Wife of Judah:	326
75.	Sisera's Mother:	329
76.	Solomon's wives – Pharaoh's Daughter, Moabites, Ammonites, Edomites, Sodomans and Hittites	331
77.	Susanna and Other Women:	332
78.	Tabitha or Dorcas:	334
79.	Tamar – The Sister of Absalom:	337
80.	Tamar – the Wife of Er:	342

81.	The Canaanite Woman and her Daughter:	349
82.	The Daughter of Jesse - Abigail:	353
83.	The Daughter of Jesse - Zeruiah:	354
84.	The Elect Lady:	355
85.	The Ruler's Daughter	358
86.	The Daughters of Zelophehad: Mahlah, Noah, Hoglah, Milcah and Tirzah:	362
87.	The Widow of Zarephath:	366
88.	The Widow and Oil:	371
89.	The Wives of Ashur the father of Tekoa:	375
90.	The Wife of Haman – Zeresh:	376
91.	The Witch of Endor:	378
92.	The Wives for the Benjaminites (Judges 21:1 - 25)	381
93.	The Concubine of Caleb –Ephah:	382
94.	The Daughter of Caleb – Acsah:	383
95.	The Woman from Tekoa:	384
96.	The Woman With The Issue of Bleeding:	387
97.	Zebidah – The Mother of Jehoiakim:	393
98.	Zeruah – Jeroboam's Mother:	394
99.	Zillah – Lamech's wife	395
100.	Zilpah – Leah's Maid	397
101.	Zipporah – Moses wife	400

God is the Umbrella of Women in the Bible and the World
A Protection against the Rain and the Sun

1. A Crippled Woman Healed on the Sabbath:

Who Was This Woman?

- She was in the synagogue where Jesus was teaching
- She had been crippled for eighteen years
- She was bent over
- She could not straighten up
- Jesus saw her and called her
- She was healed on the Sabbath
- The Ruler of the synagogue was not pleased

The Story:

She was a crippled woman who lived in this area for eighteen years. She was bent over so many people knew her as it was so visible to anyone that she was crippled.

She was in the synagogue where Jesus was teaching, maybe because she had heard that he was healing various people. You would think that people would have rejoiced to see her healed. Not so especially for the Ruler of the synagogue. He told her off. There are six days for you to come and be healed instead of coming to be healed on the Sabbath, he said.

Jesus just said, "Woman, you are set free from your infirmity." There and then she was healed.

He then told the people that if they saw their ox or donkey thirsty on a Sabbath would they not give it water to drink. You would think that people would have been pleased but they were not.

She was freed and praised God.

The Bible and the Crippled Woman Healed on the Sabbath:

On a Sabbath Jesus was teaching in one of the synagogues, and a woman was there who had been crippled by a spirit for eighteen years. She was bent over and could not straighten up at all. When Jesus saw her, he called her forward and said to her, "Woman, you are set free from your infirmity." Then he put his hands on her, and immediately she straightened up and praised God.

Indignant because Jesus had healed on the Sabbath, the synagogue ruler said to the people, "There are six days for work. So come and be healed on those days, not on the Sabbath."

The Lord answered him; "You hypocrites" Doesn't each of you on the Sabbath untie his ox or donkey from the stall and lead it out to give it water? Then should not this woman, a daughter of Abraham, whom Satan has kept bound for eighteen long years, be set free on the Sabbath day from what bound her?"

When he said this, all his opponents were humiliated, but the people were delighted with all the wonderful things he was doing. (Luke 13:10 – 17)

Lessons to Learn:

- Why is it that people rejoice at the misfortunes of others?
- Would it have crossed your mind that someone was being healed on the Sabbath?
- Are people happy to see the Blind see?
- Are people happy to see the Lame walk?
- Are people happy to see the sick Healed?
- Are people happy to see the Deaf hear?
- Why is it people want to discourage believers from believing that they can be healed?
- Do you think if the synagogue Ruler was the one healed he would have worried about the Sabbath?
- Was Jesus right to call these people Hypocrites?
- Have you ever commented on someone's healing?
- Have you ever discouraged someone who believed that he was healed?

The Bible has powerful teaching on how we can all believe in what Jesus was doing!

God is the Umbrella of Women in the Bible!

2. A Levite Concubine:

In those days Israel had no king, now a Levite who lived in a remote area in the hill country of Ephraim took a concubine from Bethlehem in Judah. But she was unfaithful to him. She left him and went back to her father's house, in Bethlehem Judah. After she had been there four months, her husband went to her to persuade her to return; He had with him his servant and two donkeys. She took him into her father's house, and when her father saw him, he gladly welcomed him. His father-in-law, the girl's father, prevailed upon him to stay; so he remained with him three days, eating and drinking and sleeping there.

On the fourth day they got up early and he prepared to leave, but the girl's father said to his son-in-law: "Refresh yourself with something to eat; then you can go." So the two of them sat down to eat and drink together. Afterward the girl's father said, "Please stay tonight and enjoy yourself." And when the man got up to go his father-in-law persuaded him, so he stayed there that night. On the morning of the fifth day when he rose to go, the girl's father said, "Refresh yourself, so the two of them ate together.

Then when the man, with his concubine and his servant, got up to leave, his father-in-law, the girl's father said, "Now look its almost evening, Spend the night here; the day is nearly over. Stay and enjoy yourself. Early tomorrow morning you can get up and be on your way," But unwilling

God is the Umbrella of Women in the Bible

to stay another night, the man left and went towards Jebus. (that is Jerusalem, with his two saddled donkeys and his concubine.

When they were near Jebus and the day was almost gone, the servant said to his master, "Come let's stop at this city of the Jebusites and spend the night."

His Master replied, "No, we won't go into an alien city, whose people are not Israelites. We will go on to Gibeah." He added, let's try to reach Gibeah or Ramah and spend the night in one of those places." So they went on and the sun set as they neared Gibeah in Benjamin. There they stopped to spend the night. They went and sat in the city square, but no one took them into his home for the night.

That evening an old man from the hill country of Ephraim, who was also living in Gibeah (the men of the place were Benjaminites), came in from his work in the fields; When he looked and saw the traveler in the city square, the old man asked, "Where are you going? Where did you come from?

He answered, "We are on our way from Bethlehem in Judah to a remote area in the hill country of Ephraim where I live. I have been to Bethlehem in Judah and now I am going to the house of the LORD. No one has taken me into his house. We have both straw and fodder for our donkeys and bread and wine for ourselves your servants – me, your maidservant and the young man with us. We don't need anything."

You are welcome at my house, the old man said, and 'Let me supply whatever you need. Only don't spend the night in the square." So he took him into his house and fed his donkeys. After they had washed their feet they had something to eat and drink.

While they were enjoying themselves, some of the wicked men of the city surrounded the house. Pounding on the door; they shouted to the old man who owned the house, "Bring out the man who came to your house so we can have sex with him.

The owner of the house went outside and said to them, "No, my friends don't be so vile. Since this man is my guest, don't do this disgraceful thing. Look, here is my virgin daughter, and his concubine. I will bring them out to you now, and you can use them and do to them whatever you wish. But to this man, don't do such a disgraceful thing

But the men would not listen to him. So the man took his concubine and sent her outside to them, and they raped her and abused her. Throughout the night and at dawn they let her go. At day break the woman went back to the house where her master was staying, fell down at the door and lay there until daylight.

When her master go up in the morning and opened the door of the house and stepped out to continue on his way, there lay his concubine, fallen in the doorway of the house, with her hands on the threshold. He said to her, "Get up; let's go." But there was no answer. Then the man put her on his donkey and set out for home.

When they reached home, he took a knife and cut up his concubine, limb by limb, into twelve parts and sent them into all the areas of Israel. Everyone who saw it said, "Such a thing has never been seen or done, not since the day the Israelites came up out of Egypt. Think about it! Consider it! Tell us what to do!"

(Judges 19) also Read (Judges 20 and 21)

God is the Umbrella of Women in the Bible!

3. A Wise Woman – In Abel Beth Maacah:

All the troops with Joab came and besieged Sheba in Abel Beth Maacah. They built a siege ramp up to the city, and it stood against the outer fortifications. While they were battering the wall to bring it down, a wise woman called from the city, "Listen! Listen! Tell Joab to come here so I can speak to him." He went toward her, and she asked, "Are you Joab?" She said, "Listen to what your servant has to say." "I am," he answered. She continued, "Long ago they used to say, 'Get your answer at Abel,' and that settled it. We are the peaceful and faithful in Israel. You are trying to destroy a city that is a mother in Israel. Why do you want to swallow up the LORD's inheritance?

"Far be it from me!" Joab replied, "Far be it from me to swallow up or destroy! That is not the case. A man named Sheba son of Bicri, from the hill country of Ephraim, has lifted up his hand against the king, against David. Hand over this one man, and I'll withdraw from the city." The woman said to Joab, "His head will be thrown to you from the wall."

Then the woman went to all the people with her wise advice, and they cut off the head of Sheba son of Bicri and threw it to Joab. So he sounded the trumpet, and his men dispersed from the city, each returning to his home. And Joab went back to the king in Jerusalem.

Joab was over Israel's entire army; Benaiah son of Jehoiada was over the Kerethites and Pelethites; Adoniram was in charge of forced labour; Jehoshaphat son of Ahilud was recorder; Sheva was secretary; Zadok and Abiathar were priests; and Ira the Jairite was David's priest. (2 Samuel 20:15 – 26)

Lessons to Learn:

- Is there a situation that has or is developing around you?
- What action do you think you can take?
- This woman approached Joab, talked to him!
- She went back to all her people with some wise advice.
- They accepted her advice and took action.
- The problem was solved.
- Can we get back what we have lost over the years?
- The wise woman did!
- In the bible most wise women spoke to God first.
- Speak to God before attempting some of these situations for guidance.

God is the Umbrella of Women in the Bible!

4. Abigail – (1 Samuel 25:1 – 42)

Who Was This Woman?

- She was Nabal's wife and later became David's wife
- She was intelligent and beautiful but her husband, a Calebite, was surly and mean in his dealings.
- She had foresight. We have a saying in Shona that says "Kandiro kanoenda kunobva kamwe" which means "A small plate is sent to where another small plate came from" or "A good deed deserves another"
- She was an organized woman as she quickly took two hundred loaves of bread, two skins of wine, five dressed sheep, five seahs of roasted grain, a hundred cakes of raisins and two hundred cakes of pressed figs, and loaded them on donkeys.
- She told her servants, to go ahead and that she would follow.

- She humbled herself for when she saw David she quickly got off the donkey and bowed down before David with her face to the ground.
- She fell at his feet and said: "My lord, let the blame be on me alone. Please let your servant speak to you; hear what your servant has to say. May my lord pay no attention to that wicked man Nabal? He is just like his name – his name is Fool, and folly goes with him.
- She exonerated herself and said: "As for me your servant, I did not see the men my master sent."

The Story:

Abigail was an intelligent and beautiful woman who was married to a surly and mean man whose name was Nabal. Nabal was wealthy he owned one thousand goats and three thousand sheep.

At one time David was in the desert, he heard that Nabal was shearing sheep. So he sent ten young men to Nabal. David must have thought that since he had done well to Nabal's men when they came to Carmel; Nabal would do the same for him and his men. Therefore he sent his men to him asking for a return favour.

He told his men to go and say: "Now I hear that it is sheep shearing time. When your shepherds were with us, we did not mistreat them, and the whole time they were at Carmel nothing of theirs was missing. Ask your own servants and they will tell you. Therefore be favorable toward my young men, since we come at a festive time. Please give your servants and your son David whatever you can find for

God is the Umbrella of Women in the Bible

them." So the men went to Nabal and gave him the message that David had told them to deliver.

Nabal then refused to give any type of assistance to David and his men. He was sarcastic and he said: "Who is this David? Who is this son of Jesse? Many servants are breaking away from their masters these days. Why should I take my bread and water, and the meat I have slaughtered for my shearers, and give it to men coming from who knows where?"

David's men turned around and went back. When they arrived, they reported every word. David said to his men, "Put on your swords!" So they put on their swords, and David put on his. About four hundred men went up with David, while two hundred stayed with the supplies.

However, Abigail was told by one of her servants what her husband had done. He said, "David sent messengers from the desert to give our master his greetings, but he hurled insults at them. Yet these men were very good to us. They did not mistreat us, and the whole time we were out in the fields near them nothing was missing. Night and day they were a wall around us all the time we were herding our sheep near them. Now think it over and see what you can do, because disaster is hanging over our master and his whole household. He is such a wicked man that no one can talk to him."

Abigail lost no time. She took two hundred loaves of bread, two skins of wine, five dressed sheep, five seahs of roasted grain, a hundred cakes of raisins and two hundred cakes of pressed figs, and loaded them on donkeys. Then she told her servants, "Go on ahead I'll follow you." But she did not tell her husband Nabal.

As she came riding her donkey into a mountain ravine, there was David and his men descending toward her, and she met them. David had just said, "It's been useless- all my watching over this fellow's property in the desert so that nothing of his was missing. He has paid me back evil for good. May God deal with David, be it ever so severely, if by morning I leave alive one male of all who belong to him.

When Abigail saw David, she quickly got off the donkey and bowed down before David with her face to the ground. She fell at his feet and said: "My lord, let the blame be on me alone. Please let your servant speak to you; hear what your servant has to say. May my lord pay no attention to that wicked man Nabal. He is just like his name – his name is Fool, and folly goes with him. But as for me your servant, I did not see the men my master sent.

"Now since the Lord had kept you, my master, from bloodshed and from avenging yourself with your own hands, as surely as the Lord lives and as you live, may your enemies and all who intend to harm my master be like Nabal. And let this gift, which your servant has brought to my master, be given to the men who follow you.

Please forgive your servant's offense, for the Lord will certainly make a lasting dynasty for my master, because he fights the Lord's battles. Let no wrong doing be found in you as long as you live. Even though someone is pursuing you to take your life, the life of my master will be bound securely in the bundle of the living by the Lord your God. But the lives of your enemies he will hurl away as from the pocket of a sling. When the Lord has done for my master every good thing he promised concerning him and has appointed him leader over Israel, my master will not have on his conscience the staggering burden of needless bloodshed or of having avenged himself. And when the Lord has brought my master success, remember your servant.

David changed his mind and went back. After the death of Nabal, David sent for her and she became his wife.

The Bible and Abigail

Now Samuel died, and all Israel assembled and mourned for him; and they buried him at his home in Ramah.

Then David moved down into the Desert of Maon. A certain man in Maon, who had property there at Carmel, was very wealthy. He had a thousand goats and three thousand sheep, which he was shearing in Carmel. His name was Nabal and his wife's name was Abigail. She was an intelligent and beautiful woman, but her husband, a Calebite, was surly and mean in his dealings.

While David was in the desert, he heard that Nabal was shearing sheep, So he sent ten young men and said to them, "Go up to Nabal at Carmel and greet him in my name. Say to him, "Long life to you! Good health to you and your household! And good health to all that is yours.

"'Now I hear that it is sheep shearing time. When your shepherds were with us, we did not mistreat them, and the whole time they were at Carmel nothing of theirs was missing. Ask your own servants and they will tell you. Therefore be favorable toward my young men, since we come at a festive time. Please give your servants and your son David whatever you can find for them.'"

When David's men arrived, they gave Nabal this message in David's name. Then they waited.

Nabal answered David's servants, "Who is this David? Who is this son of Jesse? Many servants are breaking away from their masters these days. Why should I take my bread and water, and the meat I have slaughtered for my shearers, and give it to men coming from who knows where?"

David's men turned around and went back. When they arrived, they reported every word. David said to his men, "Put on your swords!" So they put on their swords, and

David put on his. About four hundred men went up with David, while two hundred stayed with the supplies.

One of the servants told Nabal's wife Abigail: "David sent messengers from the desert to give our master his greetings, but he hurled insults at them. Yet these men were very good to us. They did not mistreat us, and the whole time we were out in the fields near them nothing was missing. Night and day they were a wall around us all the time we were herding our sheep near them. Now think it over and see what you can do, because disaster is hanging over our master and his whole household. He is such a wicked man that no one can talk to him.

Abigail lost no time. She took two hundred loaves of bread, two skins of wine, five dressed sheep, five seahs of roasted grain, a hundred cakes of raisins and two hundred cakes of pressed figs, and loaded them on donkeys. Then she told her servants, "Go on ahead I'll follow you." But she did not tell her husband Nabal.

As she came riding her donkey into a mountain ravine, there were David and his men descending toward her, and she met them. David had just said, "It's been useless- all my watching over this fellow's property in the desert so that nothing of his was missing. He has paid me back evil for good. May God deal with David, be it ever so severely, if by morning I leave alive one male of all who belong to him.

When Abigail saw David, she quickly got off the donkey and bowed down before David with her face to the ground. She fell at his feet and said: "My lord, let the blame be on me alone. Please let your servant speak to you, hear what your servant has to say. May my lord pay no attention to that wicked man Nabal. He is just like his name – his name is Fool, and folly goes with him. But as for me your servant, I did not see the men my master sent.

"Now since the Lord had kept you, my master, from bloodshed and from avenging yourself with your own hands, as surely as the Lord lives and as you live, may your enemies and all who intend to harm my master be like Nabal. And let this gift, which your servant has brought to my master, be given to the men who follow you.

Please forgive your servant's offense, for the Lord will certainly make a lasting dynasty for my master, because he fights the Lord's battles. Let no wrong doing be found in you as long as you live. Even though someone is pursuing you to take your life, the life of my master will be bound securely in the bundle of the living by the Lord your God. But the lives of your enemies he will hurl away as from the pocket of a sling. When the Lord has done for my master every good thing he promised concerning him and has appointed him leader over Israel, my master will not have on his conscience the staggering burden of needless bloodshed or of having avenged himself. And when the Lord has brought my master success, remember your servant.

David said to Abigail, "Praise be to the Lord, the God of Israel, who has sent you today to meet me. May you be blessed for your good judgment and for keeping me from bloodshed this day and from avenging myself with my own hands. Otherwise, as surely as the Lord, the God of Israel lives, who has kept me from harming you, if you had not come quickly to meet me, not one male belonging to Nabal would have been left alive by daybreak.

Then David accepted from her hand what she had brought him and said, "Go home in peace, I have heard your words and granted you request."

When Abigail went to Nabal, he was in the house holding a banquet, like that of a king. He was in high spirits and very drunk. So she told him nothing, until daybreak. Then in the morning, when Nabal was sober, his wife told him all these things, and his heart failed him and he became like a stone. About ten days later the Lord struck Nabal and he died.

When David heard that Nabal was dead, he said, "Praise be to the Lord, who has upheld my cause against Nabal for treating me with contempt. He has kept his servant from doing wrong and has brought Nabal's wrong doing down on his own head."

Then David sent word to Abigail, asking her to become his wife. His servants went to Carmel and said to Abigail, "David has sent us to you to take you to become his wife."

She bowed down with her face to the ground and said, "Here is your maidservant, ready to serve you and wash the feet of my master's servants." Abigail quickly got on a donkey and, attended by her five maids, went with David's messengers and became his wife. David had also married Ahinoam of Jezreel, and they both were his wives. But Saul had given his daughter Michal, David's wife to Paltiel, son of Laish, who was from Gallim. (1 Samuel 25:1 – 42)

David and his men settled in Gath with Achish. Each man had his family with him, and David had his two wives: Ahinoam of Jezreel and Abigail of Carmel the widow of Nabal. (1 Samuel 27:3)

Lessons to Learn:

- Have you ever done something that averted some sort of disaster either in your family, among friends, or in your church?
- What do you think of bowing down your face to the ground?
- What do you see in your life and in other people's life?

- Abigail actually saw David as King of Israel and wanted him to remember her!
- How did you meet your spouse?
- David was already married to Ahinoam of Jezreel and to Michal, Saul's daughter so she was the third wife.

God is the Umbrella of Women in the Bible!

5. Abihail the Wife of Abishur the son of Shammai:

The sons of Onam: Shammai and Jada; the sons of Shammai: Nadab and Abishur; Abishur's wife was named Abihail, who bore him Ahban and Molid.
(1 Chronicles 2:29)

God is the Umbrella of Women in the Bible!

6. Abijah the Wife of Hezron.

Later, Hezron lay with the daughter of Makir the father of Gilead (he had married her when he was sixty years old), and she bore him Segub. Segub was the father of Jair, who controlled twenty-three towns in Gilead. (But Geshur and Aram captured Havvoth Jair, as well as Kenath with its surrounding settlements – sixty towns.) All these were descendants of Makir the father of Gilead.

After Hezron died in Caleb Ephrathah, Abijah the wife of Hezron bore him Ashur the father of Tekoa. (1 Chronicles 2:21 – 24)

God is the Umbrella of Women in the Bible!

7. Abishag – Warmth for King David

Who Was This Woman?

- She was a young virgin girl
- She was beautiful throughout Israel
- She was a Shunammite
- She was obedient
- She provided warmth for the King David

The Story:

Abishag's story begins with the desire of David's servants to please their master. They were working for David and they knew and saw what was going on in his household. David's wives included: Ahinoam of Jezreel, Abigail of Carmel, Maacah daughter of Talmai king of Geshur, Haggith, Abital, Eglah, and Bathsheba daughter of Ammiel.

All these women were not providing the warmth that the servants of David thought was sufficient for their king. So they decided to look for a young virgin girl who would take that place. This is where Abishag comes in to fulfill the servants' to see their king well and warm.

The servants of King David made a plan to look for a young virgin, who could attend the king and take care of him. She was to act like a hot water bottle to the king. The girl had to be a virgin and be beautiful. So they went throughout Israel in search of this beautiful girl and guess what, they found Abishag, a Shunammite virgin and brought her to the king. She did what she was told warm King David despite that he had his own wives. The king was kind to her and was not intimate with her.

There are a lot of services that Abishag provided for King David. She was there the whole day with him taking care of him. Seeing that he woke up well, in the morning, since she was in bed with him. If anything happened to him at night she would be the one to report it to others. Probably, making sure that he had breakfast, lunch and supper everyday. That he was dressed well as he was quite old at that time.

The Bible and Abishag:

When King David was old and well advanced in years, he could not keep warm even when they put covers over him. So his servants said to him, "Let us look for a young virgin to attend the king and take care of him. She can lie beside him so that our lord the king may keep warm."

Then they searched throughout Israel for a beautiful girl and found Abishag, A Shunammite, and brought her to the king. The girl was very beautiful; she took care of the king and waited on him, but the king had no intimate relations with her. (1 Kings 1:1 – 4)

So Bathsheba went to see the aged king in his room, where Abishag the Shunammite was attending him. Bathsheba bowed low and knelt before the king; "What is it you want?" the king asked. (1 Kings 1:15 – 16)

Lessons to Learn:

- Have you ever been placed into a situation where you were unable to make your own decisions?
- Would you provide warmth to anyone without being asked to?
- Abishag did her Job and King David was pleased
- He said "I thank God who has made me see my successor seating on my throne."
- How do you treat your spouse when he is old?
- Would you allow anyone to come and sleep with him/her like Abishag did?
- Where were all the wives of King David?
- What do you think of the action taken by the Servants of David?

God is the Umbrella of Women in the Bible!

8. Adah – Lamech's wife

Who Was This Woman?

- She was Lamech's wife
- Adah was a great and blessed woman.
- She was one of the two wives of Lamech
- She was the mother of Jabal the father of those who live in the tents and raise livestock
- She was also the mother of Jubal the father of all who play the harp and flute
- Her husband told her that he had killed a man for wounding him, a young man for injuring him and if Cain is avenged seven times, then Lamech seventy-seven times."

The Story

Cain lay with his wife, and she gave birth to Enoch. Cain was building a city, and he named it Enoch. To Enoch was born Irad and Irad was the father of Mehujael, and Mehujael was the father of Methushael, and Methushael was the father of Lamech. Lamech married Adah and Zillah. At 182 years he had a son. He named him Noah saying,

"He will comfort us in the labour and painful toil of our hands caused by the ground the LORD has cursed." After Noah, Lamech lived 595 years, and had sons and daughters. Lamech lived 777 years.

Lamech married two women, one named Adah and the other Zillah. Adah gave birth to Jabal; he was the father of those who live in the tents and raise livestock. His brother's name was Jubal; he was the father of all who play the harp and flute. Zillah also had a son, Tubal-Cain, who forged all kinds of tools out of bronze and iron. Tubal-Cain's sister was Naamah.

Adah is the great, great, grandmother of farmers such as those who live in tents and raise livestock. The Masai people of Kenya come to mind and of course other places too. She also is the great, great, grandmother of musicians especially those who play the harp and flute. Think of the Opera musicians do you think they come from her? The black-smiths come from Zillah.

The Bible and Adah

Lamech married two women, one named Adah and the other Zillah. Adah gave birth to Jabal; he was the father of those who live in the tents and raise livestock. His brother's name was Jubal; he was the father of all who play the harp and flute. Zillah also had a son, Tubal-Cain, who forged all kinds of tools out of bronze and iron. Tubal-Cain's sister was Naamah.

Lamech said to his wives, "Adah and Zillah listen to me, wives of Lamech, hear my words. I have killed a man for wounding me, a young man for injuring me.

If Cain is avenged seven times, then Lamech seventy-seven times."

(Genesis 4:19 – 24)

Lessons to Learn:

- Her son Jabal is the father of all those who live in tents and raise livestock
- Her second son Jubal is the father of all those who play the harp and flute
- She gave birth to two extremely talented sons.
- If you look around today we have people who lived in tents and are still living in tents.
- Though, nowadays some tents are used for leisure such as camping out in the woods.
- Those who raise livestock owe it to Adah too.
- Imagine those who play the harp – a musical instrument made up of strings stretched across a frame and plucked by the fingers.
- As well as those who play the flute – a musical instrument made up of a long pipe with holes that are stopped by fingers or keys.

God is the Umbrella of Women in the Bible!

9. Adah/Judith – the Wife of Esau:

Who Was This Woman?

- She was the daughter of Elon the Hittite
- She was the mother of Eliphaz born in Canaan
- She was the grandmother of Teman, Omar, Zepho, Gatam and Kenaz
- She was also grandmother of Amalek from Eliphaz's concubine Timna

The Story:

Parents hope that their children will turn out right. Their sons should marry the right girls, and daughters to marry the right boys. Rebekah and Isaac's first son Esau married Hittite women when he was forty one years old; Judith and Basemath. Then later, he woke up to the fact that his two wives were a source of grief for his parents. He tried to salvage the situation by marrying his father's brother's daughter Mahalath. His younger brother Jacob had obeyed his mother and father, who had told him not to marry a Canaanite woman.

The Bible and Judith:

When Esau was forty years old, he married Judith daughter of Beeri the Hittite, and also Basemath daughter of Elon the Hittite. They were a source of grief to Isaac and Rebekah. (Genesis 26:34)

Then Rebekah said to Isaac, "I'm disgusted with living because of these Hittite women. If Jacob takes a wife from among the women of this land, from Hittite women like these, my life will not be worth living." (Genesis 27:46)

The LORD said to her, "Two nations are in your womb, and two peoples from within you will be separated; one people will be stronger than the other, and the older will serve the younger." (Genesis 25:23)

Now Esau learned that Isaac had blessed Jacob and had sent him to Paddan Aram to take a wife from there, and that when be blessed him he commanded him, "Do not marry a Canaanite woman," and that Jacob had obeyed his father and mother and had gone to Paddan Aram. Esau then realized how displeasing the Canaanite women were to his father Isaac; so he went to Ishmael and married Mahalath, the sister of Nebaioth and daughter of Ishmael son of Abraham in addition to the wives he had already.

When Esau was forty years old, he married Judith daughter of Beeri the Hittite, and also Basemath daughter of Elon the Hittite. They were a source of grief to Isaac and Rebekah. (Genesis 26:34)

Lessons to Learn:

- From what Rebekah said, it would seem that Judith was not a good daughter-in-law.
- She was a source of grief to both Isaac and Rebekah.
- She married Esau who was the older twin of Rebekah

God is the Umbrella of Women in the Bible!

10. Aiah – Who bore Rizpah – Saul's Daughter:

During the reign of David there was a famine for three successive years; so David sought the face of the LORD. The LORD said, "It is on account of Saul and his blood-stained house; it is because he put the Gibeonites to death.

The king summoned the Gibeonites and spoke to them. (Now the Gibeonites were not a part of Israel but were survivors of the Amorites; the Israelites had sworn to spare them, but Saul in his zeal for Israel and Judah had tried to annihilate them.) David asked the Gibeonites, "What shall I do for you? How shall I make amends so that you will bless the LORD's inheritance?"

The Gibeonites answered him, "We have no right to demand silver or gold from Saul or his family, nor do we have the right to put anyone in Israel to death."

"What do you want me to do for you? David asked. They answered the king, "As for the man who destroyed us and plotted against us so that we have been decimated and have no place anywhere in Israel, let seven of his male descendants be given to us to be killed and exposed before the LORD at Gibeah of Saul – the LORD's chosen one."

So the king said, "I will give them to you." The king spared Mephibosheth son of Jonathan, the son of Saul, because of the oath before the LORD between David and Jonathan son of Saul. But the king took Armoni and

Mephibosheth, the two sons of Aiah's daughter Rizpah, whom she had borne to Saul, together with the five sons of Saul's daughter Merab, whom she had borne to Adriel son of Barzillai the Meholathite. He handed them over to the Gibeonites, who killed and exposed them on a hill before the LORD. All seven of them fell together; they were put to death during the first days of the harvest, just as the barley harvest was beginning.

Rizpah daughter of Aiah took sackcloth and spread it out for herself on a rock. From the beginning of the harvest till the rain poured down from the heavens on the bodies, she did not let the birds of the air touch them by day or the wild animals by night. When David was told what Aiah's daughter Rizpah, Saul's concubine, had done, he went and took the bones of Saul and his son Jonathan from the citizens of Jabesh Gilead. (They had taken them secretly from the public square at Beth Shan, where the Philistines had hung them after they struck Saul down on Gilboa.) David brought the bones of Saul and his son Jonathan from there, and the bones of those who had been killed and exposed were gathered up.

They buried the bones of Saul and his son Jonathan in the tomb of Saul's father Kish, at Zela in Benjamin, and did everything the king commanded. After that, God answered prayer in behalf of the land. (2 Samuel 21:1 - 14)

God is the Umbrella of Women in the Bible!

11. Anna – the Prophetess:

Who Was This Woman?

- She was a Prophetess
- The daughter of Phanuel
- She was widowed after seven years of marriage
- She worshiped God night and day
- She fasted and prayed
- She never left the temple
- She gave thanks to God and spoke about Jesus
- She spoke to all who were looking for redemption

The Story:

The prophetess, Anna, was the daughter of Phanuel, of the tribe of Asher. She had been married when she was young. She had lived with her husband seven years after her marriage. Then her husband passed away and then was a widow. She was very old when Mary and Joseph brought Jesus to the temple; she was eighty-four years of age.

She never left the temple but worshiped night and day, fasting and praying. She was expecting God to send someone to redeem Jerusalem. She was at the temple when Mary and Joseph brought Jesus.

She saw them coming up to them at that very moment, she gave thanks to God and spoke about the child to all who were looking forward to the redemption of Jerusalem.

The Bible and Anna the Prophetess

On the eighth day, when it was time to circumcise him, he was named Jesus, the name the angel had given him before he had been conceived.

When the time of their purification according to the Law of Moses had been completed, Joseph and Mary took him to Jerusalem to present him to the Lord (as it is written in the Law of the Lord, "Every firstborn male is to be consecrated to the Lord"), and to offer a sacrifice in keeping with what is said in the Law of the Lord: "a pair of doves or two young pigeons."

Now there was a man in Jerusalem called Simeon, who was righteous and devout. He was waiting for the consolation of Israel, and the Holy Spirit that he would not die before he had seen the Lord's Christ. Moved by the Spirit, he went into the temple courts. When the parents brought in the child Jesus to do for him what the custom of the Law required, Simeon took him in his arms and praised God, saying:

"Sovereign Lord, as you have promised, you now dismiss your servant in peace. For my eyes have seen your salvation, which you have prepared in the sight of all people, a light for revelation to the Gentiles and for Israel."

The child's father and mother marveled at what was said about him. Then Simeon blessed them and said to Mary, his mother: "This child is destined to cause the falling and rising of many in Israel, and to be a sign that will be spoken against, so that the thoughts of many hearts will be revealed. And a sword will pierce your own soul too."

There was also a prophetess, Anna, the daughter of Phanuel, of the tribe of Asher. She was very old; she had lived with her husband seven years after her marriage, and then was a widow until she was eighty-four. She never left the temple but worshiped night and day, fasting and praying. Coming up to them at that very moment, she gave thanks to God and spoke about the child to all who were looking forward to the redemption of Jerusalem.

When Joseph and Mary had done everything required by the Law of the Lord, they returned to Galilee to their own town of Nazareth. And the child grew and became strong. He was filled with wisdom, and the grace of God was upon him. (Luke 2:36 – 38)

Lessons to Learn:

- An amazing Widow
- A Prophetess
- An example of fasting and Praying
- She saw the Lord Jesus Christ
- Gave thanks to the Lord
- Spoke about the child to all who were looking for the Redemption of Jerusalem

God is the Umbrella of Women in the Bible!

12. Asenath – Joseph's Wife

Who Was This Woman?

- She was the daughter of Potiphera, priest of On
- Pharaoh gave Asenath to Joseph to be his wife
- She was the mother of Manasseh and Ephraim
- She was married to a powerful man in the land of Egypt

The Story:

When Pharaoh saw that he had a good man in charge of his country, he decided to give him a good wife. Therefore after all the arrangements Asenath was given to Joseph by Pharaoh. She is an example of a supporting wife. She did not choose Joseph but he was given to her by Pharaoh. Why? Because Pharaoh knew that Joseph needed a good strong woman to rally behind him while he is doing his duties. She is one of the great women in the bible, who is behind a successful man. Both her children were also blessed by Jacob.

The Bible and Asenath:

So Pharaoh said to Joseph, "I hereby put you in charge of the whole land of Egypt." Then Pharaoh took his signet ring from his finger and put it on Joseph's finger. He dressed him in robes of fine linen and put a gold chain around his neck. He had him ride in a chariot as his second-in-command, and men shouted before him. "Make way!" Thus he put him in charge of the whole land of Egypt.

Then Pharaoh said to Joseph, "I am Pharaoh, but without your word no one will lift hand or foot in all Egypt. Pharaoh gave Joseph the name Zaphenath-Panea and gave him Asenath daughter of Potiphera, priest of On, to be his wife. And Joseph went throughout the land of Egypt. (Genesis 41:41 – 45)

Before the years of famine came, two sons were born to Joseph by Asenath daughter of Potiphera, priest of On. Joseph named his firstborn Manasseh and said, "It is because God has made me forget all my trouble and all my father's household." The second son he named Ephraim and said, "It is because God has made me fruitful in the land of my suffering." (Genesis 41:50 – 52)

The sons of Jacob's wife Rachel: Joseph and Benjamin. In Egypt Manasseh and Ephraim were born to Joseph by Asenath daughter of Potiphera, priest of On.

The sons of Benjamin: Bela Beker, Ashbel, Gera, Naaman, Ehi, Rosh,

These were the sons of Rachel who were born to Jacob – fourteen in all. (Genesis 46:19 – 27)

Then he blessed Joseph and said: "May the God before whom my fathers Abraham and Isaac walked, the God who has been my Shepherd all my life to this day, the angel who has delivered me from all harm – may he bless these boys. May they be called by my name and the names of my fathers Abraham and Isaac, and may they increase greatly upon the earth."

When Joseph saw his father placing his right hand on Ephraim's head he was displeased; so he took hold of his father's hand to move it from Ephraim's head to Manasseh's head. Joseph said to him, "No, my father, this one is the firstborn; put your right hand on his head."

But his father refused and said, "I know my son, I know. He too will become a people, and he too will be come great. Nevertheless, his younger brother will be greater than he, and his descendants will become a group of nations." He blessed them that day and said, "In your name will Israel pronounce this blessing: 'May God make you like Ephraim and Manasseh.'"

So he put Ephraim ahead of Manasseh. Then Israel said to Joseph, "I am about to die, but God will be with you and take you back to the land of your fathers. And to you, as one who is over your brothers, I give the ridge of land I took from the Amorites with my sword and my bow." (Genesis 48:15 – 22)

Lessons to Learn:

Even today we hear of arranged marriages for people in royal and other families. Sometimes we tend to worry about issues that really do not deserve our worrying about. If we would pay attention to what our parents and society want us to become, we may end up appreciating some of these situations. This is what happened in Joseph's case. He was royalty and Pharaoh knew that. Asenath was the mother of Manasseh and Ephraim and became the grandmother of Makir, Manasseh's son and great grandmother of Makir's children. She was a blessed woman and daughter-in-law of Jacob. Her children were blessed and Ephraim was put before Manasseh. When you wait and do well, the right person will come your way. Her children were called by Israel's name and the names of his fathers Abraham and Isaac. Identify areas that you may think that it was God's plan for her to have an arranged marriage to Joseph.

God is the Umbrella of Women in the Bible!

13. Atarah – the Wife of Jerahmeel the son of Hezron:

The sons of Jerahmeel the firstborn of Hezron; Ram his firstborn, Bunah, Oren, Ozem and Ahijah. Jerahmeel had another wife, whose name was Atarah; she was the mother of Onam. (1 Chronicles 2:25)

God is the Umbrella of Women in the Bible!

14. Athaliah – the Mother of Ahaziah:

Who Was This Woman?

- The Mother of Ahaziah
- The Wife of Jehoshaphat
- The grandmother of Omri
- She encouraged her son to do wrong
- Ahazia was killed by Jehu
- When she saw that her son was dead she proceeded to destroy the whole royal family of the house of Judah
- Jehosheba the daughter of king Jehoram took Joash son of Ahaziel and stole him away from the royal princes who were about to be murdered and put him and his nurses in a bedroom
- Jehosheba was the wife of Jehoida the priest
- Jehosheba was also the daughter of king Jehoram
- Jehosheba was the sister of Ahaziah
- Jehosheba hid Joash from Athaliah

- Joash was hidden at the Temple of the LORD for six years
- Athaliah went to the Temple of the LORD
- She looked and there was the king standing by the pillar at the entrance
- All people were rejoicing and blowing trumpets, and singers with musical instruments were leading praised
- Athaliah tore her robe and shouted Treason, Treason
- Jehoidah the priest said: "Bring her out through the ranks and put to the sword anyone who follows her.
- The Commanders seized her as she reached the entrance to the Horse Gate on the Palace grounds, and there they put her to death
- And the city was quiet, because Athalia had been slain with the sword.
- (2 Chronicles Chapters 22 and 23)

The Bible and Athaliah:

The people of Jerusalem made Ahaziah, Jehoram's youngest son, king in his place, since the raiders who came with the Arabs into the camp, had killed all the older sons. So Ahaziah son of Jehoram king of Judah began to reign.

Ahaziah was twenty-two years old when he became king, and he reigned in Jerusalem one year. His mother's name was Athaliah, a granddaughter of Omri.

He too walked in the ways of the house of Ahab, for his mother encouraged him in going wrong. He did evil in the eyes of the LORD, as the house of Ahab had done, for after his father's death they became his advisers, to his undoing. He also followed their counsel when he went with Joram son of Ahab king of Israel to war against Hazael king of Aram at Ramoth Gilead. The Arameans wounded Joram; so he returned to Jezreel to recover from the wounds they had inflicted on him at Ramoth in his battle with Hazael king of Aram.

Then Ahazia son of Jehoram king of Judah went down to Jezreel to see Joram son of Ahab because he had been wounded.

Through Ahaziah's visit to Joram, God brought about Ahaziah's downfall. When Ahaziah arrived, he went out with Joram to meet Jehu son of Nimshi, whom the LORD had anointed to destroy the house of Ahab, he found the princes of Judah and the sons of Ahaziah's relatives, who had been attending Ahaziah, and he killed them. He then went in search of Ahaziah and his men captured him while he was hiding in Samaria. He was brought to Jehu and put to death. They buried him for they said, "He was a son of Jehoshaphat, who sought the LORD with all his heart." So there was no one in the house of Ahaziah powerful enough to retain the kingdom.

When Athaliah the mother of Ahaziah saw that her son was dead, she proceeded to destroy the whole royal family of the house of Judah. But Jehosheba, the daughter of King Jehoram, took Joash son of Ahazia and stole him away from among the royal princes who were about to be murdered and put him and his nurse in a bedroom. Because Jehosheba, the daughter of King Jehoram wife of the priest Jehoiada, was Ahaziah's sister, she hid the child from Athaliah so she could not kill him. He remained hidden with them at the temple of God for six years while Athaliah ruled the land. (2 Chronicles 22:1 – 12)

Jehoiada and his sons brought out the king's son and put the crown on him; they presented him with a copy of the covenant and proclaimed him king. They anointed him and shouted, "Long live the king!"

When Athalia heard the noise of the people running and cheering the king, she went to them at the temple of the LORD. She looked. And there was the king, standing by his pillar at the entrance. The officers and the trumpeters were beside the king, and all the people of the land were rejoicing and blowing trumpets, and singers with musical instruments were leading the praises. Then Athalia tore her robes and shouted, "Treason! Treason!"

Jehoiada the priest sent out the commanders of units of a hundred, who were in charge of the troops, and said to them: "Bring her out between the ranks and put to the sword anyone who follows her." For the priest had said, "Do not put her to death at the temple of the LORD." So they seized her as she reached the entrance of the Horse Gate on the palace grounds, and there they put her to death.

Jehoiada then made a covenant that he and the people and the king would be the LORD's people. All the people went to the temple of Baal and tore it down. They smashed the altars and idols and killed Mattan the priest of Baal in front of the alters.

Then Jehoiada placed the oversight of the temple of the LORD in the hands of the priests, who were Levites, to whom David had made assignments in the temple, to present the burnt offerings of the LORD as written in the Law of Moses, with rejoicing and singing, as David had ordered. He also stationed doorkeepers at the gates of the LORD's temple so that no one who was in any way unclean might enter.

He took with him the commanders of hundreds, the nobles, the rulers of the people and all the people of the land and brought the king down from the temple of the LORD. They went into the palace through the Upper Gate and seated the king on the royal throne, and all the people of the land rejoiced. And the city was quiet, because Athalia had been slain with the sword. (2 Chronicles 23:11-21)

Lessons to Learn:

- Cruelty does not pay and God will always take action when he promises to.
- Is there a Joash in your life?
- Someone who has been hidden waiting for his or her turn to come back and take over what you took from him or her?
- How long has it been since you took over? – Joash was hidden for six years!
- Who is your Priest's wife?
- Do an exercise on wives of some prominent people you know!
- It is like the African Chiefs – They are descendants of Chiefs – As time goes, each house will have a turn on the throne, and there are those who know exactly whose turn it is.
- Athalia thought she had it all bagged up and sealed but Joash was there waiting.
- The way she murdered the royal princes is the way she was also killed by the sword.

God is the Umbrella of Women in the Bible!

15. Basemath – the Wife of Esau

Who Was This Woman?

- She was Esau's second wife
- Esau was the elder twin of Rebekah and Isaac
- Rebekah had been told by God that there were two nations in her womb
- Rebekah was disgusted because of Basemath
- She was a source of grief to Isaac and Rebekah
- She was the Daughter of Elon the Hittite

The Story:

Parents hope that their children will turn out right. Their sons should marry the right girls, and daughters to marry the right boys. Rebekah and Isaac's first son Esau married Hittite women when he was forty one years old; Judith and Basemath. Then later, he woke up to the fact that his two wives were a source of grief for his parents. He tried to salvage the situation by marrying his father's brother's daughter Mahalath. His younger brother Jacob had obeyed his mother and father, who had told him not to marry a Canaanite woman.

God already knew what type of people these twins were going to be. One was going to be stronger than the other. The older was going to serve the younger.

The Bible and Basemath:

The LORD said to her, "Two nations are in your womb, and two peoples from within you will be separated; one people will be stronger than the other, and the older will serve the younger." (Genesis 25:23)

When Esau was forty years old, he married Judith daughter of Beeri the Hittite, and also Basemath daughter of Elon the Hittite. They were a source of grief to Isaac and Rebekah. (Genesis 26:34)

Then Rebekah said to Isaac, "I'm disgusted with living because of these Hittite women. If Jacob takes a wife from among the women of this land, from Hittite women like these, my life will not be worth living." (Genesis 27:46)

Now Esau learned that Isaac had blessed Jacob and had sent him to Paddan Aram to take a wife from there, and that when be blessed him he commanded him, "Do not marry a Canaanite woman," and that Jacob had obeyed his father and mother and had gone to Paddan Aram. Esau then realized how displeasing the Canaanite women were to his father Isaac; so he went to Ishmael and married Mahalath, the sister of Nebaioth and daughter of Ishmael son of Abraham in addition to the wives he had already. (Genesis 28:6 – 90)

Lessons to Learn:

- From what Rebekah said, it would seem that Basemath was not a good daughter-in-law.
- She was a source of grief to both Isaac and Rebekah
- She married Esau who was the older twin of Rebekah, about whom the LORD had said the older will serve the younger
- Do you think you should be influenced by your parents in who you should marry?
- Do you have any examples of marriages against parent's wishes?
- Have they been successful or disastrous like Basemath and Esau's?
- Do you think marrying Ishmael's daughter was of any help?
- Who influenced you in marrying your spouse?

God is the Umbrella of Women in the Bible!

16. Bathsheba – the Mother of King Solomon:

Who was this Woman?

- She was a soldier's wife
- She was beautiful
- The daughter of Eliam
- She was bathing in a place where she could be seen
- She had purified herself
- She slept with King David
- She became pregnant2
- Caused the death of her husband Uriah
- Her baby that she had as a result died
- She became King David's wife
- She is the mother of King Solomon
- She is a powerful woman in the bible

The Story:

King David was actually supposed to have been fighting with his army; but for some reason he decided to stay behind and thence the following unfolded in the life of Bathsheba.

Her husband Uriah had gone to war, she was bathing in an open roofed area of her house. At that same time King David was also strolling on the rooftop of the Palace. At this time he saw a naked Bathsheba and lusted for her.

Bathsheba was the wife of Uriah. Uriah was one of King David's Special Force members and was very brave. He was a skilled and loyal warrior. Unfortunately he was killed while fighting for his country; because David had slept with his wife.

When David knew that Bathsheba was pregnant he designed a plan. He sent for Uriah to come back from the war; so that he could spend sometime with his wife. This was so that Bathsheba could say it was Uriah's pregnancy. But this was not to be so. Despite all his tactics Uriah refused to go to his house but slept with others at the palace.

David then wrote a letter commanding that Uriah must be put in the forefront of the war so that he can be killed. This was done and Uriah was killed. Thereafter David took Bathsheba and made her his wife. This is in addition to his three wives: Ahinoam, Abigail and Michal. Bathsheba became the fourth wife of David.

God however punished him for this behaviour and Bathsheba's son with him died. She later gave birth to Solomon who later became King of Israel after David.

Bathsheba's son Solomon was made king by his father king David. "Then King David said, "Call in Bathsheba." So she came into the king's presence and stood before him. The king then took an oath: "As surely as the Lord lives, who has delivered me out of every trouble, I will surely carry out today what I swore to you by the Lord, the God of Israel: Solomon your son shall be king after me, and he will sit on my throne in my place.

The Bible and Bathsheba:

In the spring, at the time when kings go off to war, David sent Joab out with the king's men and the whole Israelite army. They destroyed the Ammonites and besieged Rabbah. But David remained in Jerusalem.

One evening David got up from his bed and walked around on the roof of the palace. From the roof he saw a woman bathing. The woman was very beautiful, and David sent someone to find out about her. The man said, "Isn't this Bathsheba, the daughter of Eliam and the wife of Uriah the Hittite?" Then David sent messengers to get her. She came to him, and he slept with her. (She had purified herself from her uncleanness.) Then she went back home. The woman conceived and sent word to David, saying "I am pregnant."

So David sent this word to Joab: "Send me Uriah the Hittite." And Joab sent him to David. When Uriah came to him, David asked him how Joab was how the soldiers were and how the war was going. Then David said to Uriah "Go down to your house and wash your feet." So Uriah left the palace, and a gift from the king was sent after him. But Uriah slept at the entrance to the palace with all his master's servants and did not go down to his house.

When David was told, "Uriah did not go home," he asked him, "Haven't you just come from a distance? Why didn't you go home?"

Uriah said to David, "The ark and Israel and Judah are staying in tents and my master Joab and my lord's men are camped in the open fields. How could I go to my house to eat and drink and lie with my wife? As surely as you live, I will not do such a thing!"

Then David said to him, "Stay here one more day, and tomorrow I will send you back." So Uriah remained in Jerusalem that day and the next day. At David's invitation, he ate and drank with him, and David made him drunk. But in the evening Uriah went out to sleep on his mat among his master's servants; he did not go home.

In the morning David wrote a letter to Joab and sent it with Uriah. In it he wrote, "Put Uriah in the front line where the fighting is fiercest. Then withdraw from him so that he will be struck down and die."

So while Joab had the city under siege, he put Uriah at a place where he knew the strongest defenders were. When the men of the city came out and fought against Joab, some of the men in David's army fell; moreover Uriah the Hittite died.

Joab sent a full account of the battle. He instructed the messenger: "When you have finished giving the king this account of the battle, the king's anger may flare up, and he may ask you, 'Why did you get so close to the city to fight? Didn't you know they would shoot arrows from the wall? Who killed Abimelech son of Jerub-Besheth? Didn't a woman throw an upper millstone on him from the wall, so that he died in Thebez? Why did you get so close to the wall? If he asks you this, then say to him, 'Also, your servant Uriah the Hittite is dead.'"

The messenger set out, and when he arrived he told David everything Joab had sent him to say. The messenger said to David "The men over powered us and came out against us in the open, but we drove them back to the entrance to the city gate. Then the archers shot arrows at your servants from the wall, and some of the king's men died. Moreover, your servant Uriah the Hittite is dead."

David told the messenger, "Say this to Joab: 'Don't let this upset you; the sword devours one as well as another. Press the attack against the city and destroy it' Say this to encourage Joab."

When Uriah's wife heard that her husband was dead, she mourned for him. After the time of mourning was over. David had her brought to his house, and she became his wife and bore him a son. But the thing David had done displeased the Lord. (2 Samuel 11)

Then David comforted his wife Bathsheba, and he went to her and lay with her. She gave birth to a son, and they named him Solomon. The LORD loved him; and because the LORD loved him, he sent word through Nathan the prophet to name him Jedidah. (2 Samuel 12:24 – 25).

When King David was old and well advanced in years, he could not keep warm even when they put covers over him. So his servants said to him, "Let us look for a virgin to attend the king and take care of him. She can lie beside him so that our lord the king may keep warm." Then they searched throughout Israel for a beautiful girl and found Abishag, a Shunammite, and brought her to the king. The girl was very beautiful; she took care of the king and waited on him, but the king had no intimate relations with her.

Now Adonijah, whose mother was Haggith, put himself forward and said, "I will be king. So he got chariots and horses ready, with fifty men to run ahead of him. (His father had never interfered with him by asking "Why do you behave as you do?" He was also very handsome and was born next after Absalom.)

Adonijah conferred with Joab son of Zeruiah and with Abiathar the priest, and they gave him their support. But Zadok the priest, Benaiah son of Jehoiada, Nathan the prophet, Shimei and Rei and David's special guard did not join Adonijah.

Adonijah then sacrificed sheep, cattle and fattened calves at the Stone of Zoheleth near En Rogel. He invited all his brothers, the king's sons, and all the men of Judah who were royal officials, but he did not invite Nathan the prophet or Benaiah or the special guard or his brother Solomon.

Then Nathan asked Bathsheba, Solomon's mother, "Have you not heard that Adonijah, the son of Haggith, has become king without our lord David's knowing it? Now then let me advise you how you can save your own life and the life of your son Solomon. Go in to King David and say to him, 'My lord the king, did you not swear to me your servant: "Surely Solomon your son shall be king after me, and he will sit on my throne? Why then has Adonijah become king?' While you are still there talking to the king, I will come in and confirm what you have said."

So Bathsheba went to see the aged king in his room, where Abishag the Shunammite was attending him. Bathsheba bowed low and knelt before the king. "What is it you want?" the king asked. She said to him, "My lord, you yourself swore to me your servant by the LORD your God: 'Solomon your son shall be king after me, and he will sit on my throne.' But now Adonijah has become king, and you, my lord the king, do not know about it. He has sacrificed great numbers of cattle, fattened calves, and sheep, and has invited all the king's sons, Abiathar the priest and Joab the commander of the army, but he has not invited Solomon your servant. My lord the king, the eyes of all Israel are on you, to learn from you who will sit on the throne of my lord the kind after him. Otherwise, as soon as my lord the king is laid to rest with his fathers, I and my son Solomon will be treated as criminals.

While she was still speaking with the king, Nathan the prophet arrived. And they told the king, "Nathan the prophet is here." So he went before the king and bowed with his face to the ground.

Nathan said, "Have you my lord the king, declared that Adonijah shall be king after you, and that he will sit on your throne? Today he had gone down and sacrificed great numbers of cattle, fattened calves, and sheep. He has invited all the king's sons, the commanders of the army and Abiathar the priest. Right now they are eating and drinking with him and saying, 'Long live King Adonijah!' But me your servant, and Zadok the priest, and Benaiah son of Jehoiada, and your servant Solomon he did not invite. Is this something my lord the king has done without letting his servants know who should sit on the throne of my lord the king after him?

Then King David said, "Call in Bathsheba." So she came into the king's presence and stood before him. The king then took an oath: "As surely as the LORD lives, who delivered me out of every trouble, I will surely carry out today what I swore to you by the LORD the God of Israel: Solomon your son shall be king after me, and he will sit on my throne in my place."

Then Bathsheba bowed low with her face to the ground and, kneeling before the king, said, "May my lord King David live forever!"

King David said, "Call in Zadok the priest, Nathan the prophet and Benaiah son of Jehoiada." When they came before the king, he said to them: "Take your lord's servants with you and set Solomon my son on my own mule and take him down to Gihon. There shall Zadok the priest and Nathan the prophet anoint him king over Israel. Blow the trumpet and shout, "Long live King Solomon!" Then you are to go up with him and he is to come and sit on my throne and reign in my place. I have appointed him ruler over Israel and Judah.

Benaiah son of Jehoiada answered the king, "Amen! May the Lord, the God of my lord the king so declare it. As the Lord was with my lord the king, so may he be with Solomon to make his throne even greater than the throne of my lord King David!"

So Zadok the priest, Nathan the prophet, Benaiah son of Jehoiada, the Kerethites and the Pelethites went down and put Solomon on King David's Mule and escorted him to Gihon. Zadok the priest took the horn of oil from the sacred tent and anointed Solomon. Then they sounded the trumpet and all the people shouted, "Long live King Solomon!" And all the people went up after him, playing flutes and rejoicing greatly, so that the ground shook with the sound. (1 Kings 1:1 – 40)

Lessons to Learn:

- David sinned against God by sleeping with Bathsheba
- Her husband Uriah was killed
- God sent Nathan to rebuke David – (2 Samuel 21:1 – 25)
- Her son with David died as a punishment from God
- Solomon was later born
- She became one of David's Wives after Ahoniham of Jezreel, Abigail the widow of Nabal of (Carmel 2 Samuel 2:2) and Michal daughter of Saul (2 Samuel 3:13 – 14)

God is the Umbrella of Women in the Bible!

17. Bilhah – the Mother of Dan and Naphtali:

- Rachel gave her to Jacob
- Dan – Was her first son whom she birthed for Rachel
- Naphtali – Was her second son whom she birthed for Rachel

The Story:

Bilhah was also Laban's servant. She was given to Rachel as her servant when she married Jacob. When Rachel saw that she could not have children she forced her husband to give her children through Bilhah. Jacob slept with her and she had two sons for Rachel. Their names were Dan and Naphtali.

The Bible and Bilhah:

When Rachel saw that she was not bearing Jacob any children, she became jealous of her sister. So she said to Jacob, "Give me children, or I'll die!"

Jacob became angry with her and said, "Am I in the place of God, who has kept you from having children?"

Then she said, here is Bilhah, my maidservant. Sleep with her so that she can bear children for me and that through her I too can build a family."

So she gave him her servant Bilhah as a wife, Jacob slept with her, and she became pregnant and bore him a son. Then Rachel said, "God has vindicated me; he has listened to my plea and given me a son." Because of this she named him Dan.

Rachel's servant Bilhah conceived again and bore Jacob a second son. Then Rachel said, "I have had a great struggle with my sister and I have won." So she named him Naphtali.

When Leah saw that she had stopped having children, she took her maidservant Zilpah and gave her to Jacob as a wife. Leah's servant Zilpah bore Jacob a son. Then Leah said, "What good fortune!" So she named him Gad.

Leah's servant Zilpah bore Jacob a second son. Then Leah said, "How happy I am!" The women will call me happy." So she named him Asher.

During wheat harvest, Reuben went out into the fields and found some mandrake plants, which he brought to his mother Leah. Rachel said to Leah, "Please give me some of your son's mandrakes."

But she said to her, "Wasn't it enough that you took away my husband? Will you take my son's mandrakes too?"

"Very well," Rachel said, "he can sleep with you tonight in return for your son's mandrakes." So when Jacob came in from the fields that evening, Leah went out to meet him. "You must sleep with me," she said, "I have hired you with my son's mandrakes." So he slept with her that night.

God listened to Leah, and she became pregnant and bore Jacob a fifth son. Then Leah said, "God has rewarded me for giving my maidservant to my husband." So she named him Issacher.

Some time later she gave birth to a daughter and named her Dinah.

Then God remembered Rachel; he listened to her and opened her womb. She became pregnant and gave birth to a son and said, "God has taken away my disgrace." She named him Joseph, and said "May the Lord add to me another son." (Genesis 30:1 – 24)

Lessons to Learn:

- "God has vindicated me; he has listened to my plea and given me a son."
- She had two sons with Jacob for Rachel
- Her sons were Dan and Naphtali
- What do you think about what Rachel did?
- Do you know of any of this happening today?
- Would you call this polygamism or mere assistance?
- Would you still call her a Maid or a Wife of Jacob?

God is the Umbrella of Women in the Bible!

18. Candace, queen of the Ethiopians: (Acts 8:26 - 32

God is the Umbrella of Women in the Bible!

19. Deborah – the Prophetess:

Who Was This Woman?

- She was the wife of Lappidoth
- She was a Prophetess
- God spoke to her
- She ruled Israel
- She went to war
- She gave instructions from God to Barak to go and fight Sisera
- Barak did not want to go without her

The Story:

Deborah was one of Israel's most charismatic leaders. She was a prophet as well as a judge. She was the wife of Lappidoth. Her court was held between Ramah and Bethel under the Palm of Deborah, in the hill country of Ephraim.

Deborah told Barak the son of Naphtali that: "The LORD, the God of Israel commands you: Go, take with you ten thousand men of Naphtali and Zebulum and lead the way to Mount Tabor. I will lure Sisera, the commander of

Jabin's army, with his chariots and his troops to the Kishon River and give him into your hands."

Barak said to her, "If you go with me, I will go, but if you can't go with me, I won't go."

By this Barak showed that he was afraid and could not take God's word spoken through the prophetess Deborah.

Deborah agreed to go with him but told him that he would not have the honour of killing Sisera but a woman would kill him.

When they told Sisera that Barak son of Abinoam had gone up to Mount Tabor, Sisera gathered together his nine hundred iron chariots and all the men with him, from Harosheth Haggoyim to the Kishon River.

Then Debora said to Barak, "Go! This is the day the LORD has given Sisera into your hands. Has not the LORD gone ahead of you?"

So Barak went down Mount Tabor, followed by ten thousand men. At Barak's advance the LORD routed Sisera and all his chariots and army by the sword, and Sisera abandoned his chariot and fled on foot. But Barak pursued the chariots and army as far as Harosheth Haggoyim. All troops of Sisera fell by the sword not a man was left. (Judges 4 and 5)

The Bible and Deborah:

After Ehud died, the Israelites once again did evil in the eyes of the LORD. So the LORD sold them into the hands of Jabin, a king of Canaan, who reigned in Hazor.

The commander of his army was Sisera, who lived in Harosheth Haggoyim. Because he had nine hundred iron chariots and had cruelly oppressed the Israelites for twenty years, they cried to the LORD for help.

Deborah, a prophetess, the wife of Lappidoth, was leading Israel at that time. She held court under the Palm of Deborah between Ramah and Bethel in the hill country of Ephraim, and the Israelites came to her to have their disputes decided. She sent for Barak son of Abinoam from Kedesh in Naphtali and said to him, "The LORD, the God of Israel, commands you: 'Go, take with you ten thousand men of Naphtali and Zebulum and lead the way to Mount Tabor. I will lure Sisera, the commander of Jabin's army with his chariots and his troops to the Kishon River and give him into your hands,"

Barak said to her, "If you go with me, I will go; but if you don't go with me, I won't go" Very well Deborah said, "I will go with you. But because of the way you are going about this, the honour will not be yours, for the LORD will hand Sisera over to a woman." So Deborah went with Barak to Kedesh, where he summoned Zebulun and Naphtali. Ten thousand men followed him, and Deborah also went with him.

When they told Sisera that Barak son of Abinoam had gone up to Mount Tabor, Sisera gathered together his nine hundred iron chariots and all the men with him, from Harosheth Haggoyim to the Kishon River.

Then Deborah said to Barak, "Go! This is the day the LORD has given Sisera into your hands. Has not the LORD gone ahead of you?" So Barak went down Mount Tabor, followed by ten thousand men. At Barak's advance, the LORD routed Sisera and all his chariots and army by the sword, and Sisera abandoned his chariot and fled on foot. But Barak pursued the chariots and army as far as Harosheth Haggoyim. All the troops of Sisera fell by the sword; not a man was left.

Sisera, however, fled on foot to the tent of Jael, the wife of Heber the Kenite; because there were friendly relations between Jabin king of Hazor and the clan of Heber the Kenite.

Jael went out to meet Sisera and said to him, "Come, my lord, com right in. Don't be afraid." So he entered her tent, and she put a covering over him. "I'm thirsty," he said, "Please give me some water." She opened a skin of milk, gave him a drink, and covered him up.

Stand in the doorway of the tent," he told her. "If someone comes by and asks you, 'Is anyone here?' say 'No'"

But Jael, Heber's wife, picked up a tent peg and a hammer and went quietly to him while he lay fast asleep, exhausted. She drove the peg through his temple into the ground, and he died.

Barak came by in pursuit of Sisera, and Jael went out to meet him. "Come" she said, "I will show you the man you're looking for." So he went in with her, and there lay Sisera with the tent peg through his temple – dead. On that day God subdued Jabin, the Canaanite king, before the Israelites. And the hand of Israelites grew stronger and stronger against Jabin, the Canaanite king, until they destroyed him. (Judges 4:1 -24)

Lessons to Learn:

- Barak did not get the honour of killing Sisera
- Jael a woman was given the honour of killing Sisera
- Israel was led by her
- Disputes were settled under the Palm of Deborah
- She was a woman of God

- Are there any such women who come to your mind today?
- Women who speak to God?
- Commanders of Armies?
- Judges?

God is the Umbrella of Women in the Bible!

20. Dinah – the Daughter of Leah:

Who Was This Woman?

- She was Leah and Jacob's daughter
- She was defiled by Shechem the son of Hamor the Hivite.
- Intermarriages were not allowed and what Shechem had done to her was disgraceful in Israel
- Hamor went to talk with Jacob
- Her brothers were filled with grief and fury
- She was the only daughter of Jacob born to him by Leah

The Story:

I remember how I used to feel when I was the only girl with five brothers. Dinah was the only girl with twelve brothers. Brothers are always very protective of their sister, especially if she is the only one they had. She was also the only daughter of Jacob and Leah. Her brothers were: Reuben, Simeon,

Levi, Judah, Dan, Naphtali, Gad, Asher, Issacher, Zebulum, Joseph and Benjamin. They were extremely protective of their sister. So when they heard that Dinah was defiled by Shechem; they were filled with grief and fury. They felt that a thing like this should not have been done.

We can't give our sister to a man who is not circumcised they said. But Hamor said to them, "My son Shechem has his heart set on your daughter. Please give her to him as his wife. Intermarry with us; give us your daughters and take our daughters for yourselves. You can settle among us, the land is open to you. Live in it, trade in it, and acquire property in it. Then Shechem said to Dinah's father and brothers, "Let me find favor in your eyes, and I will give you whatever you ask. Make the price for the bride the gift I am to bring as great as you like and I'll pay whatever you ask me. Only give me the girl as my wife.

We will give our consent to you on one condition only; that you become like us by circumcising all your males. Then we will give you our daughters and take your daughters for ourselves. We'll settle among you and become one people with you. But if you will not agree to be circumcised, we'll take our sister and go.

Their proposal seemed good to Hamor and his son Shechem. So Hamor and his son Shechem went to their fellow townsmen. "These men are friendly toward us," they said. "Let them live in our land and trade in it; the land has plenty of room for them. We can marry their daughters and they can marry ours. But the men will consent to live with us as one people only on the condition that our males are circumcised, as they themselves are. So let us give our consent to them, and they will settle among us." Their people agreed to perform the circumcision of all the males in their clan. All the men who went out of the city gate agreed with Hamor and his son Shechem, and every male in the city was circumcised. That was their downfall; Dinah's brothers came and killed all of them.

The Bible and Dinah:

Sometime later Leah gave birth to a daughter and named her Dinah. (Genesis 30:21)

Now Dinah, the daughter Leah had borne to Jacob, went out to visit the women of the land. When Shechem son of Hamor the Hivite, the ruler of that area, saw her, he took her and violated her. His heart was drawn to Dinah daughter of Jacob, and he loved the girl and spoke tenderly to her. And Shechem said to his father Hamor, "Get me this girl as my wife."

When Jacob heard that his daughter Dinah had been defiled, his sons were in the fields with his livestock; so he kept quiet about it until they came home.

Then Shechem's father Hamor went out to talk with Jacob. Now Jacob's sons had come in from the fields as soon as they heard what had happened. They were filled with grief and fury, because Shechem had done a disgraceful thing in Israel, by lying with Jacob's daughter – a thing that should not be done.

But Hamor said to them, "My son Shechem has his heart set on your daughter. Please give her to him as his wife. Intermarry with us; give us your daughters and take our daughters for yourselves. You can settle among us, the land is open to you. Live in it, trade in it, and acquire property in it

Then Shechem said to Dinah's father and brothers, "Let me find favor in your eyes, and I will give you whatever you ask. Make the price for the bride the gift I am to bring as great as you like and I'll pay whatever you ask me. Only give me the girl as my wife.

Because their sister Dinah had been defiled, Jacob's sons replied deceitfully as they spoke to Shechem, and his father Hamor. They said to them," We can't do such a thing; we can't give out sister to a man who is not circumcised. That would be a disgrace to us. We will give our consent to you our consent to you on one condition only; that you become like us by circumcising all your males. Then we will give you our daughters and take your daughters for ourselves. We'll settle among you and become one people with you. But if you will not agree to be circumcised, we'll take our sister and go.

Their proposal seemed good to Hamor and his son Shechem. The young man, who was the most honored of all his father's household, lost to time in doing what they said, because he was delighted with Jacob's daughter. So Hamor and his son Shechem went to the gate of their city to speak to their fellow townsmen.

"These men are friendly toward us," they said. "Let them live in our land and trade in it; the land has plenty of room for them. We can marry their daughters and they can marry ours. But the men will consent to live with us as one people only on the condition that our males are circumcised, as they themselves are. Won't their livestock, their property and all their other animals become ours? So let us give our consent to them, and they will settle among us."

All the men who went out of the city gate agreed with Hamor and his son Shechem, and every male in the city was circumcised.

Three days later while all men were still in pain, two of Jacob's sons, Simeon and Levi, Dinah's brothers, took their swords and attacked the unsuspecting city, killing every male. They put Hamor and his son Shechem to the sword and took Dinah from Shechem's house and left. The sons of Jacob came upon the dead bodies and looted the city where their sister had been defiled. They seized their flocks and herds and donkeys and everything else of theirs in the city and out in the fields. They carried off all their wealth and all their women and children, taking as plunder everything in the houses. Then Jacob said to Simeon and Levi," You have brought trouble on me by making me a stench to the Canaanites and Perizzites, the people living in this land. We are few in number and if they join forces against me and attack me, I and my household will be destroyed. But they replied, "Should he have treated our sister like a prostitute?" (Genesis 34:1 – 31)

Lessons to Learn:

It is not good to defile other people's daughters. How would you have handled the situation if Shechem was your son? How would you have handled the situation if Shechem was your brother? How would you have handled the situation if Dinah was your sister? How would you have handled the situation if Dinah was your daughter? How would you have handled the situation if you were Hamor's clan? Dinah's brothers took their swords and attacked the unsuspecting city, killing every male.

They put Hamor and his son Shechem to the sword. They took Dinah from Shechem's house and left. The sons of Jacob came upon the dead bodies and looted the city where their sister had been defiled. They seized their flocks and herds and donkeys and everything else of theirs in the city and out in the fields. They carried off all their wealth and all their women and children, taking as plunder everything in the houses.

Then Jacob said to Simeon and Levi," You have brought trouble on me by making me a stench to the Canaanites and Perizzites, the people living in this land. We are few in number and if they join forces against me and attack me, I and my household will be destroyed. But they replied, "Should he have treated our sister like a prostitute?"

God is the Umbrella of Women in the Bible!

21. Elizabeth – the Mother of John the Baptist:

Who Was This Woman

- She was the wife of Zechariah
- She was a priests wife
- She was barren
- She was old
- The Angel Gabriel appeared to Zechariah and told them that they were going to have a child
- He did not believe the angel
- He was made dumb until the child was born
- He was told to name the child John
- She became pregnant
- She secluded herself for five months
- She gave birth to John
- She gave him the name John
- Zechariah wrote the name John on a tablet
- He then started to speak
- Elizabeth praised God for this favour

- The angel Gabriel also told Mary the Mother of Jesus about Elizabeth's pregnancy

The Story:

Elizabeth was a descendant of Aaron and was married to a priest named Zechariah. She and her husband were upright people in the eyes of the Lord. They kept all the Lord's commandments and regulations. They were both fairly old, and Elizabeth was barren.

Once when Zechariah's division was on duty and he was serving as priest before God, he was chosen by lot, according to the custom of the priesthood, to go into the temple of the Lord and burn incense. And when the time for the burning of incense came, all the assembled worshipers were praying outside.

Then an angel of the Lord appeared to him, standing at the right side of the alter of incense. When Zechariah saw him, he was startled and was gripped with fear. But the angel said to him: "Do not be afraid, Zechariah; your prayer has been heard. Your wife Elizabeth will bear you a son, and you are to give him the name John. He will be a joy and delight to you, and many will rejoice because of his birth, for he will be great in the sight of the Lord. He is never to take wine or other fermented drink, and he will be filled with the Holy Spirit even from birth. Many of the people of Israel will he bring back to the Lord their God. And he will go on before the Lord, in the spirit and power of Elijah, to turn the hearts of the fathers to their children and the disobedient to the wisdom of the righteous - to make ready a people prepared for the Lord."

Zechariah told the angel that he was an old man and his wife was well along in years. He asked the angel how he could be sure of this

The angel then said, "I am Gabriel, I stand in the presence of God, and I have been sent to speak to you and to tell you this good news. And now you will be silent and not able to speak until the day this happens, because you did not believe my words, which will come true at their proper time."

He returned home. Later his wife Elizabeth became pregnant and for five months remained in seclusion. She said. "The Lord had done this for me; in these days he has shown his favour and taken away my disgrace among the people."

The angel of the Lord also told Mary, the Mother of Jesus that "Even Elizabeth your relative is going to have a child in her old age, and she who was said to be barren is in her sixth month. For nothing is impossible with God."

At that time Mary got ready and hurried to a town in the hill country of Judea, where she entered Zechariah's home and greeted Elizabeth. When Elizabeth heard Mary's greeting, the baby leaped in her womb, and Elizabeth was filled with the Holy Spirit. In a loud voice she exclaimed:

Then Elizabeth said to Mary: "Blessed are you among women, and blessed is the child you will bear! But why am I so favoured, that the mother of my Lord should come to me? As soon as the sound of your greeting reached my ears, the baby in my womb leaped for joy. Blessed is she who has believed that what the Lord has said to her will be accomplished!"

When it was time for Elizabeth to have her baby, she gave birth to a son. Her neighbours and relatives heard that the Lord had shown her great mercy, and they shared her joy.

On the eighth day they came to circumcise the child, and they were going to name him after his father Zechariah, but his mother spoke up and said, "No! He is to be called John."

They said to her, "There is no one among your relatives who has that name."

Then they made signs to his father, to find out what he would like to name the child. He asked for a writing tablet, and to everyone's astonishment he wrote, "His name is John." Immediately his mouth was opened and his tongue was loosed, and be began to speak, praising God. The neighbours were all filled with awe, and throughout the hill country of Judea people were talking about these things. Everyone who heard about this wondered about it, asking, "What then is this child going to be?" For the Lord's hand was with him

The Bible and Elizabeth:

In the time of Herod king of Judea there was a priest named Zechariah, who belonged to the priestly division of Abijah; his wife Elizabeth was also a descendant of Aaron. Both of them were upright in the sight of God, observing all the Lord's commandments and regulations blamelessly. But they had no children, because Elizabeth was barren; and they were both well along in years.

Once when Zechariah's division was on duty and he was serving as priest before God, he was chosen by lot, according to the custom of the priesthood, to go into the temple of the Lord and burn incense. And when the time for the burning of incense came, all the assembled worshipers were praying outside.

Then an angel of the Lord appeared to him, standing at the right side of the alter of incense. When Zechariah saw him, he was startled and was gripped with fear. But the angel said to him: "Do not be afraid, Zechariah; your prayer has been heard. Your wife Elizabeth will bear you a son, and you are to give him the name John. He will be a joy and delight to you, and many will rejoice because of his birth, for he will be great in the sight of the Lord. He is never to take wine or other fermented drink, and he will be filled with the Holy Spirit even from birth. Many of the people of Israel will he bring back to the Lord their God. And he will go on before the Lord, in the spirit and power of Elijah, to turn the hearts of the fathers to their children and the disobedient to the wisdom of the righteous =- to make ready a people prepared for the Lord."

Zechariah asked the angel, "How can I be sure of this? I am an old man and my wife is well along in years."

The angel answered, "I am Gabriel, I stand in the presence of God, and I have been sent to speak to you and to tell you this good news. And now you will be silent and not able to speak until the day this happens, because you did not believe my words, which will come true at their proper time."

Meanwhile, the people were waiting for Zechariah and wondering why he stayed so long in the temple. When he came out, he could not speak to them. They realized he had seen a vision in the temple, for he kept making signs to them but remained unable to speak.

When his time of service was completed, he returned home. After this his wife Elizabeth became pregnant and for five months remained in seclusion.

"The Lord had done this for me," she said. "In these days he has shown his favour and taken away my disgrace among the people." (Luke 1:5 – 25)

"Even Elizabeth your relative is going to have a child in her old age, and she who was said to be barren is in her sixth month. For nothing is impossible with God." (Luke 1:36)

At that time Mary got ready and hurried to a town in the hill country of Judea, where she entered Zechariah's home and greeted Elizabeth. When Elizabeth heard Mary's greeting, the baby leaped in her womb, and Elizabeth was filled with the Holy Spirit. In a loud voice she exclaimed:

"Blessed are you among women, and blessed is the child you will bear! But why am I so favoured, that the mother of my Lord should come to me? As soon as the sound of your greeting reached my ears, the baby in my womb leaped for joy. Blessed is she who has believed that what the Lord has said to her will be accomplished!" (Luke 1:39 – 45)

When it was time for Elizabeth to have her baby, she gave birth to a son. Her neighbours and relatives heard that the Lord had shown her great mercy, and they shared her joy.

On the eighth day they came to circumcise the child, and they were going to name him after his father Zechariah, but his mother spoke up and said, "No! He is to be called John."

They said to her, "There is no one among your relatives who has that name."

Then they made signs to his father, to find out what he would like to name the child. He asked for a writing tablet, and to everyone's astonishment he wrote, "His name is John." Immediately his mouth was opened and his tongue was loosed, and be began to speak, praising God. The neighbours were all filled with awe, and throughout the hill country of Judea people were talking about these things. Everyone who heard about this wondered about it, asking, "What then is this child going to be?" For the Lord's hand was with him. (Luke 1:57 – 66)

Lessons to Learn:

- Nothing is impossible with God.
- Elizabeth was filled with the Holy Spirit.
- She had a child in her old age
- Powerful experiences of Gain and Loss
- Powerful woman
- Mary went to visit her and the child in her womb leaped or acknowledged the Mother of Jesus.

God is the Umbrella of Women in the Bible!

22. Eve –the Mother of Cain and Abel:

Who Was This Woman?

- She was the first female created by God
- She was blessed together with Adam
- She was made by the LORD God from the rib he had taken out of the man
- She was brought to the man
- Adam named his wife Eve, because she would become the mother of all the living
- She ate the forbidden fruit in the Garden of Eden
- She also gave some to her husband, who was with her, and he ate it
- She is the first married woman
- She is the mother of Cain, Abel and Seth
- She is the grandmother of Enosh, Seth's son
- When Adam was 130 years he had a son in his own likeness, In his own image, and he named him Seth

- After Seth was born Adam lived 800 years and had other sons and daughters
- Her husband died at the age of 930 years
- Then the eyes of both of them were opened, and they realized they were naked; so they sewed fig leaves together and made coverings for themselves.
- She and her husband heard the sound of the LORD God as he was walking in the garden in the cool of the day, and they hid from the LORD God among the trees of the garden.

The Story:

But for Adam no suitable helper was found. So the Lord God caused the man to fall into a deep sleep; and while he was sleeping he took one of the man's ribs and closed up the place with flesh. Then the Lord God made a woman from the rib he had taken out of the man, and he brought her to the man.

The man said, "This is now bone of my bones and flesh of my flesh, she shall be called woman."

For this reason a man will leave his father and mother and be united to his wife, and they will become one flesh.

The Bible and Eve:

So God created man in his own image, in the image of God created he him; male and female he created them (Genesis 1:27)

God blessed them and said to them: "Be fruitful and increase in number; fill the earth and subdue it. Rule over the fish of the sea and the birds of the air and over every living creature that moves on the ground. (Genesis 1:28)

But for Adam no suitable helper was found. So the Lord God caused the man to fall into a deep sleep; and while he was sleeping he took one of the man's ribs and closed up the place with flesh. Then the Lord God made a woman from the rib he had taken out of the man, and he brought her to the man. The man said, "This is now bone of my bones and flesh of my flesh, she shall be called woman." For this reason a man will leave his father and mother and be united to his wife, and they will become one flesh. The man and his wife were both naked and they felt no shame. (Genesis 2:20 – 25)

Now the serpent was craftier than any of the wild animals the Lord God had made. He said to the woman, "Did God really say, 'You must not eat from any tree in the garden'?" The woman said to the serpent, "We may eat fruit from the trees in the garden, but God did say, 'You must not eat fruit from the tree that is in the middle of the garden, and you must not touch it, or you will die.'"

"You will surely not die," the serpent said to the woman. "For God knows that, when you eat of it your eyes will be opened, and you will be like God, knowing good and evil."

When the woman saw that the fruit of the tree was good for food and pleasing to the eye, and also desirable for gaining wisdom, she took some and ate it. She also gave some to her husband, who was with her, and he ate it. Then the eyes of both of them were opened, and they realized they were naked; so they sewed fig leaves together and made coverings for themselves.

Then the man and his wife heard the sound of the Lord God as he was walking in the garden in the cool of the day, and they hid from the Lord God among the trees of the garden. But the Lord God called to the man, "Where are you?"

He answered, "I heard you in the garden, and I was afraid because I was naked; so I hid." And he said, "Who told you that you were naked? Have you eaten from the tree that I commanded you not to eat from?" The Man said, "The woman you put here with me – she gave me some fruit from the tree, and I ate it."

Then the Lord said to the woman, "What is this you have done?"

The woman said, the serpent deceived me, and I ate."

So the Lord God said to the serpent, "Because you have done this, "Cursed are you above all the livestock and all the wild animals! You will crawl on your belly and you will eat dust all the days of your life. And I will put enmity between you and the woman, and between your offsprings and hers, he will crush your head and you will strike his heel." To the woman he said, "I will greatly increase your pains in childbearing, with pain you will give birth to children. Your desire will be for your husband, and he will rule over you." To Adam he said, "Because you listened to your wife and ate from the tree about which I commanded you, 'You must not eat of it.'

Cursed is the ground because of you, through painful toil you will eat of it all the days of your life. It will produce thorns and thistles for you and you will eat the plants of the field. By the sweat of your brow you will eat your food until you return to the ground, since from it you were taken, for dust you are and to dust you will return

Adam named his wife Eve, because she would become the mother of all living.

The Lord God made garments of skin for Adam and his wife and clothed them. And the Lord God said, "The man has now become like one of us, knowing good and evil. He must not be allowed to reach out his hand and take also from the tree of life and eat, and live forever." So the Lord God banished him from the Garden of Eden to work the ground from which he had been taken. After he drove the man out, he placed on the east side of the Garden of Eden Cherubim and a flaming sword flashing back and forth to guard the way to the tree of life.(Genesis 3:1 – 24)

Adam lay with his wife Eve, and she became pregnant and gave birth to Cain. She said, "With the help of the Lord I have brought forth a man." Later she gave birth to his brother Abel. (Genesis 4:1-2)

Abel kept flocks and Cain worked the soil. (Genesis 4:2)

Adam lay with his wife again, and she gave birth to a son and named him Seth, saying "God has granted me another child in place of Abel, since Cain killed him. (Genesis 4:25)

When Adam had lived 130 years, he had a son in his own likeness, in his own image, and he named him Seth. After Seth was born Adam lived 800 years and had other sons and daughters. He died at the age of 930 years. (Genesis 5:1 – 4)

"But at the beginning of creation God made them male and female. For this reason man will leave his father and mother and be united to his wife, and the two will come one flesh. So they are no longer two, but one. Therefore what God and joined together, let man not separate?" (Mark 10:6 -9)

Anyone who divorces his wife and marries another woman commits adultery against her. And if she divorces her husband and marries another man, she commits adultery.

Lessons to Learn:

When God had finished creating man and animals and plants he saw that there was something missing from man. The LORD said it is not good for man to be alone. I will make a helper suitable for him. Then the LORD God made a woman from the rib he had taken out of the man and brought her to the man. Then the man said, this is now bone of my bones and flesh of my flesh; she shall be called woman for she was taken from man. For this reason a man will leave his father and mother and be united to his wife and they will become one flesh.

Have you ever been the only one in a situation? The only son in your family? The only daughter in your family? The only woman in your company? The only man in your company? The only child in your family? What about helping, would you say women are helpers to their husbands?

God is the Umbrella of Women in the Bible!

23. Hagar – the Mother of Ishmael:

Who Was This Woman

- An Egyptian
- She was Sarai's maidservant
- She was obedient and agreed to sleep with Abram
- She was fruitful in that her son Ishmael had several children
- She despised Sarai as soon as she knew she was pregnant
- She is the mother of Ishmael

The Story:

Hagar was an Egyptian maidservant of Sarai. She was made to sleep with Abram to build a family as Sarai was barren. Abram agreed and Hagar became pregnant and began to despise Sarai. Sarai complained and was told that Hagar was hers and she could do whatever she thought well. Sarai mistreated her and she fled. The Angel of the LORD met her and told her to go back to her mistress as she was pregnant. She said "You are the God who sees me." She bore a son and Abram named him Ishmael. Abram was eighty-six years old then.

Even in her situation, God sent his angel to go and speak to her and she spoke to God.

The Bible and Hagar:

Now Sarai, Abram's wife, had borne him no children. But she had and Egyptian maidservant named Hagar, so she said to Abram, "The Lord has kept me from having children. Go, sleep with my maidservant; perhaps I can build a family through her."

Abram agreed to what Sarai said. So after Abram had been living in Canaan ten years, Sarai his wife took her Egyptian maidservant Hagar and gave her to her husband to be his wife. He slept with Hagar, and she conceived.

When she knew she was pregnant, she began to despise her mistress. Then Sarai said to Abram, "You are responsible for the wrong I am suffering. I put my servant in your arms, and now that she knows she is pregnant, she despises me. May the LORD judge between you and me?"

Your servant is in your hands," Abram said, "Do with her whatever you think best." Then Sarai mistreated Hagar, so she fled from her.

The angel of the Lord found Hagar near a spring in the desert; it was the spring that is beside the road to Shur. And he said, "Hagar, servant of Sarai, where have you come from, and where are you going?" "I'm running away from my mistress Sarai," she answered.

"Then the angel of the Lord told her, "Go back to your mistress and submit to her." The angel added, "I will so increase your descendants that they will be too numerous to count." The angel of the Lord also said told her: "You are now with child and you will have a son. You shall name him Ishmael, for the Lord has heard of your misery. He will be a wild donkey of a man; his hand will be against everyone and everyone's hand against him, and he will live in hostility toward all his brothers."

She gave this name to the Lord who spoke to her: "You are the God who sees me," for she said, "I have now seen the One who sees me." That is why the well was called Beer Lahai Roi; it is still there, between Kadesh and Bered. So Hagar bore Abram a son, and Abram gave the name Ishmael to the son she had born. Abram was eighty-six years old when Hagar bore him Ishmael.. (Genesis 16:1 - 16)

This is the account of Abraham's son Ishmael, whom Sarah's maidservant, Hagar the Egyptian, bore to Abraham.

These are the names of the sons of Ishmael, listed in the order of their birth: Nebaioth the first born of Ishmael, Kedar, Adbeel, Mibsam, Mishma, Dumah, Massa, Hadad, Tema, Jetur, Naphish and Kademah.

These were the sons of Ishmael, and these are the names of the twelve tribal rulers according to their settlements and camps. Altogether, Ishmael lived a hundred and thirty-seven years. Be breathed his last and died, and he was gathered to his people. His descendants settled in the area from Havilah to Shur, near the border of Egypt, as you go toward Asshur. And they lived in hostility toward all their brothers. (Genesis 25:12 – 18)

These were their descendants: Nebaioth the first born of Ishmael, Kedar, Adbeel, Mibsam, Mishma, Dumah, Massa, Hadad, Tema, Jetur, Naphish and Kademah. These were sons of Ishmael. (1 Chronicles 1:29 – 30)

Lessons to Learn:

Think of a situation that can be assisted by Hagar's story, and take action to rectify or solve a problem that you or someone else might be facing. Her son Ishmael is thought to be the father of the Arab nations. What would it tell you? God does not give up on anyone. Imagine her son also had twelve sons: Nebaioth, Kedar, Adbeel, Mibsam, Mishma, Dumah, Massa, Hadad, Tema, Jetur, Naphish and Kademah.

God is the Umbrella of Women in the Bible!

24. Hamutal the Daughter of Jeremiah:

Who Was This Woman?

- She was the mother of Jehoahaz and Zedekiah
- She was the daughter of Jeremiah
- She was from Libnah
- She was the wife of Josiah

The Bible and Hamutal:

Jehoahaz was twenty-three years old when he became king and he reigned in Jerusalem three months. His mother's name was Hamutal daughter of Jeremiah; she was from Libnah. (2 Kings 23:31)

Zedekiah was twenty-one years old when he became king, and he reigned in Jerusalem eleven years. His mother's name was Hamutal daughter of Jeremiah; she was from Libnah.

25. Hannah – the Mother of Samuel:

Who Was this Woman?

- She was barren
- Her husband loved her
- She meant more than ten sons to him
- Her husband took a second wife Peninnah
- She was provoked by Peninnah
- She prayed, fasted and wept
- She was persistent
- She made a vow to the LORD
- She believed in God
- She became pregnant
- She gave birth to a son- Samuel
- She gave him back to the LORD

The Story:

Hannah's story is an extremely challenging one to all the peoples of the world. She was married to a certain man. The story is not about this man but a lot of information is given about him: For example:

He was from Ramathaim
He was a Zuphite from the hill country of Ephraim
His name was Elkanah
He was the son of Jeroham
His father was the son of Elihu
His grandfather was the son of Tohu
His grandfather was the son of Zuph
Zuph was an Ephramite

Hannah's information is that Elkanah had two wives. The first wife was Hannah and the second wife was Peninnah. Hannah was barren and had no children, while Peninnah had several children.

Thus her story unravels, for several years Hannah went to Shiloh with her husband to worship and sacrifice to the Mighty God. Elkanah always gave portions of the meat to his family, Peninnah, her sons and daughters and Hannah. To Hannah he always gave a double portion. This was a sign of favoritism because he loved her. Then you wonder whether he loved Peninnah!

The Bible says God had closed her womb. God always has a purpose for everything. God knows everything and God is everywhere and sees everything that is going on.

But Peninnah used to ridicule her and frustrate her on a daily basis, may be reminding her that she had no children. She provoked Hannah and made sure she was irritated. This went on year after year. Even when she was at the house of the LORD; Peninnah continued to provoke her until she cried and would not eat. Then Peninnah was happy with her actions.

Elkanah would notice that Hannah was crying and would come over to comfort her. He knew the problem of not having children was bothering her. He would ask her why she was weeping. He would ask why she was not eating and why she was downhearted. He thought he meant more to her than ten sons. Surely, Elkanah was not enough for her. When you want a child you want a child. No matter how much the husband loves you, you still want a child. Even men want children too and they can go to all extends to get them. In Hannah's case Elkanah had several children from Peninnah.

At one time they were at Shiloh, after they had finished eating and drinking Hannah stood up. She made up her mind that she was going to speak to the LORD about her problem. She wept in bitterness of soul and she said: "O LORD Almighty, if you would only look upon your servant's misery, and remember me, and not forget your servant but give her a son, then I will give him to the LORD for all the days of his life, no razor will ever be used on his head."

When you are serious words just come out of your mouth from your heart. Hannah did:

- Look upon me – my misery
- Remember me
- Do not forget me
- Give me a son
- I will give him back to you
- No razor will be used on his head

Once you make up your mind as to what you want God to do for you; you will be able to spell it out. At that point you will come out of your comfort zone and you will really know that it is between you and God. You will not care who is looking at you or what you are doing. You will be in another place altogether. A place where you know God is there for you and you can say anything to him he is your father.

Eli the priest was sitting on a chair by the doorpost of the LORD's temple, and he observed that Hannah's mouth was moving. Hannah was praying in her heart but her lips were moving, but her voice was not being heard. God only was hearing what she was saying. Eli asked her how long she was going to keep on getting drunk; and asked her to get rid of the wine.

Hannah explained to Eli that she was greatly troubled that she had not been drinking wine or beer. She told him that she was pouring out her soul to the LORD. She was not a wicked woman. She told him that she was praying out of great anguish and grief (deep sorrow).

The priest told her to go in peace and he also prayed that the God of Israel may grant her what she had asked of him.

Hannah was grateful and said to Eli "May your servant find favour in your eyes." She actually was no more downcast. The power of prayer had changed everything.

They worshipped the LORD, and left and went back to Ramah. Elkanah lay with Hannah, the LORD remembered her. In the course of time she conceived and gave birth to a son. She named him Samuel (asked God – in Hebrew) saying because she asked the LORD.

When Samuel was weaned, Hannah took him to Eli, where he lived for the rest of his life.

The LORD was gracious and gave Hannah more children. In the end Hannah had three more sons and two daughters. God will always listen to our prayers and also expects us to keep our part of the bargain. If you promise to do anything for God, do not slack, do it and God will bless you even more.

Sometimes when you need something seriously, you make promises to God and it is important to keep those promises when the good thing has happened to you and Hannah did. Hannah knew that if God will give her the first son, then surely she will have other children after him. She believed it.

When you read about Hannah remember that she was the mother of a Prophet, and a Circuit Judge Samuel. The Lord blessed her and she had five other children.

Even now many women who become second or third wives, as in some African marriages which allow men to have more than one wife, the first wife is always ridiculed by the second or third. Sometimes the first and second wives become friendly only when they want to fight against the third or fourth wife.

God created Adam and Eve and that was the type of marriage he had for mankind. However, we always end up doing the wrong thing all the time. If there was no forgiveness I wonder where we would all be.

That is Hannah's Story what's yours?

The Bible and Hannah:

There was a certain man from Ramathaim, a Zuphite from the hill country of Ephraim, whose name was Elkanah son of Jeroham, the son of Elihu, the son of Tohu, the son of Zuph, and Ephramite. He had two wives; one was called

Hannah and the other Peninnah. Peninnah had children but Hannah had none.

Year after year this man went up from his town to worship and sacrifice to the LORD Almighty at Shiloh, where Hophni and Phinehas, the two sons of Eli, were priests of the LORD. Whenever the day came for Elkanah to sacrifice, he would give portions of the meat to his wife Peninnah and to all her sons and daughters. But to Hannah he gave a double portion because he loved her, and the LORD had closed her womb, her rival kept provoking her in order to irritate her. This went on year after year. When Hannah went up to the house of the LORD, her rival provoked her till she wept and would not eat. Elkanah her husband would say to her, "Hannah, why are you weeping? Why don't you eat? Why are you downhearted? Don't I mean more to you than ten sons?"

Once when they had finished eating and drinking in Shiloh, Hannah stood up. Now Eli the priest was sitting on a chair by the doorpost of the LORD's temple. In bitterness of soul Hannah wept much and prayed to the LORD And she made a vow, saying, "O LORD Almighty, if you will only look upon your servant's misery and remember me, and not forget your servant but give her a son, then I will give him to the LORD for all the days of his life, and no razor will ever be used on his head."

As she kept on praying to the LORD, Eli observed her mouth. Hannah was praying in her heart, and her lips were moving but her voice was not heard. Eli thought she was drunk and said to her, "How long will you keep on getting drunk? Get rid of your wine."

"Not so, my lord," Hannah replied, "I am a woman who is deeply troubled. I have not been drinking wine or beer; I was pouring out my soul to the LORD. Do not take your servant for a wicked woman; I have been praying her out of my great anguish and grief;"

Eli answered, "Go in peace, and May the God of Israel grant you what you have asked of him."

She said, "May your servant find favour in your eyes." Then she went her way and ate something and her face was no longer downcast.

Early the next morning they arose and worshiped before the LORD and then went back to their home at Ramah. Elkana lay with Hannah his wife, and the LORD remembered her. So in the course of time Hannah conceived and gave birth to a son.

She named him Samuel, saying, "Because I asked the LORD for him."

When the man Elkanah went up with all his family to offer the annual sacrifice to the LORD and to fulfill his vow, Hannah did not go. She said to her husband. "After the boy is weaned, I will take him and present him before the LORD, and he will live there always."

"Do what seems best to you," Elkanah her husband told her. "Stay here until you have weaned him; only may the LORD make good his work." So the woman stayed at home and nursed her son until she had weaned him.

After he was weaned, she took the boy with her, young as he was, along with a three year old bull, an Ephah of flour and a skin of wine, and brought him to the house of the LORD at Shiloh. When they had slaughtered the bull, they brought the boy to Eli, and she said to him, "As surely as you live, my lord, I am the woman who stood here beside you praying to the LORD. I prayed for this child, and the LORD has granted me what I asked of him. So now I give him to the LORD. For the whole life he will be given over to the LORD." And he worshiped the LORD there. (1 Samuel 1:1 – 28)

But Samuel was ministering before the LORD – a boy wearing a linen ephod. Each year his mother made him a little robe and took it to him when she went up with her husband to offer the annual sacrifice. Eli would bless Elkanah and his wife, saying "May the LORD give you children by this woman to take the place of the one she prayed for and gave to the LORD." Then they would go home. And the LORD was gracious to Hannah; she conceived and gave birth to three sons and two daughters. Meanwhile, the boy Samuel grew up in the presence of the LORD.

(1 Samuel 2:18 – 21)

Then Hannah prayed and said:

My heart rejoices in the Lord, in the LORD my horn (strength) is lifted high. My mouth boasts over my enemies, for I delight in your deliverance.

There is no one holy like the LORD, there is no one besides you; there is no Rock like our God.

Do not keep talking so proudly or let your mouth speak such arrogance for the LORD is a God who knows and by him deeds are weighed.

The bows of the warriors are broken, but those who stumbled are armed with strength.

Those who were full hire themselves out for food, but those who were hungry hunger no more. She who was barren has borne seven children but she who has had many sons pines away.

The Lord brings death and makes alive, he brings down to the grave and raises up.

The LORD sends poverty and wealth; he humbles and he exalts

He raises the poor from the dust and lifts the needy from the ash heap; he seats them with princes and has them inherit a throne of honour. "For the foundations of the earth are the LORD's; upon them he has set the world;

He will guard the feet of his saints, but the wicked will be silenced in darkness;

"It is not by Strength that one prevails; those who oppose the LORD will be shattered. He will thunder against them from heaven; the LORD will judge the ends of the earth. "He will give strength to his king and exalt the horn (strength) to his anointed."

Then Elkanah went to Ramah, but the boy ministered before the LORD under Eli the priest. (1 Samuel 2:1 – 11)

Lessons to Learn:

- Hannah became the Mother of a Prophet Samuel
- Samuel was also a Judge
- She had five more children three sons and two daughters
- God Answers Prayers
- Today women still are in the habit of provoking other women is similar situations as Hannah was
- I would rather be in a monogamous marriage what about you?

God is the Umbrella of Women in the Bible!

26. Hazzelelponi – The daughter of Etam:

She was the sister of Jezreel, Ishma and Idbash, the sons of Etam. (1 Chronicles 4:3)

God is the Umbrella of Women in the Bible!

27. Herodias – the wife of Philip:

Who Was This Woman?

- She was the granddaughter of Herod the Great
- She caused the arrest of John the Baptist
- John had told Herod that it was not lawful for him to have his brother's wife
- Her daughter danced on Herod's birthday
- Herod promised to give her anything she asked for
- Herodias prompted her daughter to ask for John the Baptist's head on a platter
- Herod ordered that her request be granted
- John was beheaded in prison
- His head was brought in a platter and given to the girl
- The girl carried the head to her mother
- The disciples of John took his body and buried it

- Then they went and told Jesus

The Story:

Herodias was known for being a woman who would stop at nothing to get what she wanted. She was married in an arranged marriage to Herod the II also known as Philip. They had a daughter named Salome.

She divorced Philip and married his brother Herod, because she felt he was in better standing than her own husband. On Herod's birthday her daughter danced for them.

Herod was so pleased with the dance that he promised to give the daughter anything that she would ask for. She went and asked her mother what she could ask for. Herodias, since he did not like John the Baptist then told her to ask for his head on a platter.

Herod, who also had been told off by John the Baptist, and who privately would have loved to kill John, pretended that he could do nothing but to have John killed and his head brought to the girl.

The girl got the head on the platter and carried it to her mother. What a terrible thing to do to John the Baptist, what a terrible thing to do her own daughter. She was a mean woman and she wanted to marry her husband's brother; which was against Jewish law. If the brother had died then inheritance would be arranged but she wanted him there and then.

The Bible and Herodias:

Now Herod had arrested John and bound him and put him in prison because of Herodias, his brother Philip's wife, for

John had been saying to him: "It is not lawful for you to have her." (Matthew 14:3)

On Herod's birthday the daughter of Herodias danced for them and pleased Herod so much that he promised with an oath to give her, whatever she asked. Prompted by her mother she said, "Give me here on a platter the head of John the Baptist."

The king was distressed, but because of his oaths and his dinner guests, he ordered that her request be granted and had John beheaded in the prison. His head was brought in on a platter and given to the girl, who carried it to her mother. John's disciples came and took his body and buried it. They went and told Jesus. (Matthew 14:6 – 12)

Lessons to Learn:

- John the Baptist was beheaded
- Her husband was exiled when he could not become king

God is the Umbrella of Women in the Bible!

28. Huldah – the Prophetess:

Who Was This Woman?

- She was a Prophetess
- She was the wife of Shallum son of Tikvah, the son of Harhas, keeper of the wardrobe.
- She lived in Jerusalem, in the Second District.
- God spoke to her and she told people what He had said
- Josiah the king renewed the covenant in the presence of the LORD

The Story:

Huldah was the wife of Shullum son of Tikvah, the son of Harhas, keeper of the wardrobe. She lived in Jerusalem, in the Second District.

When King Josiah sent Hilkiah the priest, Ahikam, Acbor, Shaphan and Asaiah to speak to her she told them what the LORD, the God of Israel had said. That he was going to bring disaster on their place and their people, according to everything written in the book the king of Judah has read. Because they had forsaken God and burned incense to other gods and provoked God to anger by all the idols their hands had made, His anger was going to burn against their place and will not be quenched.'

Huldah told them to go and tell the king of Judah, who had sent them to inquire of the LORD, that "This is what the LORD, the God of Israel, says concerning the words he heard: " Because your heart was responsive and you humbled yourself before the LORD when you heard what I had spoken against this place and its people, that they would become accursed and laid waste, and because you tore your robes and wept in my presence, I have heard you, declares the LORD. Therefore I will gather you to your fathers, and you will be buried in peace. Your eyes will not see all the disaster I am going to bring on this place." Huldah sent them back to king Josiah.

The Bible and Huldah:

Josiah was eight years old when he became king and he reigned in Jerusalem thirty-one years. His mother's name was Jedidah daughter of Adaiah; she was from Bozkath. He did what was right in the eyes of the LORD and walked in all the ways of his father David, not turning aside to the right or to the left.

In the eighteenth year of his reign, King Josiah sent the secretary, Shaphan son of Azaliah, the son of Meshullum, to the temple of the LORD. He said: "Go up to Hilkiah the high priest and have him get ready the money that has been brought into temple of the LORD. Which the doorkeepers have collected from the people. Have them entrust it to the men appointed to supervise the work on the temple. And have these men pay the workers who repair the temple of the LORD - the carpenters, the builders and the masons. Also have them purchase timber and dressed stone to repair the temple. But they need not account for the money entrusted to them, because they are acting faithfully."

Hilkiah the high priest said to Shaphan the secretary, "I have found the Book of the Law in the temple of the LORD." He gave it to Shaphan, who read it. Then Shaphan the secretary went to the king and reported to him. "Your officials have paid out the money that was in the temple of the LORD and have entrusted it to the workers and supervisors at the temple." Then Shaphan the secretary informed the king, "Hilkiah the priest has given me a book." And Shaphan read from it in the presence of the king.

When the king heard the words of the Book of the Law, he tore his robes. He gave these orders to Hilkiah the priest, Ahikam son of Shaphan, Acbor son of Micaiah, Shaphan the secretary and Asaiah the king's attendant: "Go and inquire of the LORD for me and for the people and for all Judah about what is written in this book that has been found. Great is the LORD's anger that burns against us because our fathers have not obeyed the words of this book; they have not acted in accordance with all that is written there concerning us."

Hilkiah the priest, Ahikam, Acbor, Shaphan and Asaiah went to speak to the prophetess Huldah, who was the wife of Shullum son of Tikvah, the son of Harhas, keeper of the wardrobe. She lived in Jerusalem, in the Second District.

She said to them, "This is what the LORD, the God of Israel, says: Tell the man who sent you to me, 'This is what the LORD says: I am going to bring disaster on this place and its people, according to everything written in the book the king of Judah has read. Because they have forsaken me and burned incense to other gods and provoked me to anger by all the idols their hands have made, my anger will burn against this place and will not be quenched.' Tell the king of Judah, who sent you to inquire of the LORD, "This is what the LORD, the God of Israel, says concerning the words you heard: Because your heart was responsive and you humbled yourself before the LORD when you heard what I have spoken against this place and its people, that they would become accursed and laid waste, and because you tore your robes and wept in my presence, I have heard you, declares the LORD. Therefore I will gather you to your fathers, and you will be buried in peace. Your eyes will not see all the disaster I am going to bring on this place." So they took her answer back to the king. (2 Kings 22:1 – 20

Lessons to Learn:

- God spoke to her and told her everything to tell the people who had been sent to her by King Josiah. What are your experiences of God speaking to you?
- King Josiah renewed the Covenant in the presence of the LORD

God is the Umbrella of Women in the Bible!

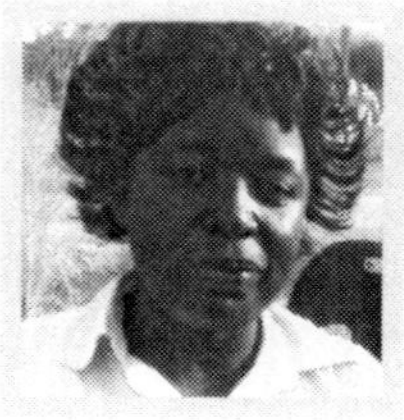
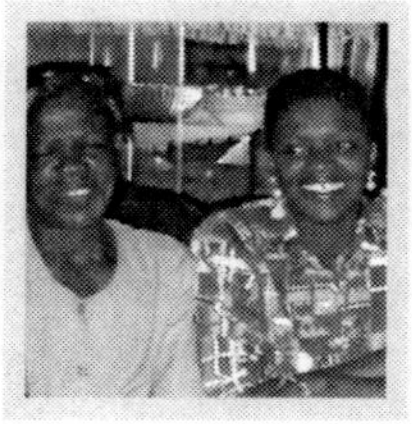
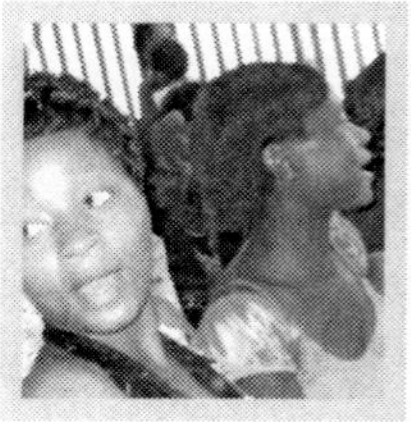
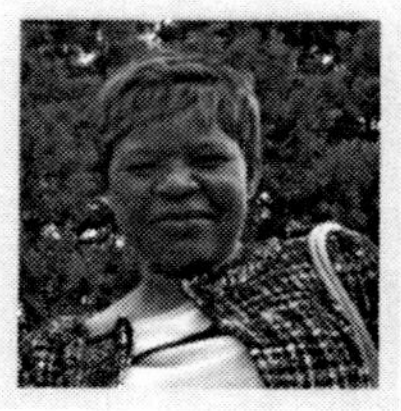
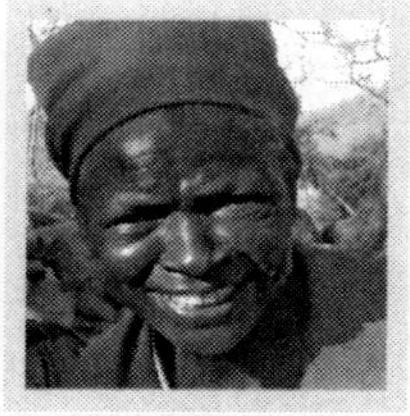
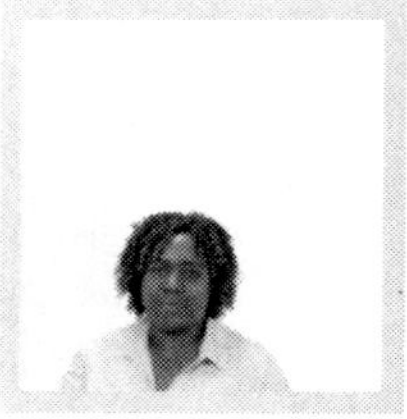
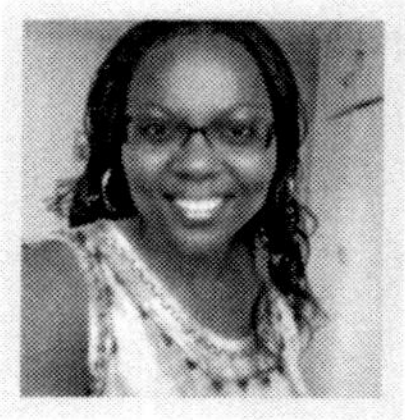
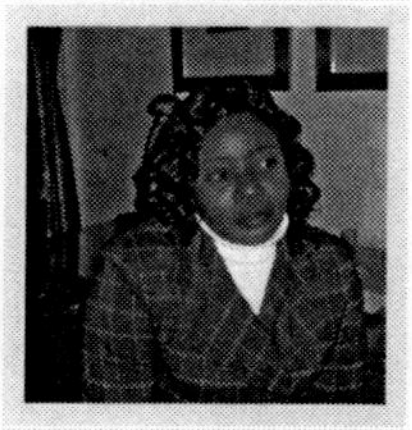
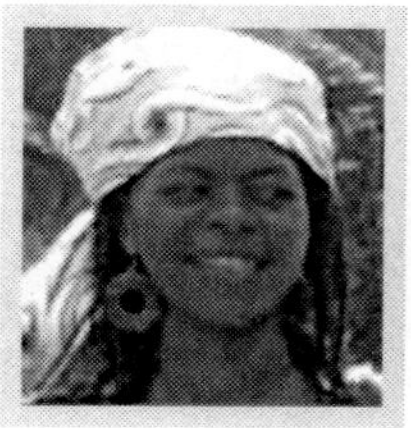
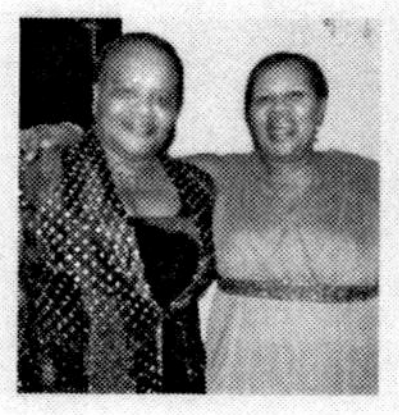
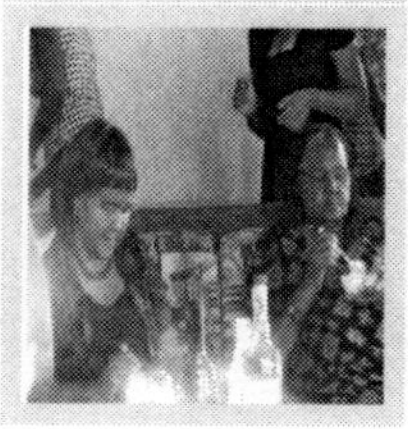
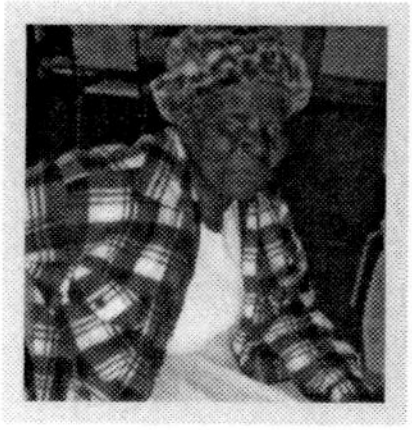

3

29. Jael - the Killer of Sisera

Who Was This Woman?

- She was the wife of Heber a Nomadic man
- She was a metal worker
- She was aware of what was happening around her
- She knew Sisera and what he was famous for
- She welcomed him
- She listened to his orders to stand in the doorway
- She gave him milk
- She drove the peg into Sisera's temple
- She killed Sisera

The Story:

Jael killed Sisera a Canaanite commander who had terrorized Israel for twenty years. God had already planned that a woman was going to kill Sisera as stated in Judges 4:9 – "Very well" Deborah said, "I will go with you but because of the way you are going about this, the honour will not be yours the LORD will hand Sisera to a woman." The woman in this case was Jael.

Jael went out to meet Sisera and said to him, "Come, my lord, come right in. Don't be afraid." So he entered her tent, and she put a covering over him. "I am thirsty," he said. "Please give me some water." She opened a skin of mild, gave him a drink, and covered him up. Stand in the doorway of the tent," he told her, "If someone comes by and asks you, 'Is anyone here?' Say 'No.'" But Jael Heber's wife picked up a tent peg and a hammer and went quietly to him while he lay fast asleep, exhausted, she drove the peg through his temple into the ground, and he died.

The Bible and Jael:

But Jael, Heber's wife, picked up a tent peg and a hammer and went quietly to him while he lay fast asleep, exhausted. She drove the peg through his temple into the ground, and he died.

Barak came by in pursuit of Sisera, and Jael went out to meet him. "Come" she said, "I will show you the man you're looking for." So he went in with her, and there lay Sisera with the tent peg through his temple – dead. On that day God subdued Jabin, the Canaanite king, before the Israelites. And the hand of Israelites grew stronger and stronger against Jabin, the Canaanite king, until they destroyed him. (Judges 4:18 – 24)

Lessons to Learn:

- Jael a woman was given the honour of killing Sisera

- Jael was aware of what was going on in her society
- Do you know what is going on around you?
- Would you know people who running away from something if you see them?
- Would you take immediate action like Jael did?
- What is important for you in society?
- Is it trying to prove to people that you are always doing what is right?
- Is it ignoring or shutting you away from general events?
- I remember people who used to believe that if you are poor you should look poor?
- What do you think?
- Was Sisera out of touch with his people here?
- God was there for Jael she was there to be used by him.

God is the Umbrella of Women in the Bible!

30. Jochebed – The Mother of Moses

Who Was This Woman

- The daughter of Levi
- Her husband was Amram
- She was Amram's father's sister
- She is the mother of three prophets
- She is a woman of faith
- She placed Moses in the basket in the River Nile
- She breastfed Moses in Pharaoh's daughter's house
- She is an important figure in the bible
- The mother of Moses
- The mother of Aaron
- The mother of Miriam
- The sister of Geshon, Kohath, Merari

The Story:

Like most people in her days Jochebed was married to Amram who was a descended of Levi who was the third son of Jacob. Jochebed was an aunt to Amram. She was his father's sister.

When the Israelites, were living in Egypt they became numerous that Pharaoh was so worried about their numbers. Firstly, he decided to work them hard so that they could die from exhaustion. However that did not work. The Israelites were a strong people. No wonder God chose them.

Then Pharaoh decided that the best thing was to throw the baby boys into the River Nile, and several were thrown into the river. Jochebed decided to keep her son for three months hidden. Then she prepared a papyrus basket and sealed it with tar. She placed her baby in it and floated it on the Nile River.

Her daughter Miriam stood at the bank of the river Nile and watched her brother floating in a basket. She was looking out for someone to pick him up.

Pharaoh's daughter came to the river to bathe with her servants. She noticed the basket and asked the servant to go and pick it up out of the water. She discovered that a baby was in the basket.

Miriam who was watching from a distance went to Pharaoh's daughter and offered to look for a Hebrew woman who could look after the baby; to which she agreed. Miriam went to her mother and told her what had happened. Then she brought her to Pharaoh's daughter.

Pharaoh's daughter instructed her to look after her baby and nurse him and bring him back when he was a little older. She did feed her own baby and returned him to Pharaoh's daughter, who named him Moses meaning that she drew him out of water.

Florence Mutambanengwe

The Bible and Jochebed:

Now a man of the house of Levi married a Levite woman, and she became pregnant and gave birth to a son. When she saw that he was a fine child, she hid him for three months. But when she could hide him no longer, she got a papyrus basket for him and coated it with tar and pitch. Then she placed the child in it and put it among the reeds along the bank of the Nile. His sister stood at a distance to see what would happen to him.

Then Pharaoh's daughter went down to the Nile to bathe, and her attendants were walking along the river back. She saw the basket among the reeds and sent her slave girl to get it. She opened it and saw the baby. He was crying, and she felt sorry for him. "This is one of the Hebrew babies," she said.

Then his sister asked Pharaoh's daughter, "Shall I go and get one of the Hebrew women to nurse the baby for you?"

"Yes, go," she answered. And the girl went and got the baby's mother. Pharaoh's daughter said to her, "Take this baby and nurse him for me, and I will pay you." So the woman took the baby and nursed him. When the child grew older she took him to Pharaoh's daughter and he became her son. She named him Moses, saying, "I drew him out of the water." (Exodus 2:1 – 10)

Jochebed was the youngest daughter of Levi, who was born in Egypt. Her marriage fell out with the laws of Moses because Amram her husband was her brother's son. She planned to save her son from being killed by placing him in a basket in the River Nile. She got employed by Pharaoh's daughter. She was the mother of Miriam, Aaron and Moses. She was buried in the tomb of the Matriarchs in Tiberius. It is important that something is written about this important woman in the bible. (Numbers 26:29)

Amram married his father's sister Jochebed, who bore him Aaron, Moses and Miriam. (Exodus 6:20)

Lessons to Learn:

- She saved Moses
- She nursed her son Moses
- Moses was used by God to liberate the Israelites
- All her children were used by God Miriam, Aaron and Moses
- She played a major role in the history of mankind.

God is the Umbrella of Women in the Bible!

31. Jehosheba – the Wife of Jehoiada the Priest:

Who Was This Woman?

- She was the daughter of King Jehoram
- She was the wife of the Priest Jehoiada
- She was Ahaziah's sister
- Ahazia was the father of Joash
- She hid the child from Athalia who was killing all princes
- She hid him for six years in the temple of the LORD

The Bible and Jehosheba:

When Athaliah the mother of Ahaziah saw that her son was dead, she proceeded to destroy the whole royal family of the house of Judah. But Jehosheba, the daughter of King Jehoram, took Joash son of Ahazia and stole him away from among the royal princes who were about to be murdered and put him and his nurse in a bedroom. Because Jehosheba, the daughter of King Jehoram wife of the priest Jehoiada, was

Ahaziah's sister, she hid the child from Athaliah so she could not kill him. He remained hidden with them at the temple of God for six years while Athaliah ruled the land.

Lessons to Learn:

- What can you do to stand up for what is right in society today?
- She risked being killed by Athalia
- Can you list any similar situations that you might have heard of?
- Jehosheba was a woman with a controlled tongue
- Can you keep a secret for six years?

God is the Umbrella of Women in the Bible!

32. Jezebel –the Wife of Ahab:

Who was this Woman?

- She worshipped the Canaanite gods Baal and Asherah
- She was a Phoenician Princess and was Ahab's wife
- She was the daughter of Ethbaal king of the Sidonians
- She almost wiped out Judaism as she killed religious leaders
- She elevated some religious leaders
- She supported a religious congress with treasury money
- 450 Baal prophets and 400 Ashera prophets
- She tried to kill God's prophets but 100 survived
- On Mount Carmel Elijah challenged the prophets of Baal and Asherah to call down fire from the sky to burn their sacrifices

- The people then killed the Baal prophets after God had sent down fire on Elijah's call
- She caused the death of Naboth

The Story:

Jezebel was the daughter of King Ethbaal and was therefore a princess. Her father was the king of the Sidonians, who lived in what is now known as Lebanon. She had grown up living in a palace with her family. She is a type of person who must have always dreamt and schemed to one day become Queen of some place and how she should rule her people ruthlessly.

King Omri of Israel arranged the marriage of his son Ahab to Jezebel. Knowing very well that it was not the right thing to do. Jezebel worshipped Baal and Asherah and as a result influenced her husband to do evil in the eyes of the LORD.

At one time Ahab asked Naboth to give him his vineyard so that he could use it for a vegetable garden. Imagine someone coming and asking you to surrender you vineyard which you have inherited from your forefathers, for that purpose. Naboth refused and Jezebel organized the stoning and killing of Naboth to get the vineyard for Ahab. This was done and a message was sent to Jezebel saying, "Naboth has been stoned and is dead." Then she told her husband to go and takeover the vineyard because Naboth was dead. You would think that Ahab would have been surprised how Naboth had died; no he went straight ahead and took over the vineyard.

Jezebel's actions caused God to send the prophet Elijah to tell Ahab that what had happened was evil and he was going to be punished for it. When Ahab was killed the dogs licked up his blood, as the word of the LORD had declared. When Jezebel died she was eaten by dogs also as the word of the LORD had also said. What a horrible end to a horrible life!

The Bible and Jezebel:

In the thirty-eighth year of Asa king of Judah, Ahab son of Omri became king of Israel, and he reigned in Samaria over Israel twenty two years. Ahab son of Omri did more evil in the eyes of the Lord than any of those before him. He not only considered it trivial to commit the sins of Jeroboam son of Nebat, but he also married Jezebel daughter of Ethbaal king of the Sidonians, and began to serve Baal and worship him. He set up an altar for Baal in the temple of Baal that he built in Samaria. Ahab also made an Asherah pole and did more to provoke the Lord, the God of Israel, to anger than did all the kings of Israel before him.

In Ahab's time, Hiel of Bethel rebuilt Jericho. He laid its foundations at the cost of his firstborn son Abiram, and he set up its gates at the cost of his youngest son Segub, in accordance with the word of the Lord spoken by Joshua son of Nun.

(1 Kings 16:29 – 34)

His wife Jezebel came in and asked him, "Why are you so sullen? Why won't you eat? He answered her, "Because I said to Naboth the Jezreelite, 'Sell me your vineyard; or if you prefer, I will give you another vineyard in its place.' But he said, 'I will not give you my vineyard.'"

Jezebel his wife said, "Is this how you act as king over Israel? Get up and eat! Cheer up. I'll get you the vineyard of Naboth the Jezreelite."

So she wrote letters in Ahab's name, placed his seal on them, and sent then to the elders and nobles who lived in Naboth's city with him. In those letters she wrote: "Proclaim a day of fasting and seat Naboth in a prominent place among the people. But seat two scoundrels opposite him and have

God is the Umbrella of Women in the Bible

them testify that he has cursed both God and the king. Then take him out and stone him to death." (1 Kings 21:5 – 10)

As soon as Jezebel heard that Naboth had been stoned to death, she said to Ahab, "Get up and take possession of the vineyard of Naboth the Jezreelite that he refused to sell you. He is no longer alive, but dead." (1 Kings 21:15)

And also concerning Jezebel the LORD says: 'Dogs will devour Jezebel by the wall of Jezreel.' "Dogs will eat those belonging to Ahab, who die in the city and the birds of the air will feed on those who die in the country."

(There was never a man like Ahab, who sold himself to do evil in the eyes of the LORD, urged on by Jezebel his wife. He behaved in the vilest manner by going after idols, like the Amorites the LORD drove out before Israel.)(1 Kings 21:26)

So the king died and was brought to Samaria, and they buried him there. They washed the chariot at a pool in Samaria (where the prostitutes bathed), and the dogs leaked up his blood, as the word of the LORD had declared. (1 Kings 22:37 – 38)

As for Jezebel, dogs will devour her on the plot of ground at Jezreel, and no one will bury her." Then he opened the door and ran. (2 Kings 9:10)

Then Jehu went to Jezreel. When Jezebel heard about it, she painted her eyes, arranged her hair and looked out of a window. As Jehu entered the gate, she asked, "Have you come in peace, Zimri, you murderer of your master?"

He looked up at the window and called out, "Who is on my side? Two or three eunuchs looked down at him. "Throw her down!" Jehu said. So they threw her down, and some of her blood spattered the wall and the horsed as they trampled her underfoot.

Jehu went in and ate and drank. "Take care of that cursed woman," he said, "and bury her, for she was a king's daughter" But when they went out to bury her, they found nothing except her skull, her feet and her hands. They went back and told Jehu, who said, "This is the word of the LORD that he spoke through his servant Elijah the Tishbite: On the plot of ground at Jezreel dogs will devour Jezebel's flesh. Jezebel's body will be like refuse on the ground in the plot at Jezreel, so that no one will be able to say: This is Jezebel'" (2 Kings 9:30 – 37)

Jehu then set out and went towards Samaria; he met some relatives of Ahaziah king of Judah and asked, "Who are you?" They said, "We are relatives of Ahaziah, and we have come down to great the families of the king and of the queen mother." (2 Kings 10:12 – 13)

Lessons to Learn:

- What goes up comes down. She was thrown down from a window
- Her flesh was eaten by dogs to the point that no one would again say this is Jezebel
- Have you had experiences where you have lived with such cruel women as Jezebel?
- Destroying families is not the answer is it?
- Destroying churches is not the answer is it?
- Destroying each other is not the answer is it?
- God sees all our actions and one day it will catch up as it did with Jezebel?

God is the Umbrella of Women in the Bible!

33. Ketura – The Wife Abraham Married after Sarah Died:

Who Was This Woman?

- She was Abraham's wife after Sarah died
- She was a Mother of six boys
- She was a grandmother

The Story:

Ketura's story starts with: Abraham took another wife, whose name was Keturah. Then it goes on to list the children she had with him which are six boys. These sons also had several children.

It is clear that Abraham took Ketura after Sarah's death. Sarah died when she was one hundred and twenty seven years old and Abraham died when he was one hundred and seventy five years old. That was a good forty-eight years after Sarah's death.

Abraham also gave gifts to her children when he was still alive and he actually sent them away to settle away from Isaac.

Florence Mutambanengwe

The Bible and Ketura:

Abraham took another wife, whose name was Keturah. She bore him Zimran, Jokshan, Medan, Midian, Ishbak and Shuah. Jokshan was the father of Sheba and Dedan; the descendants of Dedan were the Asshurites, the Letushites and the Leummites. The sons of Midian were Ephah, Epher, Hanoch, Abida and Eldaah. All these were descendants of Ketura.

Abraham left everything he owned to Isaac. But while he was still living, he gave gifts to the sons of his concubines and sent them away from his son Isaac to the land of the east.

Altogether, Abraham lived a hundred and seventy-five years. Then Abraham breathed his last and died at a good old age, an old man and full of years; and he was buried in the cave of Machpelah near Mamre, in the field of Ephron son of Zohar the Hittite, the field Abraham had bought from the Hittites. There Abraham was buried with his wife Sarah. After Abraham's death, God blessed his son Isaac, who then lived near Beer Lahai Roi. (Genesis 25:1 – 11)

The sons born to Keturah, Abraham's concubine: Zimran, Jokshan, Medan, Midian, Ishbak and Shua.

The sons of Jokshan: Sheba and Dedan.

The sons of Midian: Ephah, Epher, Hanoch. Abida and Eldaah.

All these were descendants of Ketura. (1 Chronicles 1:32 – 33)

Lessons to Learn:

- Several tribes came from Ketura's sons who are descendants of Abraham

God is the Umbrella of Women in the Bible!

34. Leah – the First Wife of Jacob:

Who Was This Woman?

- Jacob was tricked into marrying her
- The Lord opened her womb when He saw that she was not loved.
- Reuben – Was her first son, she named him that because she said the Lord had seen her misery
- Simeon – Was her second son, she named him that because she said the Lord heard that she was not loved
- Levi – Was her third son, she named him that because she said her husband will become attached to her
- Judah was her fourth son, she named him that because she said this time she would praise the Lord
- She gave her maidservant Zilpah to her husband

- Gad – Was her fifth son birthed by Zilpah, she named him that because she said what good fortune
- Asher – Was her sixth son birthed by Zilpah, she named him that because she said how happy she was and all women will call her happy
- Reuben brought some mandrake plants to his mother
- Rachel asked Leah for her son's mandrakes
- Leah gave her in exchange of sleeping with Jacob that night
- Issacher – Was her seventh son, she named him that because she said God had rewarded her for giving her maidservant to her husband
- Zebulum – Was her eighth son, she named him that because she said God had presented her with a precious gift. This time her husband would treat her with honor, because she had borne him a sixth son
- Dinah – Some time later she gave birth to a daughter and named her Dinah
- Leah had six sons and one daughter and her maidservant bore her two sons; making a total of nine children for Jacob from Leah's side (Genesis 31 and 32)

The Story:

Jacob was tricked into marrying her. The Lord opened her womb when He saw that she was not loved. Reuben – Was her first son, she named him that because she said the Lord had seen her misery. Simeon – Was her second son, she named him that because she said the Lord heard that she was not loved. Levi – Was her third son, she named him that because she said her husband will become attached to her. Judah was her fourth son, she named him that because she said this time she would praise the Lord.

She gave her maidservant Zilpah to her husband. Gad – Was her fifth son birthed by Zilpah, she named him that because she said what good fortune. Asher – Was her sixth son birthed by Zilpah, she named him that because she said how happy she was and all women will call her happy. Her son Reuben brought some mandrake plants to her. Rachel asked Leah for her son's mandrakes Leah gave her in exchange of sleeping with Jacob that night. Issacher – Was her seventh son, she named him that because she said God had rewarded her for giving her maidservant to her husband. Zebulum – Was her eighth son, she named him that because she said God had presented her with a precious gift. This time her husband would treat her with honor, because she had borne him a sixth son. Some time later she gave birth to a daughter and named her Dinah. Leah had six sons and one daughter and her maidservant bore her two sons; making a total of nine children for Jacob from Leah's

The Bible and Leah:

Then Jacob continued on his journey and came to the land of the eastern peoples. There he saw a well in the field, with three flocks of sheep lying near it because the flocks were watered from that well. The stone over the mouth of the well was large. When all the flocks were gathered there, the shepherds would roll the stone away from the well's mouth and water the sheep. Then they would return the stone to its place over the mouth of the well.

Jacob asked the shepherds, "My brothers, where are you from?"

"We are from Haran," they replied.

He said to them, "Do you know Laban, Nahor's grandson?"

"Yes, we know him," they answered.

Then Jacob asked them, "Is he well?"

"Yes, he is," they said, "and here comes his daughter Rachel with the sheep."

"Look," he said, "the sun is still high; it is not time for the flocks to be gathered. Water the sheep and take them back to pasture."

"We can't," they replied, "until all the flocks are gathered and the stone has been rolled away from the mouth of the well. Then we will water the sheep."

While he was still talking with them, Rachel came with her father's sheep, for she was a shepherdess. When Jacob saw Rachel daughter of Laban, his mother's brother, and Laban's sheep, he went over and rolled the stone away from the mouth of the well and watered his uncle's sheep. Then Jacob kissed Rachel and began to weep aloud. He had told Rachel that he was a relative of her father and a son of Rebekah. So she ran and told her father.

As soon as Laban heard the news about Jacob, his sister's son, he hurried to meet him. He embraced him and kissed him and brought him to his home, and there Jacob told him all these things. Then Laban said to him. "You are my own flesh and blood."

(Genesis 29:1 – 14)

After Jacob had stayed with him for a whole month, Laban said to him, "Just because you are a relative of mine, should you work for me for nothing? Tell me what your wages should be." Now Laban had two daughters; the name of the older was Leah, and the name of the younger was Rachel. Leah had weak eyes, but Rachel was lovely in form, and beautiful. Jacob was in love with Rachel and said, "I will work for you seven years in return for your younger daughter."

Laban said, "It's better that I give her to you than to some other man. Stay here with me." So Jacob served seven years to get Rachel, but they seemed like only a few days to him because of his love for her.

Then Jacob said to Laban, "Give me my wife. My time is completed, and I want to lie with her."

So Laban brought together all the people of the place and gave a feast. But when evening came, he took his daughter Leah and gave her to Jacob, and Jacob lay with her. And Laban gave his servant girl Zilpah to his daughter as her maidservant.

When morning came, there was Leah! So Jacob said to Laban, "What is this you have done to me? I served you for Rachel, didn't I? Why have you deceived me?"

Laban replied, "It is not our custom here to give the younger daughter in marriage before the older one. Finish this daughter's bridal week; then we will give you the younger one also, in return for another seven years of work."

And Jacob did so. He finished the week with Leah, and then Laban gave his daughter Rachel to be his wife. Laban gave his servant girl, Bilhah to his daughter Rachel as her maid servant. Jacob lay with Rachel also, and he loved Rachel more than Leah. And he worked for Laban another seven years. (Genesis 29:15 – 30)

When the LORD saw that Lear was not loved, he opened her womb, but Rachel was barren. Leah became pregnant and gave birth to a son. She named him Reuben, for she said, "It is because the LORD has seen my misery. Surely my husband will love me now."

She conceived again, and when she gave birth to a son she said, "Because the LORD heard that I am not loved, he gave me this one too." So she named him Simeon.

Again she conceived, and when she gave birth to a son she said, "Now at last my husband will become attached to me, because I have borne him three sons." So he was named Levi.

She conceived again, and when she gave birth to a son she said, "This time I will praise the LORD." So she named him Judah. Then she stopped having children. (Genesis 29:31 – 35)

When Rachel saw that she was not bearing Jacob any children, she became jealous of her sister. So she said to Jacob, "Give me children, or I'll die!"

Jacob became angry with her and said, "Am I in the place of God, who has kept you from having children?" Then she said, "Here is Bilhah, my maidservant. Sleep with her so that she can bear children for me and that through her I too can build a family."

So she gave him her servant Bilhah as a wife, Jacob slept with her, and she became pregnant and bore him a son. Then Rachel said, "God has vindicated me; he has listened to my plea and given me a son." Because of this she named him Dan.

Rachel's servant Bilhah conceived again and bore Jacob a second son. Then Rachel said, "I have had a great struggle with my sister and I have won." So she named him Naphtali.

When Leah saw that she had stopped having children, she took her maidservant Zilpah and gave her to Jacob as a wife. Leah's servant Zilpah bore Jacob a son. Then Leah said, "What good fortune!" So she named him Gad. Leah's servant Zilpah bore Jacob a second son. Then Leah said,

"How happy I am!" The women will call me happy." So she named him Asher.

During wheat harvest, Reuben went out into the fields and found some mandrake plants, which he brought to his mother Leah. Rachel said to Leah, "Please give me some of your son's mandrakes." But she said to her, "Wasn't it enough that you took away my husband? Will you take my son's mandrakes too?"

"Very well," Rachel said, "he can sleep with you tonight in return for your son's mandrakes." So when Jacob came in from the fields that evening, Leah went out to meet him. "You must sleep with me," she said, "I have hired you with my son's mandrakes." So he slept with her that night.

God listened to Leah, and she became pregnant and bore Jacob a fifth son. Then Leah said, "God has rewarded me for giving my maidservant to my husband." So she named him Issacher. Some time later she gave birth to a daughter and named her Dinah.

Then God remembered Rachel; he listened to her and opened her womb. She became pregnant and gave birth to a son and said, "God has taken away my disgrace." She named him Joseph, and said "May the Lord add to me another son." (Genesis 30:1 – 24)

Lessons to Learn:

- Leah had six sons and one daughter and her maidservant bore her two sons
- In all Leah had nine children for Jacob from her side.

God is the Umbrella of Women in the Bible!

35. Loice and Eunice – the Grandmother and Mother of Timothy:

Who Were These Women?

- Loice was the grandmother of Timothy and Eunice was the mother of Timothy
- They were women of faith and the Apostle Paul remembered them
- He mentioned them by name to Timothy

The Story:

Loice was the mother of Eunice and she passed on her faith to her. Eunice then passed on the faith that she learnt from her mother, to her son Timothy. Paul was writing to Timothy to try and encourage him in the work of God that he was doing. He therefore reminded him of his mother and his grandmother.

Today we have many young people who can learn from the faith of their mothers and their grandmothers too. Personally, I learnt from my grandfather, since all my grandmothers has passed away before I was born. My grandfather did a good job. I still remember a lot of things he taught me up to today.

He taught me that I should fear nothing because God is always there for me. In those days people used to fear evil people in the villages, but he impressed upon me that I had to fear nothing, as God was always going to protect me. He was a hard worker and I learnt that I had to work hard if I wanted to succeed in whatever I was doing. He also taught me to be self disciplined, and I am grateful that through all the years I have always remembered him when things were hard.

That is what Paul was telling Timothy, that he had a power house to fall back on, his grandmother and his mother.

The Bible and Loice and Eunice:

I thank God whom I serve, as my forefathers did, with a clear conscience, as night and day I constantly remember you in my prayers. Recalling your tears, I long to see you, so that I may be filled with joy. I have been reminded of your sincere faith, which first lived in your grandmother Lois and in your mother Eunice and, I am persuaded, now lives in you also. For this reason I remind you to fan into flame the gift of God, which is in you through the laying on of my hands. For God did not give us a spirit of timidity, but a spirit of power, of love and of self-discipline.

(2 Timothy 1:5)

Lessons to Learn:

- Do not get tired of teaching your child!

- Timothy was taught by his Grandmother Loice.
- His mother then followed through with the teaching.
- Parents must not give up on their children
- Even in these days it has become more important to teach your children

God is the Umbrella of Women in the Bible!

36. Lot's Wife:

Who Was This Woman?

- She was the wife of Lot
- She had two daughters
- She is the grandmother of the Moabites and the Ammonites
- Abraham always helped his nephew and his wife together with the women and the other people
- She turned back and looked at Sodom and Gomorrah

The Story:

Though not much is written about Lot's wife, it is clear that she was the mother of two virgin girls. She must have looked after them well in a city that was as horrible as Sodom and Gomorrah.

In here story unlike Sarah, she is not even mentioned doing any cooking. Instead it is said Lot baked the bread. Wonder what kind of woman she was!

The Bible and Lot's Wife:

This is the account of Terah: Terah became the father of Abram, Nahor and Haran. And Haran the father of Lot. While his father Terah was still alive, Haran died in Ur of the Chaldeans. In the land of his birth. Abram and Nahor both married. The name of Abram's wife was Sarai, and the name of Nahor's wife was Milcah; she was the daughter of Haran, the father of both Milcah and Iscah. Now Sarai was barren; she had no children. (Genesis 11:27 – 30)

He recovered all the goods and brought back his relative Lot and all his possessions, together with the women and the other people. (Genesis 14:16)

The two angels arrived at Sodom in the evening. Lot was sitting in the gateway of the city. When he saw them, he got up to meet them and bowed down with his face to the ground. My lords, he said, "please turn aside to your servant's house. You can wash your feet and spend the night and then go on your way early in the morning."

"No," they answered, "we will spend the night in the square."

But he insisted so strongly that they did go with him and entered his house. He prepared a meal for them, baking bread without yeast, and they ate. Before they had gone to bed all the men from every part of the city of Sodom – both young and old – surrounded the house. They called to Lot, "Where are the men who came to you tonight? Bring them out to us so that we can have sex with them."

Lot went outside to meet them and shut the door behind him and said, 'No my friends. Don't do this wicked thing. Look, I have two daughters who have never slept with a man. Let me bring them out to you, and you can do what you like with them. But don't do anything to these men, for they have come under the protection of my roof."

"Get out of our way," they replied. And they said, this fellow came here as an alien and now he wants to play the judge! We'll treat you worse than them." They kept bringing pressure on Lot and moved forward to break down the door.

But the men inside reached out and pulled Lot back into the house and shut the door. Then they struck the men who were at the door of the house, young and old with blindness so that they could not find the door.

The two men said to Lot. "Do you have anyone else here – sons-in-law, or daughters, or anyone else in the city who belongs to you? Get them out of here, because we are going to destroy this place. The outcry to the LORD against its people is so great that he has sent us to destroy it."

So Lot went out and spoke to his sons-in-law, who were pledged to marry his daughters. He said, "Hurry and get out of this place because the LORD is about to destroy the city!" But his sons-in-law thought he was joking.

With the coming of dawn, the angels urged Lot, saying "Hurry! Take your wife and your two daughters who are here, or you will be swept away when the city is punished."

When he hesitated, the men grasped his hand and the hands of his wife and of his two daughters and led them safely out of the city, for the LORD was merciful to them. As soon as they had brought them out, one of them said, "Flee for your lives! Don't look back, and don't stop any where in the plain! Flee to the mountains or you will be swept away!"

But Lot said to them, "No my lords, please! Your servant has found favour in your eyes, and you have shown great kindness to me in sparing my life. But I can't flee to the mountains; this disaster will overtake me, and I'll die. Look, here is a town near enough to run to, and it is small, let

God is the Umbrella of Women in the Bible

me flee to it – it is very small, isn't it? Then my life will be spared."

He said to him, "Very well, I will grant this request too; I will not overthrow the town you speak of. But flee there quickly, because I cannot do anything until you reach it." (That is why the town was called Zoar.)

By the time Lot reached Zoar, the sun had risen over the land. Then the LORD rained down burning sulfur on Sodom and Gomorrah – from the LORD out of the heavens. Thus he overthrew those cities and the entire plain, including all those living in the cities – and the also the vegetation in the land. But Lot's wife looked back, and she became a pillar of salt.

Early the next morning Abraham got up and returned to the place where he had stood before the LORD. He looked down toward Sodom and Gomorrah, toward all the land of the plain, and he saw dense smoke rising from the land, like smoke from a furnace.

So when God destroyed the cities of the plain, he remembered Abraham, and he brought out Lot out of the catastrophe that overthrew the cities where Lot had lived.

Lot and his two daughters left Zoar and settled in the mountains for he was afraid to stay in Zoar. He and his two daughters lived in a cave. One day the older daughter said to the younger, "Our father is old, and there is no man around here to lie with us, as is the custom all over the earth. Let's get our father to drink wine and then lie with him and preserve our family line through our father."

That night they got their father to drink wine, and the older daughter went in and lay with him. He was not aware of it when she lay down or when she got up.

The next day the older daughter said to the younger, "Last night I lay with my father. Let's get him to drink wine again tonight, and you go in and like with him so we can preserve our family line through our father." So they got their father to drink wine that night also, and the younger daughter went and lay with him. Again he was not aware of it when she lay down or when she got up.

So both of Lot's daughters became pregnant by their father. The older daughter had a son, and she named him Moab, he is the father of the Moabites of today. The younger also had a son, and she named him Ben-Ammi; he is the father of the Ammonites of today. (Genesis 19:1 – 38)

Lessons to Learn:

- She became a Pillar of salt
- Her daughters had to sleep with their father to preserve their family line
- Disobedience has its own Lessons to Learn:

God is the Umbrella of Women in the Bible!

37. Lydia – the First Convert of the Apostle Paul:

Who Was This Woman

- She was a Worshiper of God, from the city of Thyatira in the Eastern part of Macedonia
- She was converted by the Apostle Paul
- She was a business woman, who dealt in purple cloth
- She must have heard of this coming Revival
- She was waiting for it
- She was with other women
- She was among women who gathered to listen to Paul and Silas
- The LORD opened her heart to respond to Apostle Paul's message
- She was ready to receive the Apostles and she invited them
- She and members of her household were baptized
- She invited Paul and the others to her home

- She persuaded them
- Paul, Silas, Timothy and Luke stayed at her house

The Story:

Purple cloth was as expensive as it was difficult to make. The dye came from shell fish and a lot of fish was needed to die one garment. The fluid in the veins of the shell fish was white and it turned purple when exposed to the sun. Purple cloth was used mainly by royals.

From Lydia's story we learn that nothing happens for nothing. If you believe in God he will always be there for you. She had a desire for something better than she had. Being a business woman was not enough. There was something missing. She wanted to hear the word of God and be baptized. She did not only want this for herself but for her family and friends too.

Sometimes it is important to take part in events that are happening around us. Especially if they will fulfill our spiritual needs. Imagine Lydia met the Apostle Paul himself. Who is it that you have in mind to meet and to take to your home. In the group Lydia was easily recognized by Paul. God usually makes us stand out in a group if we worship him. God also works in his people. Have you ever noticed that when people want to come to God they need no persuasion, because God himself does the work in them? We just have to be there for them.

Lydia is among the first converts that Paul had. Her name is mentioned because she went further than that. She persuaded the entourage to come to her home if they considered her to be a believer. What? After baptizing her and her family surely you will go with her.

The Bible and Lydia:

From Troas we put out to sea and sailed straight for Samothrace, and the next day on to Neopolis. From there we traveled to Philippi, a Roman colony and the leading district of that city of that district of Macedonia. And we stayed there several days.

On the Sabbath we went outside the city gate to the river, where we expected to find a place of prayer. We sat down and began to speak to the women who had gathered there. One of those listening was a woman named Lydia, a dealer in purple cloth from the city of Thyatira, who was a worshiper of God. The LORD opened her heart to respond to Paul's message. When she and the members of her household were baptized, she invited us to her home. "If you consider me a believer in the LORD," she said, "come and stay at my house." And she persuaded us. (Acts 16:11 – 15)

Lessons to Learn:

- She and her family were baptized
- The Apostles accepted her invitation to stay at her house
- They considered her a believer in the LORD
- There was a demonstration of faith in the LORD
- Some Christians today still invite men and women of God to stay at their houses

God is the Umbrella of Women in the Bible!

38. Mahalath: the Daughter of Ishmael:

Who Was This Woman?

- She was Esau's third wife
- She was the daughter of Ishmael
- The sister of Nebaioth
- She was the mother of Reuel
- She was the grandmother of Chiefs Nahath, Zerah, Shammah and Mizzah
- She was used by Esau to appease Isaac and Rebekah

The Story:

Parents hope that their children will turn out right. Their sons should marry the right girls, and daughters to marry the right boys. Rebekah and Isaac's first son Esau married Hittite women when he was forty one years old; Judith and Basemath. Then later, he woke up to the fact that his two wives were a source of grief for his parents. He tried to salvage the situation by marrying his father's brother's daughter Mahalath. His younger brother Jacob had obeyed his mother and father, who had told him not to marry a Canaanite woman.

The Bible and Mahalath:

The LORD said to her, "Two nations are in your womb, and two peoples from within you will be separated; one people will be stronger than the other, and the older will serve the younger." (Genesis 25:23)

When Esau was forty years old, he married Judith daughter of Beeri the Hittite, and also Basemath daughter of Elon the Hittite. They were a source of grief to Isaac and Rebekah. (Genesis 26:34)

Then Rebekah said to Isaac, "I'm disgusted with living because of these Hittite women. If Jacob takes a wife from among the women of this land, from Hittite women like these, my life will not be worth living." (Genesis 27:46)

Now Esau learned that Isaac had blessed Jacob and had sent him to Paddan Aram to take a wife from there, and that when be blessed him he commanded him, "Do not marry a Canaanite woman," and that Jacob had obeyed his father and mother and had gone to Paddan Aram. Esau then realized how displeasing the Canaanite women were to his father Isaac; so he went to Ishmael and married Mahalath, the sister of Nebaioth and daughter of Ishmael son of Abraham in addition to the wives he had already. (Genesis 28:6 – 9)`

Lessons to Learn:

- It would seem that Mahalath brought some peace to Rebekah and Isaac as she was from the descendants of Abraham.

- She married Esau who was the older twin of Rebekah, about whom the LORD had said the older will serve the younger.
- This must have also affected her married life with Esau.

God is the Umbrella of Women in the Bible!

39. Martha the Sister of Lazarus:

Who Was This Woman?

- She opened her home to Jesus and his disciples
- She was the sister of Mary and Lazarus
- She was a hard working person
- She wanted to involve Mary in her work
- She complained about Mary to Jesus
- Jesus answered her: "Martha, Martha," "You are worried and upset about many things, but only one thing is needed.
- Martha and Mary sent word to Jesus, "Lord, the one you love is sick."
- Jesus loved Martha, her sister and Lazarus
- When Martha heard that Jesus was coming, she went out to meet him, but Mary stayed at home.
- Bethany was less than two miles from Jerusalem, and many Jews had come to Martha and Mary to comfort them in the loss of their brother.

- "Lord" Martha said to Jesus, "If you had been here, my brother would not have died. But I know that even now God will give you whatever you ask."
- Jesus said to her, "Your brother will rise again."
- Martha answered, "I know he will rise again in the resurrection at the last day."
- Jesus said to her, "I am the resurrection and the life. He who believes in me will live, even though he dies; and whoever lives and believes in me will never die. Do you believe this?"
- "Yes Lord" she told him, "I believe that you are the Christ, the Son of God, who was to come into the world."
- Martha told Mary "The Teacher is here, and is asking for you."
- Jesus, once more deeply moved, came to the tomb. It was a cave with a stone laid across the entrance. "Take away the stone," he said.
- "But, Lord," said Martha, the sister of the dead man, "by this time there is a bad odor, for he has been there four days."
- Then Jesus said, "Did I not tell you that if you believe, you would see the glory of God?"
- So they took away the stone. Then Jesus looked up and said, "Father, I thank you that you have heard me. I knew that you always hear me, but I said this for the benefit of the people standing here; that they may believe that you sent me."

Florence Mutambanengwe

The Story:

Martha lived in a village with her sister Mary and Brother Lazarus. She opened her home to Jesus and his disciples. As a result Jesus sat in her home teaching. Her sister Mary was very interested in what Jesus was saying and sat and listened to him.

Martha was more interested in the welfare of the people, what they would eat and drink. So she busied herself with that. However she also felt that her sister Mary should have come and assisted her in what she was doing. She actually complained to Jesus and said Lord, don't you care my sister has left me to do the work by myself? Tell her to help me!

However Jesus told her that she was worried and upset about many things. But May had chosen what was better and no one will take that away from her.

Sometime later Lazarus was sick and he died before Jesus came to see him. Many people had come to visit Martha and Mary as a result and Jesus arrived. Lazarus had already been in the tomb for four days. When Martha heard that Jesus was coming, she went out to meet him, but Mary stayed at home.

Martha then told Jesus that if he had been here, Lazarus would not have died. But she also told him that she knew that even then God would give him whatever he asked.

As the story goes Jesus did raise Lazarus from the dead even though he had been dead for four days. Many people who were there were amazed and believed in Jesus Christ.

The Bible and Martha the Sister of Lazarus:

As Jesus and his disciples were on their way he came to a village where a woman named Martha opened her home to him. She had a Sister called Mary, who sat at the Lord's feet listening to what he said. But Martha was distracted by all the preparations that had to be made. She came to him and asked, "Lord, don't you care my sister has left me to do the work by myself? Tell her to help me!"

"Martha, Martha," the Lord answered, "You are worried and upset about many things, but only one thing is needed. Mary has chosen what is better, and it will not be taken away from her." (Luke 10:38 – 42)

Now a man named Lazarus was sick. He was from Bethany, the village of Mary and her sister Martha. This Mary, whose brother Lazarus now lay sick, was the same one who poured perfume on the Lord and the same one who poured perfume on the Lord and wiped his feet with her hair. So the sisters sent word to Jesus, "Lord, the one you love is sick."

When he heard this, Jesus said, "This sickness will not end in death. No, it is for God's glory so that God's Son may be glorified through it." Jesus loved Martha and her sister and Lazarus. Yet when he heard that Lazarus was sick, he stayed where he was two more days.

Then he said to his disciples, "Let us go back to Judea."

"But Rabbi," they said, "a short while ago the Jew tried to stone you, and yet you are going back there?"

Jesus Answered, "Are there not twelve hours of daylight? A man who walks by day will not stumble, for he sees by this world's light. It is when he walks by night that he stumbles, for he has no light."

After he had said this, he went on to tell them, "Our friend Lazarus has fallen asleep; but I am going there to wake him up."

His disciples replied, "Lord, if he sleeps, he will get better." Jesus had been speaking of his death, but his disciples thought he meant natural sleep.

So then he told them plainly, "Lazarus is dead, and for your sake I am glad I was not there, so that you may believe. But let us go to him."

Then Thomas (called Didymus) said to the rest of the disciples, "Let us also go, that we may die with him." (John 11:1 – 16)

On his arrival, Jesus found that Lazarus had already been in the tomb for four days. Bethany was less than two miles from Jerusalem, and many Jews had come to Martha and Mary to comfort them in the loss of their brother. When Martha heard that Jesus was coming, she went out to meet him, but Mary stayed at home.

"Lord" Martha said to Jesus, "If you had been here, my brother would not have died. But I know that even now God will give you whatever you ask."

Jesus said to her, "Your brother will rise again."

Martha answered, "I know he will rise again in the resurrection at the last day."

Jesus said to her, "I am the resurrection and the life. He who believes in me will live, even though he dies; and whoever lives and believes in me will never die. Do you believe this?"

"Yes Lord" she told him, "I believe that you are the Christ, the Son of God, who was to come into the world."

And after she had said this, she went back and called her sister Mary aside. "The Teacher is here," she said, "and is asking for you." When Mary heard this, she got up quickly and went to him. Now Jesus had not yet entered the village, but was still at the place where Martha had met him. When the Jews who had been with Mary in the house, comforting her, noticed how quickly she got up and went out, they followed her, supposing she was going to the tomb to mourn there.

When Mary reached the place where Jesus was and saw him, she fell at his feet and said, "Lord, if you had been here, my brother would not have died."

When Jesus saw her weeping, and the Jews who had come along with her also weeping, he was deeply moved in spirit and troubled. "Where have you laid him?" he asked.

"Come and see, Lord," they replied.

Jesus wept.

Then the Jews said, "See how he loved him!"

But some of them said, "Could not he who opened the eyes of the blind man have kept this man from dying?" (John 11:17 – 37)

Jesus, once more deeply moved, came to the tomb. It was a cave with a stone laid across the entrance. "Take away the stone," he said.

"But, Lord," said Martha, the sister of the dead man, "by this time there is a bad odor, for he has been there four days."

Then Jesus said, "Did I not tell you that if you believe, you would see the glory of God?"

So they took away the stone. Then Jesus looked up and said, "Father, I thank you that you have heard me. I knew that you always hear me, but I said this for the benefit of the people standing here; that they may believe that you sent me."

When he said this, Jesus called in a loud voice, "Lazarus, come out!" The dead man came out, his hands and feet wrapped with strips of linen, and a cloth around his face.

Jesus said to them "Take off the grave clothes and let him go."

Therefore, many of the Jews who had come to visit Mary, and had seen what Jesus did, put their faith in him. (John 11:38 – 44)

Six days before the Passover, Jesus arrived at Bethany, where Lazarus lived, whom Jesus had raised from the dead. Here a dinner was given in Jesus' honour. Martha served while Lazarus was amongst those reclining at the table with him. Than Mary took about a pint of pure nard, an expensive perfume, she poured it on Jesus' feet and wiped his feet with her hair. And the house was filled with fragrance of perfume.

But one of the disciples, Judas Iscariot, who was later to betray him, objected. "Why wasn't this perfume sold and the money given to the poor? He did not say this because he cared about the poor but because he was a thief; as keeper of the money bag, he used to help himself to what was put into it.

"Leave her alone," Jesus replied "It was intended, that she should save this perfume for the day of my burial. You will always have the poor among you, but you will not always have me."

Meanwhile a large crowed of Jews found out that Jesus was there and came, not only because of him but also to see Lazarus, whom he had raised from the dead. So the chief priests made plans to kill Lazarus as well, for on account of him many of the Jews were going over to Jesus and putting their faith in him. (John 12:1 – 11)

Lessons to Learn:

- Hosting skills are just as important as listening skills
- Believing in the word of God always brings results
- Lazarus was raised from the dead by Jesus Christ

God is the Umbrella of Women in the Bible!

40. Mary the Sister of Lazarus:

Who Was This Woman?

- She was the sister of Lazarus
- She poured perfume on the Lord
- She wiped his feet with her hair.
- Jesus said "Mary has chosen what is better, and it will not be taken away from her."
- Mary and Martha sent word to Jesus, "Lord, the one you love is sick."
- Jesus loved Mary, her sister and Lazarus
- When Martha heard that Jesus was coming, she went out to meet him, but Mary stayed at home.
- Bethany was less than two miles from Jerusalem, and many Jews had come to Martha and Mary to comfort them in the loss of their brother.
- Martha went back and called her sister Mary aside. "The Teacher is here," she said, "and is asking for you."

God is the Umbrella of Women in the Bible

- When Mary heard this, she got up quickly and went to him. Now Jesus had not yet entered the village, but was still at the place where Martha had met him.
- When the Jews who had been with Mary in the house, comforting her, noticed how quickly she got up and went out, they followed her, supposing she was going to the tomb to mourn there.
- When Mary reached the place where Jesus was and saw him, she fell at his feet and said, "Lord, if you had been here, my brother would not have died."
- When Jesus saw her weeping, and the Jews who had come along with her also weeping, he was deeply moved in spirit and troubled. "Where have you laid him?" he asked.
- "Come and see, Lord," they replied.
- Jesus wept.
- Jesus, once more deeply moved, came to the tomb. It was a cave with a stone laid across the entrance. "Take away the stone," he said.
- But, Lord," said Martha, the sister of the dead man, "by this time there is a bad odor, for he has been there four days."
- Then Jesus said, "Did I not tell you that if you believe, you would see the glory of God?"
- So they took away the stone. Then Jesus looked up and said, "Father, I thank you that you have heard me. I knew that you always hear me, but

I said this for the benefit of the people standing here; that they may believe that you sent me."

The Story:

Martha lived in a village with her sister Mary and Brother Lazarus. She opened her home to Jesus and his disciples. As a result Jesus sat in her home teaching. Her sister Mary was very interested in what Jesus was saying and sat and listened to him.

Martha was more interested in the welfare of the people, what they would eat and drink. So she busied herself with that. However she also felt that her sister Mary should have come and assisted her in what she was doing. She actually complained to Jesus and said Lord, don't you care my sister has left me to do the work by myself? Tell her to help me!

However Jesus told her that she was worried and upset about many things. But May had chosen what was better and no one will take that away from her.

Sometime later Lazarus was sick and he died before Jesus came to see him. Many people had come to visit Martha and Mary as a result and Jesus arrived. Lazarus had already been in the tomb for four days. When Martha heard that Jesus was coming, she went out to meet him, but Mary stayed at home.

Martha then told Jesus that if he had been here, Lazarus would not have died. But she also told him that she knew that even then God would give him whatever he asked.

As the story goes Jesus did raise Lazarus from the dead even though he had been dead for four days. Many people who were there were amazed and believed in Jesus Christ.

Six days before the Passover, Jesus arrived at Bethany, where Lazarus lived, whom Jesus had raised from the dead.

Here a dinner was given in Jesus' honour. Martha served while Lazarus was amongst those reclining at the table with him. Then Mary took about a pint of pure nard, an expensive perfume, she poured it on Jesus' feet and wiped his feet with her hair. And the house was filled with fragrance of perfume.

Though one of the disciples complained Jesus told them to leave Mary alone, and said it was intended, that she should save this perfume for the day of his burial. He told them that they will always have the poor among them, but they will not always have him.

The Bible and Mary the Sister of Lazarus:

As Jesus and his disciples were on their way he came to a village where a woman named Martha opened her home to him. She had a Sister called Mary, who sat at the Lord's feet listening to what he said. But Martha was distracted by all the preparations that had to be made. She came to him and asked, "Lord, don't you care my sister has left me to do the work by myself? Tell her to help me!"

"Martha, Martha," the Lord answered, "You are worried and upset about many things, but only one thing is needed. Mary has chosen what is better, and it will not be taken away from her." (Luke 10:38 – 42)

Now a man named Lazarus was sick. He was from Bethany, the village of Mary and her sister Martha. This Mary, whose brother Lazarus now lay sick, was the same one who poured perfume on the Lord and the same one who poured perfume on the Lord and wiped his feet with her hair. So the sisters sent word to Jesus, "Lord, the one you love is sick."

When he heard this, Jesus said, "This sickness will not end in death. No, it is for God's glory so that God's Son may be glorified through it." Jesus loved Martha and her sister and Lazarus. Yet when he heard that Lazarus was sick, he stayed where he was two more days.

Then he said to his disciples, "Let us go back to Judea."

"But Rabbi," they said, "a short while ago the Jew tried to stone you, and yet you are going back there?"

Jesus Answered, "Are there not twelve hours of daylight? A man who walks by day will not stumble, for he sees by this world's light. It is when he walks by night that he stumbles, for he has no light."

After he had said this, he went on to tell them, "Our friend Lazarus has fallen asleep; but I am going there to wake him up."

His disciples replied, "Lord, if he sleeps, he will get better." Jesus had been speaking of his death, but his disciples thought he meant natural sleep.

So then he told them plainly, "Lazarus is dead, and for your sake I am glad I was not there, so that you may believe. But let us go to him."

Then Thomas (called Didymus) said to the rest of the disciples, "Let us also go, that we may die with him." (John 11:1 – 16)

On his arrival, Jesus found that Lazarus had already been in the tomb for four days. Bethany was less than two miles from Jerusalem, and many Jews had come to Martha and Mary to comfort them in the loss of their brother. When Martha heard that Jesus was coming, she went out to meet him, but Mary stayed at home.

"Lord" Martha said to Jesus, "If you had been here, my brother would not have died. But I know that even now God will give you whatever you ask."

Jesus said to her, "Your brother will rise again."

Martha answered, "I know he will rise again in the resurrection at the last day."

Jesus said to her, "I am the resurrection and the life. He who believes in me will live, even though he dies; and whoever lives and believes in me will never die. Do you believe this?"

"Yes Lord" she told him, "I believe that you are the Christ, the Son of God, who was to come into the world."

And after she had said this, she went back and called her sister Mary aside. "The Teacher is here," she said, "and is asking for you." When Mary heard this, she got up quickly and went to him. Now Jesus had not yet entered the village, but was still at the place where Martha had met him. When the Jews who had been with Mary in the house, comforting her, noticed how quickly she got up and went out, they followed her, supposing she was going to the tomb to mourn there.

When Mary reached the place where Jesus was and saw him, she fell at his feet and said, "Lord, if you had been here, my brother would not have died."

When Jesus saw her weeping, and the Jews who had come along with her also weeping, he was deeply moved in spirit and troubled. "Where have you laid him?" he asked.

"Come and see, Lord," they replied.

Jesus wept.

Then the Jews said, "See how he loved him!"

But some of them said, "Could not he who opened the eyes of the blind man have kept this man from dying?" (John 11:17 – 37)

Jesus, once more deeply moved, came to the tomb. It was a cave with a stone laid across the entrance. "Take away the stone," he said.

"But, Lord," said Martha, the sister of the dead man, "by this time there is a bad odor, for he has been there four days."

Then Jesus said, "Did I not tell you that if you believe, you would see the glory of God?"

So they took away the stone. Then Jesus looked up and said, "Father, I thank you that you have heard me. I knew that you always hear me, but I said this for the benefit of the people standing here; that they may believe that you sent me."

When he said this, Jesus called in a loud voice, "Lazarus, come out!" The dead man came out, his hands and feet wrapped with strips of linen, and a cloth around his face.

Jesus said to them "Take off the grave clothes and let him go."

Therefore, many of the Jews who had come to visit Mary, and had seen what Jesus did, put their faith in him. (John 11:38 – 44)

Six days before the Passover, Jesus arrived at Bethany, where Lazarus lived, whom Jesus had raised from the dead. Here a dinner was given in Jesus' honour. Martha served while Lazarus was amongst those reclining at the table with him. Than Mary took about a pint of pure nard, an expensive perfume, she poured it on Jesus' feet and wiped his feet with her hair. And the house was filled with fragrance of perfume.

But one of the disciples, Judas Iscariot, who was later to betray him, objected. "Why wasn't this perfume sold and the money given to the poor? He did not say this because he cared about the poor but because he was a thief; as keeper of the money bag, he used to help himself to what was put into it.

"Leave her alone," Jesus replied "It was intended, that she should save this perfume for the day of my burial. You will always have the poor among you, but you will not always have me."

Meanwhile a large crowed of Jews found out that Jesus was there and came, not only because of him but also to see Lazarus, whom he had raised from the dead. So the chief priests made plans to kill Lazarus as well, for on account of him many of the Jews were going over to Jesus and putting their faith in him. (John 12:1 – 11)

Lessons to Learn:

- Hosting skills are just as important as listening skills
- Believing in the word of God always brings results
- Lazarus was raised from the dead by Jesus Christ

God is the Umbrella of Women in the Bible!

41. Mary Mother of Jesus

Who Was This Woman?

- Time is important to God
- She was a virgin
- She was already engaged to Joseph a descendant of David
- Mary is a Greek name which means bitter or rebellious
- God sent an angel to her with a message
- She spoke to the angel of God
- Elizabeth knew what was happening with Mary
- Mary was a Composer and writer
- Mary was a Helper
- Joseph had in mind to divorce her quietly
- The angel of the Lord appeared to Joseph as well
- She is the virgin spoken of in the Old Testament

- The names were given to Mary and Joseph by God through the angel – The Son of God - Jesus - Immanuel – which means "God with us"
- She gave birth to Jesus
- She later gave birth to other children – James, Joseph, Simon and Judas
- She traveled with her husband and child to Egypt
- She traveled also from the town of Nazareth in Galilee to Judea, to Bethlehem the town of David.
- Mary was a normal woman and therefore these things also amazed her too
- She was instrumental in Jesus' first miracle at the wedding in Cana
- She quietly treasured all these things in her heart
- She performed all the motherly duties

The Story:

Mary's story starts with her being betrothed to be married by Joseph. A descendant of David.. Depending on how they did it in those days, she was waiting for the big day when Joseph would come for his bride. May be she was making preparations for the ceremony that would take place. Then everything changed. God sent the angel Gabriel to her with a message.

"Greetings, you who are highly favoured!
The Lord is with you."

She was surprised at the type of greeting, but the angel continued with his message:

"Do not be afraid, Mary, you have found favour with God. You will be with child and give birth to a son, and you are to give him the name Jesus. He will be great and will be called the Son of the Most High. The Lord God will give him the throne of his father David and he will reign over the house of Jacob forever, his kingdom will never end."

Then Mary tried to explain that she was a virgin, and how could she be with child. Again the angel proceeded with his message:

"The Holy Spirit will come upon you, and the power of the Most High will overshadow you. So, the holy one to be born, will be called the Son of God. Even Elizabeth your relative is going to have a child in her old age, and she who was said to be barren is in her sixth month. For nothing is impossible with God"

Then Mary answered: "I am the Lord's servant. May it be to me as you have said?"

Then the angel left her.

The Bible and Mary Mother of Jesus:

In the sixth month, God send the angel Gabriel to Nazareth, a town in Galilee, to a virgin pledged to be married to a man named Joseph, a descendant of David. The virgin's name was Mary. The angel went to her and said,

"Greetings, you who are highly favored!
The Lord is with you."

Mary was greatly troubled at his words and wondered what kind of greeting this might be. But the angel said to her,

"Do not be afraid, Mary, you have found favour with God. You will be with child and give birth to a son, and you are to give him the name Jesus. He will be great and will be called the Son of the Most High. The Lord God will give him the throne of his father David, and he will reign over the house of Jacob forever, his kingdom will never end."

"How will this be," Mary asked the angel, "since I am a virgin?"

The angel answered, "The Holy Spirit will come upon you, and the power of the Most High will overshadow you. So the holy one to be born will be called the Son of God. Even Elizabeth your relative is going to have a child in her old age, and she who was said to be barren is in her sixth month. For nothing is impossible with God"

"I am the Lord's servant." Mary answered. May it be to me as you have said?

Then the angel left her. (Luke 1:26 – 38)

At that time Mary got ready and hurried to a town in the hill country of Judea, where she entered Zechariah's home and greeted Elizabeth. When Elizabeth heard Mary's greeting, the baby leaped in her womb, and Elizabeth was filled with the Holy Spirit. In a loud voice she exclaimed:

"Blessed are you among women, and blessed is the child you will bear! But why am I so favored, that the mother of my Lord should come to me? As soon as the sound of your greeting reached my ears, the baby in my womb leaped for joy. Blessed is she who has believed that what the Lord has said to her will be accomplished!" (Luke 1 39 – 45)

Florence Mutambanengwe

Mary's Song

And Mary said:

"My soul glorifies the Lord and my spirit rejoices in God my Saviour,
For he has been mindful of the humble state of his servant
From now on all generations will call me blessed,
For the Mighty One has done great things for me –
Holy is his name.
His mercy extends to those who fear him, from generation to generation.
He has performed mighty deed with his arm;
He has scattered those who are proud in their inmost thoughts.
He has brought down rulers from their thrones but has lifted up the humble.
He has filled the hungry with good things but has sent the rich away empty.
He has helped his servant Israel, remembering to be merciful
To Abraham and his descendants forever, even as he said to our fathers."

Mary stayed with Elizabeth for about three months and then returned home.
(Luke 1:46 – 56)

This is how the birth of Jesus Christ came about:
His Mother Mary was pledged to be married to Joseph, but before they came together, she was found to be with child through the Holy Spirit. Because Joseph her husband

was a righteous man and did not want to expose her to public disgrace, he had in mind to divorce her quietly.

But after he considered this an angel of the LORD appeared to him in a dream and said,

"Joseph son of David, do not be afraid to take Mary home as your wife, because what is conceived in her is from the Holy Spirit. She will give birth to a son, and you are to give him the name Jesus, because he will save his people from their sins."

All this took place to fulfill what the Lord had said through the prophet:

"The virgin will be with child and will give birth to a son, and they will call him Immanuel" – which means "God with us"

When Joseph woke up, he did what the angel of the Lord had commanded him and took Mary home as his wife. But he had no union with her until she gave birth to a son. And he gave him the name Jesus. (Matthew 1:18 – 24)

On coming to the house, they saw the child with his mother Mary, and they bowed down and worshiped him. Then they opened their treasures and presented him with gifts of gold and incense and of myrrh. And having been warned in a dream not to go back to Herod, they returned to their country by another route. (Matthew 2:11 – 12)

When they had gone, an angel of the Lord appeared to Joseph in a dream. "Get up," he said, "take the child and his mother and escape to Egypt. Stay there until I tell you, for Herod is going to search for the child to kill him."

So he got up, took the child and his mother during the night and left for Egypt, where they stayed until the death of Herod. And so was fulfilled what the Lord had said through the prophet: "Out of Egypt I called my son." Matthew 2:13 – 15)

After Herod died, an angel of the Lord appeared in a dream to Joseph in Egypt and said, "Get up, take the child and his mother and go to the land of Israel, for those who were trying to take the child's life are dead." So he got up, took the child and his mother and went to the land of Israel. (Matthew 2:19 – 21)

Then Jesus' mother and brothers arrived. Standing outside, they sent someone in to call him. A crowd was sitting around him, and they told him, "Your mother and brothers are outside looking for you." "Who are my mother and brothers?" he asked. Then he looked at those seated in a circle around him and said, "Here are my mother and my brothers! Whoever does God's will is my brother and my sister and mother." (Mark 3:31 – 35)

In those days Caesar Augustus issued a degree that a census should be taken of the entire Roman world. (This was the first census that took place while Quirinius was governor of Syria.) And everyone went to his own home town to register.

So Joseph also went up from the town of Nazareth in Galilee to Judea, to Bethlehem the town of David. He went there to register with Mary, who was pledged to be married to him and was expecting a child. While they were there, the time came for the baby to be born, and she gave birth to her firstborn, a son. She wrapped him in cloths and placed him in a manger, because there was no room for them in the inn.

And there were shepherds living out in the fields nearby keeping watch over their flocks at night. An angel of the Lord appeared to them and the glory of the Lord shone around them. "Do not be afraid, I bring you good news of great joy that will be for all the people. Today in the town of David a Saviour has been born to you; he is Christ the Lord.

This will be a sign to you: You will find a baby wrapped in cloths and lying in a manger."

Suddenly a great company of heavenly host appeared with the angel, praising God and saying,

"Glory to God in the highest, and on earth peace to men on whom his favour rests."

When the angels had left them and gone into heaven, the shepherds said to one another, "Let's go to Bethlehem and see this thing that has happened which the Lord has told us about."

So they hurried off and found Mary and Joseph and the baby, who was lying in the manger. When they had seen him they spread the word concerning what had been told them about this child, and all who heard it were amazed at what the shepherds said to them. But Mary treasured up all these things and pondered them in her heart. The shepherds returned, glorifying and praising God for all the things they had heard and seen which were just as they had been told. (Luke 2:1 – 20)

On the eight day, when it was time to circumcise him, he was named Jesus, the name the angel had given him before he had been conceived.

When the time of their purification according to the Law of Moses had been completed, Joseph and Mary took him to Jerusalem to present him to the Lord (as it is written in the Law of the Lord, "Every firstborn male is to be consecrated to the Lord." And to offer a sacrifice in keeping with what is said in the Law of the Lord: "a pair of doves or two young pigeons."

Now there was a man in Jerusalem called Simeon, who was righteous and devout. He was waiting for the consolation of Israel, and the Holy Spirit was upon him. It had been revealed to him by the Holy Spirit that he would not die before he had seen the Lord's Christ; Moved by the

Spirit, he went into the temple courts. When the parents brought the child Jesus to do for him what the custom of the Law required. Simeon took him in his arms and praised God, saying:

Sovereign Lord, as you have promised you now dismiss your servant in peace.

For my eyes had seen your salvation, which you have prepared in the sight of all people, a light for revelation to the Gentiles and for glory to your people Israel."

The child's father and mother marveled at what was said about him. Then Simeon blessed them and said to Mary, his mother: "This child is destined to cause the falling and rising of many in Israel, and to be a sign that will be spoken against, so that the thoughts of many hearts will be revealed. And a sword will pierce your soul too."

There was also a prophetess, Anna, the daughter of Phanuel, of the tribe of Asher. She was very old; she had lived with her husband seven years after her marriage, and then was a widow until she was eighty-four. She never left the temple but worshiped night and day, fasting and praying. Coming up to them at that very moment, she gave thanks to God and spoke about the child to all who were looking forward to the redemption of Jerusalem.

When Joseph and Mary had done everything required by the Law of the Lord, they returned to Galilee to their own town of Nazareth. And the child grew and became strong; he was filled with wisdom, and the grace of God was upon him.

Every year his parents went to Jerusalem for the Feast of the Passover. When he was twelve years old, they went up to the Feast, according to their custom. After the Feast was over, while his parents were returning home, the boy Jesus stayed behind in Jerusalem, but they were unaware of it. Thinking he was in their company, they traveled on for a day. Then they began looking for him among their relatives and friends. When they did not find him, they went back to Jerusalem to look for him. After three days they found him in the temple courts, sitting among the teachers, listening to them and asking them questions. Everyone who heard him was amazed at his understanding and his answers. When his parents saw him, they were astonished. His mother said to him, "Son, why have you treated us like this? Your father and I have been anxiously searching for you."

"Why were you searching for me?" He asked. "Didn't you know I had to be in my Father's house?" But they did not understand what he was saying.

Then he went down to Nazareth with them and was obedient to them. But his mother treasured all these things in her heart. And Jesus grew in wisdom and stature, and in favour with God and men.. (Luke 2:21 – 52)

Isn't this the carpenter's son? Isn't his mother's name Mary, and aren't his brothers James, Joseph, Simon and Judas? Aren't all his sisters with us? Where did this man get all these things? (Matthew 13:55 – 56)

On the third day a wedding took place at Cana in Galilee, Jesus' mother was there, and Jesus and his disciples had also been invited to the wedding. When the wine was gone, Jesus' mother said to him, "They have no more wine."

"Dear woman, why do you involve me?" Jesus replied "My time has not yet come."

His mother said to the servants, "Do whatever he tells you." (John 2:1 – 5)

Lessons to Learn:

- Jesus was born by Mary in a manger which is a trough in a stable for horses or cattle to feed from.
- Jesus came down from heaven to save us
- We were given the name above all names

God is the Umbrella of Women in the Bible!

42. Mary Magdalene

Who Was This Woman?

- She had seven demons removed from her by Jesus
- She traveled with Jesus
- She supported the Ministry of Jesus out of her own means
- She went to the tomb, while it was still dark, on the first day of the week
- She saw that the stone had been removed from the entrance of the tomb
- She came running to Simon Peter and the other disciple, the one Jesus loved
- "They have taken the Lord out of the tomb, and we don't know where they have put him!" She said
- The disciples went back to their homes
- Mary stood outside the tomb crying
- She bent over to look into the tomb
- She saw two angels in white seated where Jesus' body had been

- One angel at the head and the other at the foot
- She had a discussion with the angels
- "They have taken my Lord away," she said "and I don't know where they have put him."
- At this she turned around and saw Jesus standing there, but she did not realize that it was Jesus.
- She was the first person to see Jesus after his resurrection
- "Woman," he said, "why are you crying? Who is it you are looking for?"
- Thinking he was the gardener, she said, "Sir, if you have carried him away tell me where you have put him, and I will get him."
- Jesus said to her, "Mary."
- She turned toward him and cried out in Aramaic, "Rabboni!" (which means Teacher)
- Jesus said, "Do not hold on to me, for I have not yet returned to the Father. Go instead to my brothers and tell them, 'I am returning to my Father and your Father, to my God and your God.'"
- Mary Magdalene went to the disciples with the news: "I have seen the Lord!" And she told them that he said these things to her.

The Story:

Mary Magdalene early in the morning on the first day of the week went to the tomb where Jesus had been buried.

She discovered that the stone had been removed from the entrance. Then she came back running to tell the other disciples of Jesus what she had seen. She told them that they had taken the Lord out of the tomb and that she did not know where they had taken the body.

The other disciples then ran to the tomb to see for themselves what had happened to Jesus. They looked around and found that the tomb was open. Then they went back. But Mary lingered on. She was extremely worried and wanted some answers as to what had happened to Jesus.

Mary stood outside the tomb crying. As she wept, she bent over to look into the tomb and saw two angels in white, seated where Jesus' body had been, one at the head and the other at the foot.

Then they asked her why she was crying. She told them that they had taken her Lord away, and she did not know where they had put him. And then she turned around and saw Jesus standing there, but she did not realize that it was Jesus.

"Woman," he said, "why are you crying? Who is it you are looking for?"

Thinking he was the gardener, Mary said Sir, if you have carried him away tell me where you have put him, and I will get him.

Jesus said to her, "Mary."

She turned toward him and cried out in Aramaic, "Rabboni!" (This means Teacher)

Jesus said, "Do not hold on to me, for I have not yet returned to the Father. Go instead to my brothers and tell them, 'I am returning to my Father and your Father, to my God and your God.'" Mary Magdalene went to the disciples with the news that she had seen the Lord! And she told them what he had said to her.

Florence Mutambanengwe

The Bible and Mary Magdalene:

Early on the first day of the week, while it was still dark, Mary Magdalene went to the tomb and saw that the stone had been removed from the entrance. So she came running to Simon Peter and the other disciple, the one Jesus loved, and said, "They have taken the Lord out of the tomb, and we don't know where they have put him!"

So Peter and the other disciple started for the tomb. Both were running, but the other disciple outran Peter and reached the tomb first. He bent over and looked in at the strips of linen lying there but did not go in. Then Simon Peter, who was behind him, arrived and went into the tomb. He saw the strips of linen lying there, as well as the burial cloth that had been around Jesus' head. The cloth was folded up by itself, separate from the linen. Finally the other disciple, who had reached the tomb, first, also went inside. He saw and believed. (They still did not understand from Scripture that Jesus had to rise from the dead.)

Then the disciples went back to their homes, but Mary stood outside the tomb crying. As she wept, she bent over to look into the tomb and saw two angels in white, seated where Jesus' body had been, one at the head and the other at the foot.

They asked her "Woman, why are you crying?"

"They have taken my Lord away," she said "and I don't know where they have put him." At this she turned around and saw Jesus standing there, but she did not realize that it was Jesus.

"Woman," he said, "why are you crying? Who is it you are looking for?"

Thinking he was the gardener, she said, "Sir, if you have carried him away tell me where you have put him, and I will get him."

Jesus said to her, "Mary."

She turned toward him and cried out in Aramaic, "Rabboni!" (Which means Teacher?)

Jesus said, "Do not hold on to me, for I have not yet returned to the Father. Go instead to my brothers and tell them, 'I am returning to my Father and your Father, to my God and your God.'"

Mary Magdalene went to the disciples with the news: "I have seen the Lord!" And she told them that he said these things to her. (John 20:1 – 18)

After this, Jesus traveled about from one town and village to another, proclaiming the good news of the kingdom of God. The twelve were with him, and also some women who had been cured of evil spirits and diseases: Mary (called Magdalene from whom seven demons had come out; Joanna the wife of Cuza, the manager of Herod's household; Susanna and many others. These women were helping to support them out of their own means.

Lessons to Learn:

- The first to get to the tomb early in the morning
- The first to see Jesus after his resurrection
- A great woman of faith
- Healed from demonic attacks
- A strong woman follower of Jesus Christ

God is the Umbrella of Women in the Bible!

43. Matred – The Mother of Mehetabel, The Wife of Hadad:

When Baal – Hanan died, Hadad succeeded him as king. His city was named Pau, and his wife's name was Mehetabel daughter of Matred, the daughter of Me-Zahab. Hadad also died. (1 Chronicles 1:50 – 51)

God is the Umbrella of Women in the Bible!

44. Mehetabel – The Wife of Hadad:

When Baal – Hanan died, Hadad succeeded him as king. His city was named Pau, and his wife's name was Mehetabel daughter of Matred, the daughter of Me-Zahab. Hadad also died. (1 Chronicles 1:50 – 51)

God is the Umbrella of Women in the Bible!

45. Merab – Saul's Daughter: (See Aiah)

God is the Umbrella of Women in the Bible!

46. Michal – the Wife of David:

Who Was This Woman?

- She was the second daughter of Saul
- She loved David
- She seems to be the first love of David before Ahinoam and Abigail
- She even lied to Saul to save David
- She was taken away from Paltiel and given back to David
- She was Merab's sister

The Story:

Saul wanted to give his daughter Merab to David in marriage. This was not a genuine interest in David, but just to get him near in order to kill him. So when David was told of this offer he turned it down and then Merab was later given to Adriel of Meholah in marriage.

Still Saul kept on pursuing his desire to give one of his daughters to David. His servants told him that his daughter

Michal was in love with David. Then Saul told them to go and entice David to marry Michal. But David said that it was no easy thing, to become the king's son-in-law. Who can blame him coming from his back ground? He said, "I am only a poor man and little known." It is like from a Jack to a King.

When the attendants of the king told him, he said he only wanted a hundred foreskins of the Philistines. He did not anything else. He actually thought that David would now be killed by the Philistines.

This was no hard task for David, remember he had killed a lion, killed Goliath, and the LORD was on his side. David organized with his men and two hundred Philistines and brought their foreskins to Saul.

Then Saul had no alternative he had to give his daughter Michal to David to marry.

She loved David to the extent that at one time when Saul sent his men to get David, she lied and said that he was not well and was in bed. They went back without him, and she let David down through a window and he escaped. However Saul sent for him to be brought in his bed. Michal however had placed a doll in the bed. She had even put goat's hair on the doll and covered it with a garment pretending it was David.

When her father asked her why she had lied to him, she told him that David had said: "Let me get away. Why should I kill you?

She was at one time married to Paltiel son of Laish but David asked that she be brought back to him. Though Paltiel cried for her it was to no avail as David had betrothed her with the foreskins of the Philistines.

One day when the LORD's Ark was being brought, David was dancing and praising the LORD; Michal looked through the window and laughed. She was punished later for that.

The Bible and Michal:

Saul said to David, "Here is my older daughter Merab. I will give her to you in marriage; only serve me bravely and fight the battles of the LORD." For Saul said to himself, I will not raise a hand against him. Let the Philistines do that."

Bur David said to Saul, "Who am I, and what is my father's clan in Israel, that I should become the king's son-in-law?" So when the time came for Merab, Saul's daughter, to be given to David, she was given in marriage to Adriel of Meholah.

Now Saul's daughter Michal was in love with David, and when they told Saul about it, he was pleased. "I will give her to him," he thought, "so that she may be a snare to him and so that the hand of the Philistines may be against him." So Saul said to David, "Now you have a second change to become my son-in-law."

Then Saul ordered his attendants: "Speak to David privately and say, 'Look the king is pleased with you, and his attendants all like you, now become his son-in-law.'"

They repeated these words to David. But David said, "Do you think it's a small matter to become the king's son-in-law? I am only a poor

When Saul's servants told him what David had said, Saul replied, "Say to David, 'The king wants no other price for the bride than a hundred Philistine foreskins, to take revenge on his enemies.'" Saul's plan was to have David fall by the hands of the Philistines.

When the attendants told David these things, he was pleased to become the king's son-in-law. So before the allotted time elapsed, David and his men went out and killed two hundred Philistines. He brought their foreskins and presented the full number to the king so that he might become the king's son-in-law. Then Saul gave him his daughter Michal in Marriage. When Saul realized that the LORD was with David and that his daughter Michal loved David, Saul became still more afraid of him, and he remained his enemy the rest of his days. (1 Samuel 18:17 – 29) (1 Samuel 19:11-17) (1 Samuel 30:4) (2 Samuel 3:13 – 21)

Lessons to Learn:

Hers is a story of love
- A father who wanted to kill her husband
- What do you do in a situation like hers?
- Due to being separated from David, she married another man!
- What could she have done?
- Waited for David's return, not knowing when?

47. Milcah – the Wife of Nahor:

Who Was This Woman?

- She was the mother of Nahor's sons
- She married Abraham's brother Nahor
- She had eight sons: Uz, Buz, Kennel (the father of Aram), Kesed, Hazo, Pildash, Jidlaph, Bethuel – the father of Rebekah
- Nahor was Abraham's brother

The Story:

Milcah was the daughter of Haran, the brother of Abraham and Nahor. She was married to Nahor her uncle or her father's brother. Milcah had eight sons namely, Uz, Buz, Kemuel, Kesed, Hazo, Pildash, Jidlaph and Bethuel. Bethuel is the father of Rebekah the wife of Isaac the son of Abraham. Milcah therefore was the grandmother of Rebeka and great grandmother of Esau (Edom) and Jacob (Israel). (Genesis 32:28) and (Genesis 35:9)

Florence Mutambanengwe

The Bible and Milcah:

After Terah had lived 70 years, he became the father of Abraham, Nahor and Haran. This is the account of Terah. Terah became the father of Abram, Nahor and Haran. And Haran became the father of Lot. While his father Terah was still alive, Haran died in Ur of the Chaldeans, in the land of his birth. Abram and Nahor both married. The name of Abram's wife was Sarai, and the name of Nahor's wife was Milcah; she was the daughter of Haran, the father of both Milcah and Iscah. Now Sarai was barren; she had no children.

Terah took his son Abram, his grandson Lot son of Haran, and his daughter-in-law Sarai, the wife of his son Abram, and together they set out from Ur of the Chaldeans to go to Canaan. But when they came to Haran, they settled there. Terah lived 205 years, and he died in Haran. (Genesis 11:26 – 32)

Some time later Abraham was told, "Milcah is also a mother; she has borne sons to your brother Nahor: Us the firstborn, Buz his brother, Kemuel (the father of Aram), Kesed, Hazo, Pildash, Jidlaph and Bethuel." Bethuel became the father of Rebekah. Milcah bore these eight sons to Abraham's brother Nahor. His concubine, whose name was Reumah, also had sons: Tebah, Gaham, Tahash and Maacah. (Genesis 22:20 – 24)

She answered him, "I am the daughter of Bethuel, the son that Milcah bore to Nahor. (Genesis 24:24)

"I asked her, 'Whose daughter are you?' "She said, 'The daughter of Bethuel son of Nahor, whom Milcah bore to him.'" (Genesis 24:47)

Lessons to Learn:

- Her children are so numerous.
- What a pleasure it was to Abraham to know that his brother had sons born by Milcah.
- He got Rebekah from them.

God is the Umbrella of Women in the Bible!

48. Miriam – The Older Sister of Aaron and Moses

Who Was This Woman?

- She was the daughter of Amram and Jochebed
- She was the eldest child
- She was the sister of Aaron and Moses
- She followed Moses as he floated in the River Nile
- She offered Pharaoh's daughter to get a Hebrew woman
- She brought Jochebed to Pharaoh's daughter
- She was a musician
- She was a prophetess
- She was jealous of Moses
- She had leprosy
- Moses prayed for her and God forgave her

The Story:

Miriam was the oldest daughter of Amram and Jochebed. Amram was a descended of Levi who was the third son of Jacob. Her mother was her father's aunt. She was the eldest child and her young brothers were Moses and Aaron.

At one point in the history of the Israelites, they were living in Egypt and became numerous that Pharaoh was so worried about their numbers. Firstly, he decided to work them hard so that may be they could just die from exhaustion. This did not work. They were a strong people. No wonder God chose them.

Then Pharaoh decided that the best thing was to throw the baby boys into the River Nile, and several were thrown into the river. Miriam's mother however decided to keep her son for three months hidden. Then she prepared a papyrus basket and sealed it with tar. She placed her baby in it and floated it on the Nile River.

Miriam stood at the bank of the river Nile and watched her brother floating in a basket. She was looking out for whether the Egyptian princess would pick him up.

Pharaoh's daughter came to the river to bathe with her servants. She noticed the basket and asked the servant to go and pick it up out of the water. She discovered that a baby was in the basket.

Of course she did and Miriam offered to look for a Hebrew woman who would look after the baby

Miriam was watching from a distance went to Pharaoh's daughter and asked her whether she could find a nurse for her child; to which she agreed. Miriam went and brought Jochebed the mother of the child, to Pharaoh's daughter.

Pharaoh's daughter instructed the mother to look after her baby and nurse him and bring him back when he was a little older. She did feed her own baby and returned him to Pharaoh's daughter, who named him Moses meaning that she drew him out of water.

Miriam was just as human as many women and behaved like some of us do. She became jealous of her brothers leadership and complained that she was just a prophet like Moses was. She also complained about the wife of Moses saying Moses married a "Cushite". Here she could have been referring to Zipporah, Moses wife or to a second wife from some North African or some Arabian country.

God however straightened Miriam and Aaron in this case. Miriam had leprosy. Though Moses cried out to God to save Miriam; God insisted that Miriam should be left out for a week, before she could be healed. God said he actually spoke to Moses face to face while to other prophets he spoke in dreams and visions.

After crossing the Red Sea, Miriam led the Hebrew women in singing and praising God. And Miriam the prophetess, the sister of Aaron, took a timbrel in her hand; and all the women went out after her with timbrels and with dances. And Miriam answered them, "Sing ye to the Lord, for he hath triumphed gloriously; the horse and his rider hath he thrown into the sea."

The Bible and Miriam:

Amram married his father's sister Jochebed who bore him Aaron and Moses. (Exodus 6:20)

Then Miriam the prophetess, Aaron's sister, took a tambourine in her hand; and all the women followed her with tambourines and dancing. Miriam sang to them:

Sing to the Lord, for he is highly exalted. The horse and its rider he has hurled into the sea. (Exodus 15:20 – 21)

Miriam and Aaron began to talk against Moses because of his Cushite wife, for he had married a Cushite. "Has the LORD spoken only through Moses?" They asked, "Hasn't he also spoken through us?" And the LORD heard this.

(Now Moses was a very humble man, more humble than anyone else on the face of the earth.) At once the LORD said to Moses, Aaron and Miriam, "Come out to the Tent of Meeting, all three of you." So, the three of them came out. Then the LORD came down in a pillar of cloud; he stood at the entrance to the Tent and summoned Aaron and Miriam. When both of them stepped forward, he said "Listen to my words:

When a prophet of the LORD is among you, I reveal myself to him in visions. I speak to him in dreams. But this is not true of my servant Moses; he is faithful in all my house. With him I speak face to face. Clearly and not in riddles; he sees the form of the LORD. Why then were you not afraid to speak, against my servant Moses?"

The anger of the LORD burned against them,. And he left them.

When the cloud lifted from above the Tent, there stood Miriam – leprous, like snow. Aaron turned toward her and saw that she had leprosy; and he said to Moses, "Please, my lord, do not hold against us the sin we have so foolishly committed. Do not let her be like a stillborn infant coming from its mother's womb with it flesh half eaten away.

So Moses cried out to the LORD. "O God, please heal her!"

The LORD replied to Moses, "If her father had spit in her face, would she not have been in disgrace for seven days? Confine her outside the camp for seven days, after that she can be brought back." So Miriam was confined outside the camp for seven days, and the people did not move on till she was brought back. After that the people left Hazeroth and encamped in the Desert of Paran. (Numbers 12:1 – 16)

God however straightened Miriam and Aaron in this case. Miriam had leprosy. Though Moses cried out to God to save Miriam; God insisted that Miriam should be left out for a week, before she could be healed. God said he actually spoke to Moses face to face while to other prophets he spoke in dreams and visions. (Numbers 12)

Miriam is a lesson to many members of the Body of Christ.

Lessons to Learn:

- Moses was breast fed by his mother until he was sent to Pharaoh's daughter
- God meted punishment to her as a result of her talking down upon Moses
- She was a Prophetess despite it all

God is the Umbrella of Women in the Bible!

49. Naomi –Elimelech's Wife

Who Was This Woman?

- In the days when the judges ruled, there was a famine in the land and a man from Bethlehem in Judah together with his wife and two sons went to live for a while in the country of Moab.
- They were Ephrathites from Bethlehem, Judah
- She was the wife of Elimelech
- She had two sons with Elimelech
- Her husband died and she remained with her two sons
- They both married Moabitess women
- Mahlon and Kilion were her sons
- After ten years her sons both died
- Naomi left Moab for her country
- Then Naomi said to her two daughters-in-law, "Go back, each of you, to your mother's home. May the Lord Show kindness to you, as you have shown to your dead and to me. May the Lord grant that each of you will find rest in the home of another husband.

- Then she kissed them and they wept aloud and said to her, "We will go back with you to your people."
- But Naomi said, "Return home, my daughters. Why would you come with me? Am I going to have any more sons, who could become your husbands? Return home, my daughters. I am too old to have another husband. Even if I thought there was still hope for me – even if I had a husband tonight and then gave birth to sons – would you wait until they grew up? No, my daughters. It is more bitter for me than for you, because the Lord's hand has gone out against me!" At this they wept again.
- Then Orpah kissed her mother-in-law good-by, but Ruth clung to her.
- "Look," said Naomi, your sister-in-law is going back to her people and her gods. Go back with her."
- But Ruth replied, "Don't urge me to leave you or to turn back from you. Where you go, and where you stay I will stay. Your people will be my people and your God my God. Where you die I will die, and there I will be buried. May the Lord deal with me, be it ever so severely, if any thing but death separates you and me."
- When Naomi realized that Ruth was determined to go with her, she stopped urging her.
- So the two women went on until they came to Bethlehem.

- When they arrived in Bethlehem, the whole town was stirred because of them, and the women exclaimed, "Can this be Naomi?"
- "Don't call me Naomi," she told them, "Call me Mara, because the Almighty had made my life very bitter. I went away full, but the Lord had brought me back empty. Why call me Naomi? The Lord had afflicted me; the Almighty has brought misfortune upon me.
- So Naomi returned from Moab accompanied by Ruth the Moabitess, her daughter
- Many people travel from their countries of birth with their families to various parts of the world today
- Mostly in search of something better than what is in their own country
- Many have had success and many have failed
- Either way there comes a time when they want to return to their original home country
- Some bring back a Boaz and some do not
- Some like Naomi go through a lot of suffering, they lose not only their belongings but their families as well
- I remember in my own country they have various sayings about people who went to South Africa and came back with nothing – "Vakachona" "A Phiri anabwera" which means literally "They stayed long" "Mr. Phiri came back"
- It takes someone like Naomi to make the decision to return home

- We have a saying that says "There is nothing like home"
- There is always rejection in foreign countries yet many have succeeded with perseverance
- Orpah remained in her own homeland, many have left behind memories of their lives in those countries
- Ruth followed Naomi and today there are many foreign women who follow their husbands to their own countries
- There is a Boaz waiting for you on the other side
- It is up to you to show up
- Learn to do right! Seek justice, encourage the oppressed, defend the cause of the fatherless, plead the cause of the widow. (Isaiah 1:17)

The Story:

There was famine in Bethlehem thus Elimelech, Naomi and their two sons Mahlon and Kilion went from Bethlehem to the land of Moab.

What type of famine has caused you to move from one place to another? Famine is a very bad shortage of food in an area. I can also think of it a very bad shortage of something in an area just to make it interesting.

When she and her family got to Moab they settled there, hoping to be there until the end of the famine. However, it was not to be, as her husband died, living her with her two sons.

The two sons then got married to Moabite women. This is very common even today our find that people visit other countries for various reasons and end up marrying local women. In my family there is a belief that our Great, great, great grandmother must have been born from a foreign nationality, because she is always described as very light in complexion with very long hair and of course very beautiful. The beautiful Mrs. Saurombe.

The two sons married Orpah and Ruth and they had not children. After ten years the two sons both died, living Naomi with her two daughters-in-law. She was greatly devastated; imagine coming with your husband and two children and then remaining with two daughters-in-law who have no children.

She then heard that the LORD had come to the aid of his people and provided them with food and she decided to go back. She told her daughters-in-law and they prepared to go with her back home. They packed whatever they could carry and set off for Bethlehem.

In my culture when a woman loses her husband and is still of child-bearing age, she is given a choice whether to remain in the family or go back to her family where she will be free to remarry. If she decides to remain in the family she may be given another relative to marry her or she can just remain to look after her own children.

In this case Naomi put it before the two women that they could go to their homes where they could stay with them and remarry. She told them that she could not promise them each a husband in Bethlehem, because she had no other sons, and she had been away for so long she was not sure how she would be received going back without her husband and two sons.

Orpah kissed her mother-in-law good by but Ruth clung to her. So Naomi went to Bethlehem with Ruth. When they arrived in Bethlehem, the whole town was stirred because of them, and women exclaimed, "Can this be Naomi!" The name Naomi means 'pleasant' in Hebrew.

She told them not to call her Naomi but to call her Mara which means bitter. She said because the Almighty has made my life very bitter. She said she went to Moab full and came back empty. Why should you call me Naomi? The LORD has afflicted me; the Almighty had brought misfortune upon me.

The Bible and Naomi

In the days when the judges ruled, there was a famine in the land and a man from Bethlehem in Judah together with his wife and two sons went to live for a while in the country of Moab.

The man's name was Elimelech, his wife's name was Naomi, and the names of his two sons were Mahlon and Kilion. They were Ephrathites from Bethlehem, Judah.

Now Elimelech, Naomi's husband, died, and she was left with her two sons.

They married Moabite women, one named Orpah and the other Ruth.

After they had lived there about ten years both Mahlon and Kilion also died and Naomi was left without her two sons and her husband.

When she heard in Moab that the Lord had come to the aid of his people by providing food for them, Naomi and her daughters-in-law prepared to return home from there.

With her two daughters-in-law she left the place where she had been living and set out on the road that would take them back to the land of Judah.

Then Naomi said to her two daughters-in-law, "Go back, each of you, to your mother's home. May the Lord show kindness to you, as you have shown to your dead and to me. May the Lord grant that each of you will find rest in the home of another husband. Then she kissed them and they wept aloud and said to her, "We will go back with you to your people."

But Naomi said, "Return home, my daughters. Why would you come with me? Am I going to have any more sons, who could become your husbands? Return home, my daughters. I am too old to have another husband. Even if I thought there was still hope for me – even if I had a husband tonight and then gave birth to sons – would you wait until they grew up? No, my daughters. It is more bitter for me than for you, because the Lord's hand has gone out against me!"

At this they wept again.

Then Orpah kissed her mother-in-law good-by, but Ruth clung to her.

"Look," said Naomi, your sister-in-law is going back to her people and her gods. Go back with her."

But Ruth replied, "Don't urge me to leave you or to turn back from you. Where you go, and where you stay I will stay. Your people will be my people and your God my God. Where you die I will die, and there I will be buried. May the Lord deal with me, be it ever so severely, if any thing but death separates you and me."

When Naomi realized that Ruth was determined to go with her, she stopped urging her.

So the two women went on until they came to Bethlehem. When they arrived in Bethlehem, the whole town was stirred because of them, and the women exclaimed, "Can this be Naomi?"

"Don't call me Naomi," she told them, "Call me Mara, because the Almighty had made my life very bitter. I went away full, but the Lord had brought me back empty. Why call me Naomi? The Lord had afflicted me; the Almighty has brought misfortune upon me.

So Naomi returned from Moab accompanied by Ruth the Moabitess, her daughter-in-law, arriving in Bethlehem as the barley harvest was beginning. (Ruth 1:1 – 27)

Ruth Meets Boaz

Now Naomi had a relative on her husband's side, from the clan of Elimelech, a man of standing, whose name was Boaz.

And Ruth the Moabitess said to Naomi, "Let me go to the fields and pick up the leftover grain behind anyone in whose eyes I find favour." Naomi said to her, "Go ahead, my daughter."

So she went out and began to glean in the fields behind the harvesters. As it turned out, she found herself working in a field belonging to Boaz, who was from the clan of Elimelech.

Just then Boaz arrived from Bethlehem and greeted the harvesters, "The Lord be with you!" "The Lord bless you!" they called back.

Boaz asked the foreman of his harvesters, "Whose young woman is that?"

The foreman replied, "She is the Moabitess who came back from Moab with Naomi.

She said, 'Please let me glean and gather among the sheaves behind the harversters.' She went into the field and has worked steadily from morning till now, except for a short rest in the shelter."

So Boaz said to Ruth, "My daughter, listen to me. Don't go and glean in another field and don't go away from here. Stay here with my servant girls.

Watch the field where the men are harvesting, and follow along after the girls. I have told the men not to touch you. And whenever you are thirsty, go and get a drink from the water jars the men have filled;"

At this, she bowed down with her face to the ground. She exclaimed, "Why have I found such favour in your eyes that you notice me – a foreigner?"

Boaz replied, "I've been told all about what you have done for your mother-in-law since the death of your husband – how you left your father and mother and your homeland and came to live with a people you did not know before.

May the Lord repay you for what you have done. May you be richly rewarded by the Lord, the God of Israel, under whose wings you have come to take refuge."

"May I continue to find favour in your eyes, my lord," she said. "You have given me comfort and have spoken kindly to your servant – though I do not have the standing of one of your servant girls."

At mealtime Boaz said to her, "Come over her. Have some bread and dip it in the wine vinegar." When she sat down with the harvesters, he offered her some roasted grain. She ate all she wanted and had some left over.

As she got up to glean, Boaz gave orders to his men, "Even if she gathers among the sheaves, don't embarrass her.

Rather, pull out some stalks for her from the bundles and leave them for her to pick up, and don't rebuke her."

So Ruth gleaned in the field until evening. Then she threshed the barley she had gathered, and it amounted to about an Ephah.

She carried it back to town, and her mother-in-law saw how much she had gathered. Ruth also brought out and gave her what she had left over after she had eaten enough.

Her mother-in-law asked her, "Where did you glean today? Where did you work? Blessed be the man who took notice of you!" Then Ruth told her mother-in-law about the one at whose place she had been working. "The name of the man I worked with today is Boaz," she said.

"The Lord bless him!" Naomi said to her daughter-in-law. "He has not stopped showing his kindness to the living and the dead." She added, "That man is our close relative; he is one of our kinsman-redeemers."

Then Ruth the Moabitess said, "He even said to me, 'Stay with my workers until they finish harvesting all my grain.' "

Naomi said to Ruth her daughter-in-law, "It will be good for you, my daughter, to go with his girls, because in someone else's field you might be harmed."

So Ruth stayed close to the servant girls of Boaz to glean until the barley and wheat harvests were finished. And she lived with her mother-in-law. (Ruth 2:1 – 23)

Ruth and Boaz at the Threshing-Floor

One day Naomi her mother-in-law said to her, "My daughter, should I not try to find a home for you, where you will be well provided for?

Is not Boaz, with whose servant girls you have been, a kinsman of ours? Tonight he will be winnowing barley on the threshing-floor.

Wash and perfume yourself, and put on your best clothes. Then go down to the threshing-floor, but don't let him know you are there until he has finished eating and drinking.

When he lies down, note the place where he is lying. Then go and uncover his feet and lie down. He will tell you what to do."

"I will do whatever you say," Ruth answered.

So she went down to the threshing-floor and did everything her mother-in-law told her to do.

When Boaz had finished eating and drinking and was in good spirits, he went over to lie down at the far end of the grain pile. Ruth approached quietly, uncovered his feet and lay down.

In the middle of the night something startled the man, and he turned and discovered a woman lying at his feet.

"Who are you?" he asked; "I am your servant Ruth," she said; "Spread the corner of your garment over me, since you are a kinsman-redeemer."

"The Lord bless you, my daughter," he replied. "This kindness is greater than that which you showed earlier: You have not run after the younger men, whether rich or poor.

And now, my daughter, don't be afraid. I will do for you all you ask. All my fellow townsmen know that you are a woman of noble character.

Although it is true that I am near of kin, there is a kinsman-redeemer nearer than I.

Stay here for the night, and in the morning if he wants to redeem, good; let him redeem. But if he is not willing, as surely as the Lord lives I will do it. Lie here until morning."

So she lay at his feet until morning, but got up before anyone could be recognized; and he said, "Don't let it be known that a woman came to the threshing-floor."

He also said, "Bring me the Shawl you are wearing and hold it out." When she did so, he poured into it six measures of barley and put it on her. Then he went back to town.

When Ruth came to her mother-in-law, Naomi asked, "How did it go, my daughter?" Then she told her everything Boaz had done for her

And added, "He gave me these six measures of barley, saying, 'Don't go back to your mother-in-law empty-handed.'
"

Then Naomi said, "Wait, my daughter, until you find out what happens. For the man will not rest until the matter is settled today." (Ruth 3:1 - 18

Boaz Marries Ruth

Meanwhile Boaz went up to the town gate and sat there. When the kinsman-redeemer he had mentioned came along, Boaz said, "Come over here, my friend, and sit down." So he went over and sat down.

Boaz took ten of the elders of the town and said, "Sit here," and they did so.

Then he said to the kinsman-redeemer, "Naomi, who has come back from Moab, is selling the piece of land that belonged to our brother Elimelech.

I thought I should bring the matter to your attention and suggest that you buy it in the presence of these seated here and in the presence of the elders of my people. If you will redeem it, do so. But if you will not, tell me, so I will know. For no-one has the right to do it except you, and I am next in line." "I will redeem it," he said.

Then Boaz said, "On the day you buy the land from Naomi and from Ruth the Moabitess, you acquire the dead man's widow, in order to maintain the name of the dead with his property."

At this, the kinsman-redeemer said, "Then I cannot redeem it because I might endanger my own estate. You redeem it yourself. I cannot do it."

(Now in earlier times in Israel, for the redemption and transfer of property to become final, one party took off his sandal and gave it to the other. This was the method of legalizing transactions in Israel.)

So the kinsman-redeemer said to Boaz, "Buy it yourself." And he removed his sandal.

Then Boaz announced to the elders and all the people, "Today you are witnesses that I have bought from Naomi all the property of Elimelech, Kilion and Mahlon.

I have also acquired Ruth the Moabitess, Mahlon's widow, as my wife, in order to maintain the name of the dead with his property, so that his name will not disappear from among his family or from the town records. Today you are witnesses!"

Then the elders and all those at the gate said, "We are witnesses. May the Lord make the woman who is coming into your home like Rachel and Leah, who together built up the house of Israel. May you have standing in Ephrata and become famous in Bethlehem.

Through the offspring the Lord gives you by this young woman, may your family be like that of Perez, whom Tamar bore to Judah."

The Genealogy of David

So Boaz took Ruth and she became his wife. Then he went to her, and the Lord enabled her to conceive, and she gave birth to a son.

The women said to Naomi: "Praise be to the Lord, who this day has not left you without a kinsman-redeemer. May he become famous throughout Israel!

He will renew your life and sustain you in your old age. For your daughter-in-law, who loves you and who is better to you than seven sons, has given him birth."

Then Naomi took the child, laid him in her lap and cared for him.

The women living there said, "Naomi has a son." And they named him Obed. He was the father of Jesse, the father of David.

- This, then is the family line of Perez: Perez was the father of Hezron,
- Hezron the father of Ram, Ram the father of Amminadab,
- Amminadab the father of Nahshon, Nahshon the father of Salmon,
- Salmon the father of Boaz, Boaz the father of Obed,
- Obed the father of Jesse, and Jesse the father of David. (Ruth 4:1 - 22)

Lessons to Learn:

- Then Naomi took the child, laid him in her lap and cared for him.
- The women living there said, "Naomi has a son." And they named him Obed. He was the father of Jesse, the father of David.
- This, then is the family line of Perez: Perez was the father of Hezron,
- Hezron the father of Ram, Ram the father of Amminadab,
- Amminadab the father of Nahshon, Nahshon the father of Salmon,

- Salmon the father of Boaz, Boaz the father of Obed,
- Obed the father of Jesse, and Jesse the father of David.

God is the Umbrella of Women in the Bible!

50. Noah's Wife:

Who Was This Woman?

- She was the mother of Shem – the line of Abram
- She was the mother of Ham
- She was the mother of Japheth
- She was there every day when Noah was building the Ark

The Story:

Noah's wife, though not mentioned by name was present. She was working behind the scene, doing all the chores that a normal house wife will do. May be she even assisted her husband in the collecting of the materials used for the building. Preparing meals for the family and looking after them. She must have even heard God speaking to her husband about the Ark. Of course she was making the family too.

The Bible and Noah's Wife:

After Noah was 500 years old he became the father of Shem, Ham and Japheth (Genesis 5:32)

But I will establish my covenant with you, and you will enter the ark – you and your sons and your wife and your sons' wives with you. (Genesis 6:18)

And Noah and his sons and his wife and his sons' wives entered the ark to escape the waters of the flood. (Genesis 7:7)

On that very day Noah and his sons, Shem, Ham and Japheth, together with his wife and the wives of his three sons, entered the ark. (Genesis 7:13)

So Noah came out. Together with his sons and his wife and his sons' wives.

(Genesis 8:18)

Lessons to Learn:

- She was just there for Noah and her sons.

God is the Umbrella of Women in the Bible!

51. Orpah – the Wife of Mahlon:

Who Was This Woman?

- She was the wife of Mahlon the son of Elimelech and Naomi
- She was a Moabitess woman
- She had no children with Mahlon
- Mahlon died
- Naomi left Moab for her country
- She remained behind when Naomi asked her to remain
- Then Naomi said to her two daughters-in-law, "Go back, each of you, to your mother's home. May the Lord show kindness to you, as you have shown to your dead and to me. May the Lord grant that each of you will find rest in the home of another husband.
- Then she kissed them and they wept aloud and said to her, "We will go back with you to your people."

- But Naomi said, "Return home, my daughters. Why would you come with me? Am I going to have any more sons, who could become your husbands? Return home, my daughters. I am too old to have another husband. Even if I thought there was still hope for me – even if I had a husband tonight and then gave birth to sons – would you wait until they grew up? No, my daughters. It is more bitter for me than for you, because the Lord's hand has gone out against me!"At this they wept again.
- Then Orpah kissed her mother-in-law good-by, but Ruth clung to her.

In the days when the judges ruled, there was a famine in the land and a man from Bethlehem in Judah together with his wife and two sons went to live for a while in the country of Moab.

The man's name was Elimelech, his wife's name was Naomi, and the names of his two sons were Mahlon and Kilion. They were Ephrathites from Bethlehem, Judah.

Now Elimelech, Naomi's husband, died, and she was left with her two sons.

They married Moabite women, one named Orpah and the other Ruth.

After they had lived there about ten years both Mahlon and Kilion also died and Naomi was left without her two sons and her husband.

When she heard, in Moab. that the Lord had come to the aid of his people, by providing food for them, Naomi and her daughters-in-law prepared to return home from there.

With her two daughters-in-law she left the place where she had been living and set out on the road that would take them back to the land of Judah.

Then Naomi said to her two daughters-in-law, "Go back, each of you, to your mother's home. May the Lord show kindness to you, as you have shown to your dead and to me. May the Lord grant that each of you will find rest in the home of another husband. Then she kissed them and they wept aloud and said to her, "We will go back with you to your people."

But Naomi said, "Return home, my daughters. Why would you come with me? Am I going to have any more sons, who could become your husbands? Return home, my daughters. I am too old to have another husband. Even if I thought there was still hope for me – even if I had a husband tonight and then gave birth to sons – would you wait until they grew up? No, my daughters. It is more bitter for me than for you, because the Lord's hand has gone out against me!"

At this they wept again.

Then Orpah kissed her mother-in-law good-by, but Ruth clung to her.

"Look," said Naomi, your sister-in-law is going back to her people and her gods. Go back with her."

But Ruth replied, "Don't urge me to leave you or to turn back from you. Where you go, and where you stay I will stay. Your people will be my people and your God my God. Where you die I will die, and there I will be buried. May the Lord deal with me, be it ever so severely, if any thing but death separates you and me."

When Naomi realized that Ruth was determined to go with her, she stopped urging her.

So the two women went on until they came to Bethlehem. When they arrived in Bethlehem, the whole town was stirred because of them, and the women exclaimed, "Can this be Naomi?"

"Don't call me Naomi," she told them, "Call me Mara, because the Almighty had made my life very bitter. I went away full, but the Lord had brought me back empty. Why call me Naomi? The Lord had afflicted me; the Almighty has brought misfortune upon me.

So Naomi returned from Moab accompanied by Ruth the Moabitess, her daughter-in-law, arriving in Bethlehem as the barley harvest was beginning.

52. Peninnah – The Second Wife of Elkanah

Who Was This Woman?

- She was the second wife of Elkanah
- She provoked Hannah the first wife
- She was a bad example of a second wife
- She had children at the time when Hannah had none
- She frustrated her husband

The Story:

Peninnah was the second wife of Elkanah. She is known only about her cruelty to Hannah the first wife of Elkanah. Peninnah had children and therefore looked down upon Hannah who was barren.

Some women like Peninnah are known only for their cruelty. What would you like to be known for? Do not wait until it is too late to rectify your behavior as it will affect generations and generations.

It would be a very good thing if people would learn to love one another; especially those that come into contact with others who have already established themselves.

Peninnah was a second wife and Hannah was the first wife. Who should harass who in this situation? Peninnah provoked and irritated Hannah in this situation.

In many cases women who come into households that had existed already usually cause confusion to both their own children and the children they find in that household. This should not be so as the children did not ask to be in those circumstances.

I know of a second wife who loved the first wife like her sister. Both her children and the first wife's children were like they came from one mother. When one of the older wife's daughters got married and was being harassed by her husband; she went and took the daughter and told the husband that he would have to contend with her. Her own mother by that time had passed away. The son-in-law later promised to look after her daughter properly and they lived well afterwards though they are both now late.

This was Peninnah problem. Elkanah already had a wife, though they had no children. The fact that she came in and had children, made her feel that she was now more important than Hannah the first wife.

What would Jesus say about Peninnah? Three things: Firstly, you are the intruder therefore be patient and willing to learn from Hannah. Secondly, listen to what her problems are and why she was in the situation that she was in and be helpful. Thirdly, encourage her and even tell her that your children are also her children since you have the same husband. This would bring peace and love to the whole household.

Instead madam Peninnah was a showy. Look I have children and I am better than you. That is why your husband took up a second wife; it is because you are barren. I am sure there are many other degrading words that came out of her mouth. God had other plans for Hannah.

The Bible and Peninnah:

There was a certain man from Ramathaim, S Zuphite from the hill country of Ephraim, whose name was Elkana son of Jeroham, the son of Elihu, the son of Tohu, the son of Zuph, and Ephramite. He had two wives; one was called Hannah and the other Peninnah. Peninnah had children but Hannah had none.

Year after year this man went up from his town to worship and sacrifice to the LORD Almighty at Shiloh, where Hophni and Phinehas, the two sons of Eli, were priests of the LORD. Whenever the day came for Elkanah to sacrifice, he would give portions of the meat to his wife Peninnah and to all her sons and daughters. But to Hannah he gave a double portion because he loved her, and the LORD had closed her womb, her rival kept provoking her in order to irritate her. This went on year after year. When Hannah went up to the house of the LORD, her rival provoked her till she wept and would not eat. Elkanah her husband would say to her, "Hannah, why are you weeping? Why don't you eat? Why are you downhearted? Don't I mean more to you than ten sons?"

Once when they had finished eating and drinking in Shiloh, Hannah stood up. Now Eli the priest was sitting on a chair by the doorpost of the LORD's temple. In bitterness of soul Hannah wept much and prayed to the LORD And she made a vow, saying, "O LORD Almighty, if you will only look upon your servant's misery and remember me, and not forget your servant but give her a son, then I will give him to the LORD for all the days of his life, and no razor will ever be used on his head."

As she kept on praying to the LORD, Eli observed her mouth. Hannah was praying in her heart, and her lips were moving but her voice was not heard. Eli thought she was drunk and said to her, "How long will you keep on getting drunk? Get rid of your wine."

"Not so, my lord," Hannah replied, "I am a woman who is deeply troubled. I have not been drinking wine or beer; I was pouring out my soul to the LORD. Do not take your servant for a wicked woman; I have been praying her out of my great anguish and grief;"

Eli answered, "Go in peace, and May the God of Israel grant you what you have asked of him."

She said, "May your servant find favour in your eyes." Then she went her way and ate something and her face was no longer downcast.

Early the next morning they arose and worshiped before the LORD and then went back to their home at Ramah. Elkana lay with Hannah his wife, and the LORD remembered her. So in the course of time Hannah conceived and gave birth to a son.

She named him Samuel, saying, "Because I asked the LORD for him."

When the man Elkanah went up with all his family to offer the annual sacrifice to the LORD and to fulfill his vow, Hannah did not go. She said to her husband. "After the boy is weaned, I will take him and present him before the LORD, and he will live there always."

"Do what seems best to you," Elkanah her husband told her. "Stay here until you have weaned him; only may the LORD make good his work." So the woman stayed at home and nursed her son until she had weaned him.

After he was weaned, she took the boy with her, young as he was, along with a three year old bull, an Ephah of flour and a skin of wine, and brought him to the house of the LORD at Shiloh. When they had slaughtered the bull, they brought the boy to Eli, and she said to him, "As surely as you live, my lord, I am the woman who stood here beside you praying to the LORD. I prayed for this child, and the LORD has granted me what I asked of him. So now I give him to the LORD. For the whole life he will be given over to the LORD." And he worshiped the LORD there.

(1 Samuel 1:1 – 28)

But Samuel was ministering before the LORD – a boy wearing a linen ephod. Each year his mother made him a little robe and took it to him when she went up with her husband to offer the annual sacrifice. Eli would bless Elkanah and his wife, saying "May the LORD give you children by this woman to take the place of the one she prayed for and gave to the LORD." Then they would go home. And the LORD was gracious to Hannah; she conceived and gave birth to three sons and two daughters. Meanwhile, the boy Samuel grew up in the presence of the LORD.

(2 Samuel 1:18 – 21)

Lessons to Learn:

- Peninnah is only known for her attitude towards Hannah and the fact that she had children while Hannah had none.
- The LORD remembered Hannah and she has several children in the end

God is the Umbrella of Women in the Bible!

53. Peter's Mother-in-Law

Who Was This Woman?

- She was in Peter's house
- She was lying in bed with fever
- Jesus touched her hand
- The fever left her
- She got up
- She waited on Jesus.
- She was part of the fulfillment of Scriptures
- She became so fit as to wait on Jesus
- Jesus carried on with his work of healing the sick

The Story:

She was lying in bed with fever at Peter's house. Jesus came into Peter's house and touched her hand and the fever left her and she got up and began to wait on him.

When evening came, many who were demon possessed were brought to him, and he drove out the spirits with a word and healed all the sick. This was to fulfill what was spoken through the prophet Isaiah: "He took up our infirmities and carried our diseases."

The Bible and Peter's Mother-in-Law

When Jesus came into Peter's house, he saw Peter's mother-in-law lying in bed with fever. He touched her hand and the fever left her and she got up and began to wait on him.

When evening came, many who were demon possessed were brought to him, and he drove out the spirits with a word and healed all the sick. This was to fulfill what was spoken through the prophet Isaiah: "He took up our infirmities and carried our diseases." (Matthew 8:14 – 17)

Lessons to Learn:

- Which house have you visited recently – Jesus went to Peter's house.
- We must pray for the sick to be healed in Jesus' Name
- He took up our infirmities and carried our diseases
- There are people who are waiting for your prayers get up and go!
- Jesus is the Healer he took up our infirmities and carried our diseases

God is the Umbrella of Women in the Bible!

54. Phoebe and the Other Women:

Who Were These Women?

- Phoebe, Mary, Tryphena, Tryphosa and Persis, Rufus' Mother, Nereus' Sister
- Servants of the Church
- Worthy of being called Saints
- Help to many people including the Apostle Paul himself
- Fellow workers in Christ Jesus
- Women who risked their lives
- The Apostle Paul and the Gentile churches were grateful to them
- They worked very hard for the Church
- They worked hard in the Lord
- They were mothers to the Apostle
- They were remembered by name by Apostle Paul

The Bible and Phoebe, Mary, Tryphena, Tryphosa and Persis, Rufus' Mother, Nereus' Sister:

I commend to you our sister Phoebe, a servant of the church in Cenchrea. I ask you to receive her in the Lord in a way worthy of the saints and to give her any help she may need from you, for she has been a great help to many people, including me.

Greet Priscilla and Aquila, my fellow workers in Christ Jesus. They risked their lives for me. Not only I but all the churches of the Gentiles are grateful to them. Greet the church that meets at their house.

Greet my dear friend Epenetus, who was the first convert to Christ in the province of Asia. Greet Mary, who worked very hard for you. Greet Andronicus and Junias, my relatives who have been in prison with me. They are outstanding among the apostles, and they were in Christ before I was.

Greet Ampliatus, whom I love in the Lord. Greet Urbanus, our fellow worker in Christ, and my dear friend Stachys. Greet Apelles, tested and approved in Christ. Greet those who belong to the household of Aristobulus. Greet Herodion, my relative. Greet those in the household of Narcissus who are in the Lord.

Greet Tryphena and Tryphosa, those women who work hard in the Lord.

Greet my dear friend Persis, another woman who has worked very hard in the lord.

Greet Rufus, chosen in the Lord, and his mother, who has been a mother to me, too.

Greet Asyncritus, Phlegon, Hermes, Patrobas, Hermas and the brothers with them. Greet Philogus, Julia, Nereus and his sister, and Olympas and all the saints with them.

Greet one another with a holy kiss. All the churches of Christ send greetings. (Romans16:1 -15)

Lessons to Learn:

- They were servants of the church
- The Apostle wanted them to be received well
- He remembered them by name
- He wanted to communicate to them in his letter
- There was a reason, he knew what they did in the church
- They were there to do the work of the Lord

God is the Umbrella of Women in the Bible!

55. Priscilla – the Wife of Aquila:

Who Was This Woman?

- A fellow worker in Christ
- A tent maker
- She participated in the Church
- She was eager to learn
- She was a good hostess
- She was a risk taker
- She was always remembered by the Apostle Paul in his letters

The Story:

Priscilla worked with her husband as tent makers. It seems they were church leaders in Rome before Claudius ordered all Jews to live Rome. She traveled with her husband to Corinth. When the Apostle Paul went to Rome he stayed with Priscilla and Aquila, because they had something in common. They were both tent makers.

Aquila reminds me of the saying "behind every successful man there is a successful woman. She was part and parcel of many discussions that must have taken place in their tent with the Apostle Paul. Paul left Priscilla and Aquila in Ephesus, where they met Apollos who was learned and had a thorough knowledge of scriptures. Priscilla and Aquila invited Apollos to their home. The type of people that Priscilla came into contact with, show you what kind of a woman she was. She must have been eager to learn and to host. The Apostle Paul himself always remembered Priscilla in his letters, he wrote: "Greet Priscilla and Aquila, my fellow workers in Christ Jesus. They risked their lives for me. Not only I but all the disciples of the Gentiles are grateful to them. Greet also the church that meets at their house.

The Bible and Priscilla:

"Greet Priscilla and Aquila, my fellow workers in Christ Jesus. They risked their lives for me. Not only I but all the Churches of the Gentiles are grateful to them. Greet also the church that meets at their house. Greet my dear friend Epenetus, who was the first convert to Christ in the province of Asia. (Romans 16:3 – .5)

Lessons to Learn:

- Included in Personal Greeting of the Apostle Paul: Do you remember anyone who included you in their greetings especially to the Church?
- Can you risk your life for anyone – discuss?
- Has the Church ever met at your house, what do you think?

- Who would you like to include in your greetings?

God is the Umbrella of Women in the Bible!

56. Puah – the Hebrew Midwife:

Who Was This Woman?

- She was one of the Hebrew midwives to whom the king of Egypt had given orders to kill the boys and save the girls
- She feared God and let the boys live
- She told the king that Hebrew women are not Egyptian women, they are vigorous and they gave birth before the midwifes arrived
- God was kind to her
- Pharaoh then ordered that every boy that was born was to be thrown into the

The Story:

When Joseph and all his brothers and all their generation had died, the Israelites had become fruitful and multiplied greatly and had become exceedingly numerous in Egypt, a new king came to power. He did not know anything about Joseph.

He then pondered a way of reducing the numbers of the Israelites. Firstly he oppressed them and worked them ruthlessly. He made their lives bitter by giving them hard labour in brick and mortar and with all kinds of work in the fields. When all this was not working he decided to go further and kill the Israelite new babies.

The Bible and Puah:

The king of Egypt said to the Hebrew midwives, whose names were Shiprah and Puah, "When you help the Hebrew women in childbirth and observe them on the delivery stool, if it is a boy, kill him, but if it is a girl let her live."

The midwives, however, feared God and did not do what the king of Egypt had told them to do; they let the boys live. Then the king of Egypt summoned the midwives and asked them, "Why have you done this? Why have you let the boys live?

The midwives answered Pharaoh, "Hebrew women are not like Egyptian women; they are vigorous and give birth before the midwives arrive.

So God was kind to the midwives and the people increased and became even more numerous. And because the midwives feared God, he gave them families of their own.

Then Pharaoh gave this order to all his people; "Every boy that is born you must throw into the Nile but let e very girl live." (Exodus 1:15 – 22)

Lessons to Learn:

- God was kind to the midwives

- The people increased and became even more numerous
- Because the midwives feared God, he gave them families of their own.
- Then Pharaoh gave this order to all his people; "Every boy that is born you must throw into the Nile but let e very girl live."
- That is the reason why Jochebed was afraid to keep her son Moses and placed him in the basket in the river Nile

God is the Umbrella of Women in the Bible!

57. Queen Esther

Who Was This Woman?

- She was a Jewish Orphan
- For 180 days the king displayed the vast wealth of his kingdom and the splendor and glory of his majesty
- King Xerxes had given a banquet for all his nobles and officials at the end of the 180 days
- This was to last for seven days on the seventh day he was in good spirits from wine; he commanded the seven eunuchs who served him to bring before him Queen Vashti
- She was supposed to come wearing her royal crown
- She was to display her beauty to the people and nobles
- The eunuchs were: Mehuman, Biztha, Harbona, Bigtha, Abagtha, Zethar and Carcas
- Queen Vashti also had given a banquet for the women

- King Xerxes wanted to show off his wife and asked that she came before him
- Queen Vashti refused to be paraded
- This was a case of law and justice now
- The king consulted the wise men who were closest to him and understood the times
- The wise men were: Carshena, Shethar, Admatha, Tarshish, Meres, Marsena and Memucan
- He consulted the seven nobles of Persia and Media who had special access to the king and were highest in the kingdom
- King Xerxes asked, "According to the law, what must be done to Queen Vashti?" "She has not obeyed the command of King Xerxes that the eunuchs have taken to her."
- Memucan replied in the presence of the king and the nobles: "Queen Vashti has done wrong not only against the king but also against the nobles and the peoples of all the provinces of King Xerxes.
- The Queens conduct will be known to all women and they will despise their husbands and say: "King Xerxes commanded Queen Vashti to be brought before him, but she would not come."
- The Persian women and the Median women of the nobility who have heard about the queen's conduct will respond to all the king's nobles in the same way. There will be no end of disrespect and discord.

- They suggested that Vashti should never again be allowed to enter the presence of King Xerxes.
- Also let the king give her royal position to some one else.
- This was given to Esther

The Story:

Her story begins after Queen Vashti had been told not to go into the presence of King Xerxes again.

It was decided and agreed that the king had to find another person to replace Vashti as queen and the following was agreed:

To search be made for beautiful young virgins for the king

To let the king appoint commissioners in every province of his realm to bring all these beautiful girls into the harem at the citadel of Susa

To let them be placed under the care of Hegai

To let beauty treatments be given to them

Then to let the girl who pleases the king become queen instead of Vashti."

The king accepted this advice as it appealed to him, and he followed it.

Now there was in the citadel of Susa a Jew of the tribe of Benjamin, named Mordecai son of Jair, the son of Shimei, the son of Kish, who had been carried into exile from Jerusalem by Nebuchadnezzar king of Babylon, among those taken captive with Jehoiachin king of Judah

Mordecai had a cousin named Hadassah, whom he had brought up because she had neither father nor mother. This girl, who was also known as Esther, was lovely in form and features, and Mordecai had taken her as his daughter when her father and mother died.

When the king's order and edict had been proclaimed, many girls were brought to the citadel of Susa and put under the care of Hegai. Esther also was taken to the king's palace and entrusted to Hegai, who had charge of the harem. She pleased him and won his favour. Immediately he provided her with her beauty treatments and special food. He assigned to her seven maids selected from the king's palace and moved her and her maids into the best place in the harem.

Esther had not revealed her nationality and family background, because Mordecai had forbidden her to do so. Every day he walked back and forth near the courtyard of the harem to find out how Esther was and what was happening to her.

Before a girl's turn came to go in to King Xerxes, she had to complete twelve months of beauty treatments prescribed for the women, six months with oil of myrrh and six with perfumes and cosmetics. And this is how she would go to the king: Anything she wanted was given her to take with her from the harem to the king's palace. In the evening she would go there and in the morning return to another part of the harem to the care of Shaashgaz, the king's eunuch who was in charge f the concubines. She would not return to the king unless he was pleased with her and summoned her by name.

When the turn came for Esther (the girl Mordecai had adopted, the daughter of his uncle Abihail) to go to the king, she asked for nothing than what Hegai, the king's eunuch who was in charge of the harem, suggested. And Esther won the favour of everyone who saw her. She was taken to King Xerxes in the royal residence in the tenth month, the month of Tebeth, in the seventh year of his reign.

Now the king was attracted to Esther more than to any of the other women, and she won his favour and approval more than any of the other virgins. So he set a royal crown on her head and made her queen instead of Vashiti. And the king gave a great banquet, Esther's banquet, for all his nobles and officials. He proclaimed a holiday throughout the provinces and distributed gifts with royal liberality.

When the virgins were assembled a second time, Mordecai was sitting at the king's gate. But Esther had kept secret her family background and nationality just as Mordecai had told her to do, for she continued to follow Mordecai's instructions as she had don when he was bringing her up.

During the time Mordecai was sitting at the king's gate, Bigthana and Teresh, two of the king's officers who guarded the doorway, became angry and conspired to assassinate King Xerxes. But Mordecai found out about the plot and told Queen Esther, who in turn reported it to the king, giving credit to Mordecai. And when the report was investigated and found to be true, the two officials were hanged on a gallows. All this was recorded in the book of the annals in the presence of the king.

The Bible and Queen Esther:

Later when the anger of King Xerxes had subsided, he remembered Vashti and what she had done and what he had decreed about her. Then the king's personal attendants proposed,

"Let a search be made for beautiful young virgins for the king. Let the king appoint commissioners in every province of his realm to bring all these beautiful girls into the harem at the citadel of Susa. Let them be placed under the care of Hegai, the king's eunuch, who is in charge of the women;

and let beauty treatments be given to them. Then let the girl who pleases the king be queen instead of Vashti."

This advice appealed to the king, and he followed it.

Now there was in the citadel of Susa a Jew of the tribe of Benjamin, named Mordecai son of Jair, the son of Shimei, the son of Kish, who had been carried into exile from Jerusalem by Nebuchadnezzar king of Babylon, among those taken captive with Jehoiachin king of Judah. Mordecai had a cousin named Hadassah, whom he had brought up because she had neither father nor mother. This girl, who was also known as Esther, was lovely in form and features, and Mordecai had taken her as his daughter when her father and mother died.

When the king's order and edict had been proclaimed, many girls were brought to the citadel of Susa and put under the care of Hegai. Esther also was taken to the king's palace and entrusted to Hegai, who had charge of the harem. The girl pleased him and won his favour. Immediately he provided her with her beauty treatments and special food. He assigned to her seven maids selected from the king's palace and moved her and her maids into the best place in the harem.

Esther had not revealed her nationality and family background, because Mordecai had forbidden her to do so. Every day he walked back and forth near the courtyard of the harem to find out how Esther was and what was happening to her.

Before a girl's turn came to go in to King Xerxes, she had to complete twelve months of beauty treatments prescribed for the women, six months with oil of myrrh and six with perfumes and cosmetics. And this is how she would go to the king: Anything she wanted was given her to take with her from the harem to the king's palace. In the evening she would go there and in the morning return to another part of the harem to the care of Shaashgaz, the king's eunuch who was in charge f the concubines. She would not return to the king unless he was pleased with her and summoned her by name.

When the turn came for Esther (the girl Mordecai had adopted, the daughter of his uncle Abihail) to go to the king, she asked for nothing than what Hegai, the king's eunuch who was in charge of the harem, suggested. And Esther won the favour of everyone who saw her. She was taken to King Xerxes in the royal residence in the tenth month, the month of Tebeth, in the seventh year of his reign.

Now the king was attracted to Esther more than to any of the other women, and she won his favour and approval more than any of the other virgins. So he set a royal crown on her head and made her queen instead of Vashiti. And the king gave a great banquet, Esther's banquet, for all his nobles and officials. He proclaimed a holiday throughout the provinces and distributed gifts with royal liberality.

When the virgins were assembled a second time, Mordecai was sitting at the king's gate. But Esther had kept secret her family background and nationality just as Mordecai had told her to do, for she continued to follow Mordecai's instructions as she had don when he was bringing her up.

During the time Mordecai was sitting at the kings gate, Bigthana and Teresh, two of the king's officers who guarded the doorway, became angry and conspired to assassinate King Xerxes. But Mordecai found out about the plot and told Queen Esther, who in turn reported it to the king, giving credit to Mordecai. And when the report was investigated and found to be true, the two officials were hanged on a gallows. All this was recorded in the book of the annals in the presence of the king. (Esther 2:1 – 23)

Lessons to Learn:

- The powerful story of Esther helps us to learn never to give up
- She was in a situation where it was difficult to talk about herself, about where she came from, yet she was an over comer. She saved he people
- What obstacles do you have in your life, is it something like what this woman went through? What can you do about it?

God is the Umbrella of Women in the Bible!

58. Queen Maacah

Who Was This Woman?

- She was Queen Mother
- She was the Mother of Abijah
- Grand Mother of King Asa
- She built an Asherah Pole
- She was Abishalom's daughter
- She was deposed from being Queen Mother by her grandson

The Story:

Maachah was the daughter of Absalom (also referred to as Abishalom) who was the son of King David. She is also referred to as the daughter of Uriel of Gibeah. Rehoboam took Mahalath the daughter of Jerimoth the son of David to wife and Abihail the daughter of Eliab the son of Jesse, he also took Maachah the daughter of Absalom which bare him Abijah and Attai and Ziza and Shelomith.

Rehoboam loved Maachah the daughter of Absalom more than all his wives and his concubines; because he had eighteen wives and threescore concubines, and had twenty and eight sons, and threescore daughters.

Rehoboam also made Abijah the son of Maachah the chief, to be ruler among his brethren as wanted to make him king. He dispersed all his children throughout all the countries of Judah and Benjamin to get them away from Abijah the son of Maachah.

She was deposed from being Queen Mother by her grandson King Asa of Judah as she had built an Asherah Pole. She was not a good grandmother as she was making idols.

The Bible and Queen Maacah:

So they strengthened the kingdom of Judah, and made Rehoboam the son of Solomon strong, three years: for three years they walked in the way of David and Solomon. And Rehoboam took him Mahalath the daughter of Jerimoth the son of David to wife, and Abihail the daughter of Eliab the son of Jesse, which bare him children; Jeush, and Shemariah, and Zaham. And after her he took Maachah the daughter of Absalom which bare him Abijah and Attai and Ziza and Shelomith. And Rehoboam loved Maachah the daughter of Absalom above all his wives and his concubines: (for he took eighteen wives and threescore concubines, and begat twenty and eight sons, and threescore daughters.)

And Rehoboam made Abijah the son of Maachah the chief, to be ruler among his brethren: for he thought to make him king. And he dealt wisely, and dispersed all his children throughout all the countries of Judah and Benjamin, unto every fenced city; and he gave them victual in abundance. And he desired many wives.

(II Chronicles 11:17 – 23)

In the eighteenth year of the reign of Jeroboam, Abijah became king of Judah, and he reigned in Jerusalem three years. His mother's name was Maacah, a daughter of Uriel of Gibeah. (2 Chronicles 13:1)

But Abijah grew in strength. He married fourteen wives and had twenty-two sons and sixteen daughters. (2 Chronicles 13:21)

In the eighteenth year of the reign of Jeroboam son of Nebat, Abijah became king of Judah, and he reigned in Jerusalem three years. His Mother's name was Maacah daughter of Abshalom. (1 Kings 15:1)

In the twentieth year of Jeroboam king of Israel, Asa became king of Judah, and he reigned in Jerusalem forty-one years. His grandmother's name was Maacah daughter of Abishalom.

Asa did what was right in the eyes of the LORD, as his father David had done. He expelled the male shrine prostitutes from the land and got rid of all the idols his fathers had made. He even deposed his grandmother Maacah from her position as queen mother, because she had made a repulsive Asherah pole. Asa cut the pole down and burned it in the Kidron Valley. (1 Kings 15:9 – 13)

Lessons to Learn:

- She caused her husband Jeroboam to make her son king
- Jeroboam dispersed all his other sons to other cities for her son's sake
- Abijah was made king because of her

- She made an Asherah pole which was destroyed by Asa
- She was deposed from being Queen Mother

God is the Umbrella of Women in the Bible!

59. Queen of Sheba

Who Was this Woman?

- Monarch of the ancient kingdom of Sheba
- Abyssinia a kingdom of the Red Sea
- In the vicinity of Ethiopia
- She is known as Balkis or Balqis
- She was a wealthy queen
- She heard about Solomon's relationship with God
- She planned to test Solomon with questions
- She organized trade for her country with King Solomon
- This particular Queen came from Sheba it is believed because she had heard of the wisdom of King Solomon.
- She was moved by the stories people were telling her about this very wise king. She must have heard about
- She visited Solomon and was well prepared for the visit, she had a large caravan with camels,

spices, and large quantities of gold and precious stones
- She was not invited, she planned it herself
- She brought with her quite a lot to impress Solomon and may be entice him to trade with her country.
- She saw all the wisdom of Solomon
- She saw the palace he had built
- She saw the food on the table
- She saw the seating of his officials
- She saw the attending servants in their robes
- She saw the cupbearers
- She saw the burnt offerings Solomon made at the temple of the LORD
- She was overwhelmed
- She did not believe it, but she saw it with her own eyes
- Not even half the Wisdom and Wealth had been told to her

The Story:

The Queen of Sheba did not believe. She decided to go and see. She did not go empty handed to King Solomon. She also had been blessed. If you hear something, why not pack your bags and go and see. Ask questions. Queen of Sheba said, "The report I heard in my own country about you, is true. But I did not believe these things until I came and saw with my own eyes." She was satisfied. Even Thomas believed Jesus after putting his finger through the Nail Hole. Move from your comfort zone; see for yourself what is happing.

The Bible and the Queen of Sheba:

How he knew the right from the wrong: "Now, O Lord my God, you have made your servant king in place of my father David. But I am only a little child and do not know how to carry out my duties. Your servant is here among the people you have chosen, a great people, too numerous to count or number. So give your servant a discerning heart to govern your people and to distinguish between right and wrong. For who is able to govern this great people of yours?" (1 Kings 3:7-9)

The prostitutes and their babies: "Then the king said, "Bring me a sword." So they brought a sword for the king. He then gave an order: "Cut the living child in two and give half to one and half to the other." The woman whose son was alive was filled with compassion for her son and said to the king, "Please, my lord, give her the living baby! Don't kill him!" But the other said, "Neither I nor you shall have him. Cut him in two!" Then the king gave his ruling: Give the living baby to the first woman. Do not kill him, she is his mother." (1Kings 3:24 – 25)

The composition of 3,000 proverbs. (The Book of Proverbs)

The composition of songs: He spoke three thousand proverbs and his songs numbered a thousand and five. (1 Kings 4:32)

His tribute to love in Ecclesiastes

His wealth and wisdom: She said to the king, "The report I heard in my own country about your achievements and your wisdom is true. But I did not believe these things until I came and saw with my own eyes. Indeed, not even half was told me; in wisdom and wealth you have far exceeded the report I heard."

(1 Kings 10:6 7)

Lessons to Learn:

- The proof of the pudding is in the eating.
- She was a powerful person
- The size of her gift was a high example of what you can give to a colleague
- Make decisions and take action
- Reciprocation is also important
- Learning never ends, she learnt a lot from King Solomon
- She set a high standard for us to follow

God is the Umbrella of Women in the Bible!

60. Queen Vashti

Who Was This Woman?

- For 180 days the king displayed the vast wealth of his kingdom and the splendor and glory of his majesty
- King Xerxes had given a banquet for all his nobles and officials at the end of the 180 days
- This was to last for seven days on the seventh day he was in good spirits from wine; he commanded the seven eunuchs who served him to bring before him Queen Vashti
- She was supposed to come wearing her royal crown
- She was to display her beauty to the people and nobles
- The eunuchs were: Mehuman, Biztha, Harbona, Bigtha, Abagtha, Zethar and Carcas
- Queen Vashti also had given a banquet for the women
- King Xerxes wanted to show off his wife and asked that she came before him

- Queen Vashti refused to be paraded
- This was a case of law and justice now
- The king consulted the wise men who were closest to him and understood the times
- The wise men were: Carshena, Shethar, Admatha, Tarshish, Meres, Marsena and Memucan
- He consulted the seven nobles of Persia and Media who had special access to the king and were highest in the kingdom
- King Xerxes asked, "According to the law, what must be done to Queen Vashti?" "She has not obeyed the command of King Xerxes that the eunuchs have taken to her."
- Memucan replied in the presence of the king and the nobles: "Queen Vashti has done wrong not only against the king but also against the nobles and the peoples of all the provinces of King Xerxes.
- The Queens conduct will be known to all women and they will despise their husbands and say: "King Xerxes commanded Queen Vashti to be brought before him, but she would not come."
- The Persian women and the Median women of the nobility who have heard about the queen's conduct will respond to all the king's nobles in the same way. There will be no end of disrespect and discord.
- They suggested that Vashti should never again be allowed to enter the presence of King Xerxes.

- Also let the king give her royal position to some one else.
- This was given to Esther

The Story:

For 180 days the king displayed the vast wealth of his kingdom and the splendor and glory of his majesty. This was to last for seven days on the seventh day he was in good spirits from wine; he commanded the seven eunuchs who served him to bring before him Queen Vashti. She was supposed to come wearing her royal crown and she was to display her beauty to the people and nobles

Queen Vashti also had given a banquet for the women who have come with their husbands. Therefore to her the invitation by the king to parade herself in front of his guests was a bit embarrassing to her and she refused to be paraded

This was not so good for the other nobles who were there and who had brought their wives too. They thought that if this case goes unchallenged their wives would in future behave in the same manner as Vashti had done.

The king consulted the wise men who were closest to him and understood the times. The wise men were: Carshena, Shethar, Admatha, Tarshish, Meres, Marsena and Memucan. He consulted the seven nobles of Persia and Media who had special access to the king and were highest in the kingdom

King Xerxes asked them what, according to the law, what must be done to Queen Vashti. She had not obeyed the command that the eunuchs had taken to her.

Then Memucan replied in the presence of the king and the nobles and said Queen Vashti had done wrong not only against the king but also against the nobles and the peoples of all the provinces of King Xerxes. He said the Queens conduct will be known to all women and they would despise their husbands and say, King Xerxes commanded Queen Vashti to be brought before him, but she would not come.

The Persian women and the Median women of the nobility who have heard about the queen's conduct would respond to all the king's nobles in the same way. He feared that there would be no end to the way they would disrespect their husbands.

They suggested that Vashti should never again be allowed to enter the presence of King Xerxes. Also let the king give her royal position to some one else. This was given to Esther after a selection later on.

The Bible and Queen Vashti:

This is what happened during the time of Xerxes, the Xerxes who ruled over 127 provinces stretching from India to Cush. At that time King Xerxes reigned from his royal throne in the citadel of Susa, and in the third year of his reign he gave a banquet for all his nobles and officials. The military leaders of Persia and Media, the princes, and the nobles of the provinces were present.

For a full 180 days he displaced the vast wealth of his kingdom and the splendor and glory of his majesty. When these days were over, the king gave a banquet, lasting seven days, in the enclosed garden of the king's palace, for all the people from the least to the greatest, who were in the citadel of Susa. The garden had hangings of white and blue linen, fastened with cords of white linen and purple material to silver rings on marble pillars. There were couches of gold and silver on a mosaic pavement of porphyry, marble, mother-of-pearl and other costly stones. Wine was served in goblets of wine was abundant, in keeping with the kings liberality. By the kings command each guest was allowed to drink in his own way, for the king all the wine stewards to serve each man what he wished.

Queen Vashti also gave a banquet for the women in the royal palace of King Xerxes. On the seventh day, when King Xerxes was in high spirits from wine, he commanded the seven eunuchs who served him – Mehuman, Biztha, Harbona, Bigtha, Abagtha, Zethar and Carcas – to bring before him Queen, wearing her royal crown, in order to display her beauty to the people and nobles, for she was lovely to look at. But when the attendants delivered the king's command, Queen Vashti refused to come.

Since it was customary for the king to consult experts in matters of law and justice, he spoke with the wise men who understood the times and were closest to the king – Carshena, Shethar, Admatha, Tarshish, Meres, Marsena and Memucan, the seven nobles of Persia and Media who has special access to the king and were highest in the kingdom.

According to law, what must be done to Queen Vashti? He asked. "She has not obeyed the command of King Xerxes that the eunuchs have taken to her."

Then Memucan replied in the presence of the king and the nobles, "Queen Vashti has done wrong, not only against the king but also against all the nobles and the peoples of all the provinces of King Xerxes. For the queen's conduct will become known to all the women, and so they will despise their husbands and say, 'King Xerxes commanded Queen Vashti to be brought before him, but she would not come. This very day the Persian and Median women of nobility who have heard about the queen's conduct will respond to all the kings' nobles in the same way. There will be no end of disrespect and discord. Therefore, if is pleases the king, let him issue a royal decree and let it be written in the laws of Persia and Media, which cannot be repeated. That Vashti is never again to enter the presence of King Xerxes. Also let the king give her royal position to someone else who is better than she. Then when the king's edict is proclaimed throughout all his vast realm, all the women will respect their husbands, from the least of the greatest."

The king and his nobles were pleased with this advice, so the king did as Memucan proposed. He sent dispatches to all parts of the kingdom, to each province in its own script and to each people in its own language, proclaiming in each people's tongue that every man should be ruler over his own household. (Ester 1:1-22)

Lessons to Learn:

- Queen Vashiti was removed from her position as Queen and Esther was crowned queen.
- How would you have handled her situation if you were in her shoes?
- Was this a good or bad decision that she made?
- How did the other women she was with advise her?
- What reaction did they have when they heard the news of their companion's downfall?

God is the Umbrella of Women in the Bible!

61. Rachel – the Wife of Jacob:

Who Was This Woman?

- She was the daughter of Laban, Rebekah's brother
- Rebekah was Jacob's Mother
- When Jacob arrived in Paddan Aram he met Rachel first
- Jacob wanted to marry Rachel
- He was tricked into marrying Leah first
- Then he married Rachel a week later
- She was jealous of Leah
- She was barren for sometime
- She gave her maidservant Bilhah to Jacob
- Dan – Was Rachel's first son birthed by Bilhah, she name her that because she said God had vindicated her
- Naphtali – Was Rachel's second son birthed by Bilhah, she named him that as she said she had won

- God remembered her; he listened to her and opened her womb.
- Joseph – was her third son whom she birthed, she named him that and said may the Lord add to me another son
- Benjamin – Was her fourth son whom she birthed and had named him Ben-Oni, but his father named him Benjamin
- Rachel died while giving birth to Benjamin
- Rachel had two sons, and her maidservant Bilhah had two sons, making a total of four sons for Jacob from Rachel's side

The Story:

When Jacob got to Arrived in Paddan Aram he met some shepherds and he asked them whether they knew Laban, Nahor's grandson. They told him that they knew him and that he was well and in fact there was his daughter Rachel coming with the sheep.

When he saw Rachel, the daughter of his mother's brother Laban, he went over and rolled the stone away from the mouth of the well and watered his uncle's sheep. Then he kissed Rachel and began to weep aloud. He told Rachel that he was a relative of her father and a son of Rebekah. Then she ran and told her father. Laban hurried to the well, embraced Jacob and kissed him and then took him home. Then Jacob explained himself to Laban who told him that he was his own flesh and blood.

After Jacob had stayed for a whole month, Laban said to him, "Just because you are a relative of mine, should you work for me for nothing? Tell me what your wages should be." Now Laban had two daughters; the name of the older was Leah, and the name of the younger was Rachel. Leah had weak eyes, but Rachel was lovely in form, and beautiful. Jacob was in love with Rachel and said, "I will work for you seven years in return for your younger daughter."

Laban said, "It's better that I give her to you than to some other man. Stay here with me." So Jacob served seven years to get Rachel, but they seemed like only a few days to him because of his love for her. Then he said to Laban, "Give me my wife. my time is completed, and I want to lie with her."

So Laban brought together all the people of the place and gave a feast. But when evening came, he took his daughter Leah and gave her to Jacob, and Jacob lay with her. And Laban gave his servant girl Zilpah to his daughter as her maidservant.

When morning came, there was Leah! So Jacob said to Laban, "What is this you have done to me? I served you for Rachel, didn't I? Why have you deceived me?"

Laban replied, "It is not our custom here to give the younger daughter in marriage before the older one. Finish this daughter's bridal week; then we will give you the younger one also, in return for another seven years of work."

And Jacob did so. He finished the week with Leah, and then Laban gave his daughter Rachel to be his wife. Laban gave his servant girl, Bilhah to his daughter Rachel as her maid servant. Jacob lay with Rachel also, and he loved Rachel more than Leah. And he worked for Laban another seven years

When Rachel saw that she was not bearing Jacob any children, she became jealous of her sister. So she said to Jacob, "Give me children, or I'll die!"

Jacob became angry with her and said, "Am I in the place of God, who has kept you from having children?" Then she said, here is Bilhah, my maidservant. Sleep with her so that she can bear children for me and that through her I too can build a family."

So she gave him her servant Bilhah as a wife, Jacob slept with her, and she became pregnant and bore him a son. Then Rachel said, "God has vindicated me; he has listened to my plea and given me a son." Because of this she named him Dan.

Rachel's servant Bilhah conceived again and bore Jacob a second son. Then Rachel said, "I have had a great struggle with my sister and I have won." So she named him Naphtali.

During wheat harvest, Reuben went out into the fields and found some mandrake plants, which he brought to his mother Leah. Rachel said to Leah, "Please give me some of your son's mandrakes." But she said to her, "Wasn't it enough that you took away my husband? Will you take my son's mandrakes too?"

"Very well," Rachel said, "he can sleep with you tonight in return for your son's mandrakes." So when Jacob came in from the fields that evening, Leah went out to meet him. "You must sleep with me," she said, "I have hired you with my son's mandrakes." So he slept with her that night.

Then God remembered Rachel; he listened to her and opened her womb. She became pregnant and gave birth to a son and said, "God has taken away my disgrace." She named him Joseph, and said "May the Lord add to me another son

Then they moved on from Bethel. While they were still some distance from Ephrath, Rachel began to give birth and had great difficulty. And as she was having great difficulty in childbirth, the midwife said to her, "Don't be afraid, for you have another son." As she breathed her last – for she was dying – she named her son Ben-Oni. But his father named him Benjamin.

Jacob had twelve sons and one daughter:

The sons of Leah: Reuben the firstborn of Jacob, Simeon, Levi, Judah, Issacher, and Zebulum. (Leah also had a daughter Dinah)
The sons of Rachel: Joseph and Benjamin.
The sons of Rachel's maidservant Bilhah: Dan and Naphtali
The sons of Leah's maidservant Zilpah: Gad and Asher.
These were the sons of Jacob born to him in Paddan Aram. Genesis 35:16 – 26)

The Bible and Rachel:

Then Jacob continued on his journey and came to the land of the eastern peoples. There he saw a well in the field, with three flocks of sheep lying near it because the flocks were watered from that well. The stone over the mouth of the well was large. When all the flocks were gathered there, the shepherds would roll the stone away from the well's mouth and water the sheep. Then they would return the stone to its place over the mouth of the well.

Jacob asked the shepherds, "My brothers, where are you from?"

"We are from Haran," they replied.

He said to them, "Do you know Laban, Nahor's grandson?"

"Yes, we know him," they answered.

Then Jacob asked them, "Is he well?"

"Yes, he is," they said, "and here comes his daughter Rachel with the sheep."

"Look," he said, "the sun is still high; it is not time for the flocks to be gathered. Water the sheep and take them back to pasture."

"We can't," they replied, "until all the flocks are gathered and the stone has been rolled away from the mouth of the well. Then we will water the sheep."

While he was still talking with them, Rachel came with her father's sheep, for she was a shepherdess. When Jacob saw Rachel daughter of Laban, his mother's brother, and Laban's sheep, he went over and rolled the stone away from the mouth of the well and watered his uncle's sheep. Then Jacob kissed Rachel and began to weep aloud. He had told Rachel that he was a relative of her father and a son of Rebekah. So she ran and told her father.

As soon as Laban heard the news about Jacob, his sister's son, he hurried to meet him. He embraced him and kissed him and brought him to his home, and there Jacob told him all these things. Then Laban said to him. "You are my own flesh and blood."

(Genesis 29:1 – 14)

After Jacob had stayed with him for a whole month, Laban said to him, "Just because you are a relative of mine, should you work for me for nothing? Tell me what your wages should be." Now Laban had two daughters; the name of the older was Leah, and the name of the younger was Rachel. Leah had weak eyes, but Rachel was lovely in form, and beautiful. Jacob was in love with Rachel and said, "I will work for you seven years in return for your younger daughter."

Laban said, "It's better that I give her to you than to some other man. Stay here with me." So Jacob served seven years to get Rachel, but they seemed like only a few days to him because of his love for her.

Then Jacob said to Laban, "Give me my wife. My time is completed, and I want to lie with her."

So Laban brought together all the people of the place and gave a feast. But when evening came, he took his daughter Leah and gave her to Jacob, and Jacob lay with her. And Laban gave his servant girl Zilpah to his daughter as her maidservant.

When morning came, there was Leah! So Jacob said to Laban, "What is this you have done to me? I served you for Rachel, didn't I? Why have you deceived me?"

Laban replied, "It is not our custom here to give the younger daughter in marriage before the older one. Finish this daughter's bridal week; then we will give you the younger one also, in return for another seven years of work."

And Jacob did so. He finished the week with Leah, and then Laban gave his daughter Rachel to be his wife. Laban gave his servant girl, Bilhah to his daughter Rachel as her maid servant. Jacob lay with Rachel also, and he loved Rachel more than Leah. And he worked for Laban another seven years. (Genesis 29:15 – 30)

When the LORD saw that Lear was not loved, he opened her womb, but Rachel was barren. Leah became pregnant and gave birth to a son. She named him Reuben, for she said, "It is because the LORD has seen my misery. Surely my husband will love me now."

She conceived again, and when she gave birth to a son she said, "Because the LORD heard that I am not loved, he gave me this one too." So she named him Simeon.

Again she conceived, and when she gave birth to a son she said, "Now at last my husband will become attached to me, because I have borne him three sons." So he was named Levi.

She conceived again, and when she gave birth to a son she said, "This time I will praise the LORD." So she named him Judah. Then she stopped having children.

(Genesis 29:31 – 35)

When Rachel saw that she was not bearing Jacob any children, she became jealous of her sister. So she said to Jacob, "Give me children, or I'll die!"

Jacob became angry with her and said, "Am I in the place of God, who has kept you from having children?" Then she said, here is Bilhah, my maidservant. Sleep with her so that she can bear children for me and that through her I too can build a family."

So she gave him her servant Bilhah as a wife, Jacob slept with her, and she became pregnant and bore him a son. Then Rachel said, "God has vindicated me; he has listened to my plea and given me a son." Because of this she named him Dan.

Rachel's servant Bilhah conceived again and bore Jacob a second son. Then Rachel said, "I have had a great struggle with my sister and I have won." So she named him Naphtali.

When Leah saw that she had stopped having children, she took her maidservant Zilpah and gave her to Jacob as a wife. Leah's servant Zilpah bore Jacob a son. Then Leah said, "What good fortune!" So she named him Gad. Leah's servant Zilpah bore Jacob a second son. Then Leah said, "How happy I am!" The women will call me happy." So she named him Asher.

During wheat harvest, Reuben went out into the fields and found some mandrake plants, which he brought to his mother Leah. Rachel said to Leah, "Please give me some of your son's mandrakes." But she said to her, "Wasn't it enough that you took away my husband? Will you take my son's mandrakes too?"

"Very well," Rachel said, "he can sleep with you tonight in return for your son's mandrakes." So when Jacob came in from the fields that evening, Leah went out to meet him. "You must sleep with me," she said, "I have hired you with my son's mandrakes." So he slept with her that night.

God listened to Leah, and she became pregnant and bore Jacob a fifth son. Then Leah said, "God has rewarded me for giving my maidservant to my husband." So she named him Issacher. Some time later she gave birth to a daughter and named her Dinah.

Then God remembered Rachel; he listened to her and opened her womb. She became pregnant and gave birth to a son and said, "God has taken away my disgrace." She named him Joseph, and said "May the Lord add to me another son." (Genesis 30:1 – 24)

Then they moved on from Bethel. While they were still some distance from Ephrath, Rachel began to give birth and had great difficulty. And as she was having great difficulty in childbirth, the midwife said to her, "Don't be afraid, for you have another son." As she breathed her last – for she was dying – she named her son Ben-Oni. But his father named him Benjamin.

So Rachel died and was buried on the way to Ephrath (that is Bethlehem). Over her tomb Jacob set up a pillar, and to this day that pillar marks Rachel's tomb. Israel moved on again and pitched his tend beyond Migdal Eder. While Israel was living in that region Reuben went in and slept with his father's concubine Bilhah and Israel heard of it.

Jacob had twelve sons:

The sons of Leah: Reuben the firstborn of Jacob, Simeon, Levi, Judah, Issacher, and Zebulum. (Leah also had a daughter Dinah)

The sons of Rachel: Joseph and Benjamin.

The sons of Rachel's maidservant Bilhah: Dan and Naphtali

The sons of Leah's maidservant Zilpah: Gad and Asher.

These were the sons of Jacob born to him in Paddan Aram. Genesis 35:16 – 26)

Lessons to Learn:

- Then God remembered Rachel; he listened to her and opened her womb
- She was Jealous of her sister since she knew that Jacob should have married her first
- She had al in all four sons; two from herself and two from Bilhah her maidservant

God is the Umbrella of Women in the Bible!

62. Rahab – the Prostitute:

Who Was This Woman?

- She was a Prostitute
- The Two Spies came directly to her house
- She was being watched
- She however assisted the spies
- She was an intelligent woman
- She was also concerned about her own family's safety
- She had heard what God had done for his people
- She certainly knew that her people were going to be destroyed
- She had heard of the way the Israelites crossed the Red Sea
- She had heard of how other kings had been conquered
- She knew what she wanted to ask for
- She knew how to keep secrets
- She saved her family

The Story:

Rahab was a Prostitute. She welcomed two spies sent by Joshua to spy Jericho. She was reported to the King by onlookers. She hid the spies and told the soldiers they had left. The soldiers chased the wind. She made a deal with the spies to save her and her family. They told her to tie a scarlet rope on the window of her house. She was saved and in the New Testament Rahab is the mother of Boaz, thus great grandmother of King David and in the family tree of Jesus. This is God's love in action for you.

The Bible and Rehab

She was either an in-keeper or a prostitute or both. However, she was at the right place at the right time. If you are well known for whatever reason people are always watching your moves. You see it with celebrities, no matter how much they try to keep things private, some media people are busy waiting for the news.

So when two spies came into Rehabs house or inn, people were watching.

"Then Joshua son of Nun secretly sent two spies from Shittim. "Go; look over the land," he said, "especially Jericho." So they went and entered the house of a prostitute named Rahab and stayed there.

The king of Jericho was told, "Look! Some of the Israelites have come here tonight to spy out the land." So the king of Jericho sent this message to Rahab: "Bring out the men who came to you and entered your house, because they have come to spy out the whole land."

But the woman had taken the two men and hidden them. She said, "Yes the man came to me, but I did not know where they had come from. At dusk, when it was time to close the city gate, the men left. I don't know which way they went. Go after them quickly. You may catch up with them." (But she had taken them up to the roof and hidden them under the stalks of flax she had laid out on the roof.) So the men set out in pursuit of the spies on the road that leads to the fords of the Jordan, and as soon as the pursuers had gone out, the gate was shut.

"Before the spies lay down for the night, she went up on the roof and said to them, I know that the Lord has given this land to you and that a great fear of you has fallen on us, so that all who live in this country are melting in fear because of you. We have heard how the Lord dried up the water of the Red Sea for you when you came out of Egypt and what you did to Sihon and Og, the two kings of the Amorites east of the Jordan, whom you completely destroyed. When we heard of it our hearts sank and everyone's courage failed because of you, for the Lord your God is God in heaven above and on the earth below.

"Now then, please swear to me by the Lord that you will show kindness to my family, because I have shown kindness to you. Give me a sure sign that you will spare the lives of my father and mother, my brothers and sisters, and all who belong to them, and that you will save us from death."

She was an intelligent woman and was aware of what was happening around her. She definitely knew that God was behind all that she had heard about.

"Our lives for your lives!" the men assured her. "If you don't tell what we are doing, we will treat you kindly and faithfully when the Lord gives us the land."

So she let them down by a rope through the window, for the house she lived in was part of the city wall. Now she said to them, "Go to the hills so the pursuers will not find you. Hide yourselves there three days until they return, and then go on your way."

The men said to her, "This oath you made us swear will not be binding on us unless, when we enter the land you have tied this scarlet cord in the window through which you let us down, and unless you have brought your father and mother, your brothers and all your family into your house. If anyone goes out of your house into the street, his blood will be on his own head, we will not be responsible. As for anyone who is in the house with you, his blood will be on our head if a hand is laid on him. But if you tell what we are doing, we will be released from the oath you made us swear."

"Agreed," she replied, "Let it be as you say." So she sent them away and they departed. And she tied the scarlet cord in the window.

When they left they went into the hills and stayed there three days, until the pursuers had searched all along the road and returned without finding them.

Then the two men started back. They went down out of the hills. Forded the river and came to Joshua Son of Nun and told him everything that had happened to them. They said to Joshua, "The Lord has surely given the whole land into our hands; all the people are melting with fear because of us. (Joshua 2)

Now Jericho was tightly shut up because of the Israelites. No one went out and no one came in.

Then the Lord said to Joshua, "See I have delivered Jericho into your hands, along with its king and its fighting men. March around the city once with all the armed men. Do this four six days. Have seven priests carry trumpets of rams' horns in front of the ark. On the seventh day, march around the city seven times , with the priests blowing the trumpets; When you hear them sound a long blast on the trumpets, have all the people give a loud shout; then the wall of the city will collapse and the people will go up, every man straight in."

So Joshua son of Nun called the priests and said to them, "Take up the ark of the covenant of the Lord and have seven priests carry trumpets in front of it." And he ordered the people, "Advance! March around the city, with the armed guard going ahead of the ark of the Lord.

When Joshua had spoken to the people, the seven priests carrying the seven trumpets before the Lord went forward, blowing their trumpets, and the ark of the Lord's covenant followed them. The armed guard marched ahead of the priests who blew the trumpets, and the rear guard followed the ark. All this time the trumpets were sounding. But Joshua had commanded the people, "Do not give a war cry, do not raise your voices, and do not say a word until the day I tell you to shout. Then shout!" So he had the ark of the Lord carried around the city circling it once. Then the people returned to camp and spent the night there.

Joshua got up early the next morning and the priests took up the ark of the Lord. The seven priests carrying the seven trumpets went forward marching before the ark of the Lord and blowing the trumpets. The armed men went ahead of them and the rear guard followed the ark of the Lord, while the trumpets kept sounding. So on the second day they marched around the city once and returned to the camp. They did this for six days.

On the seventh day, they got up at daybreak and marched around the city seven times in the same manner, except that on that day they circled the city seven times. The seventh time around, when the priests sounded the trumpet blast, Joshua commanded the people, "Shout! For the Lord had given you the city. The city and all that is in it we are to

God is the Umbrella of Women in the Bible

be devoted to the Lord. Only Rahab the prostitute and all who are with her in her house shall be spared, because she hit the spies we sent. But keep away from the devoted things, so that you will not bring about your own destruction by taking any of them. Otherwise you will make the camp of Israel liable to destruction and bring trouble on it. All the silver and gold and the articles of bronze and iron are sac red to the Lord and must go into his treasury.

When the trumpets sounded, the people shouted, and at the sound of the trumpet, when the people gave a loud shout, the wall collapsed so every man charged straight in, and they took the city. They devoted the city to the Lord and destroyed with the sword every living thing in it – men and women, young and old, cattle, sheep and donkeys.

Joshua said to the two men who had spied out the land, "Go into the prostitute's house and bring her out and all who belong to her, in accordance with your oath to her." So the young men who had done the spying went in and brought out Rahab, her father and mother and brothers and all who belong to her. They brought out her entire family and put them in a place outside the camp of Israel.

At that time Joshua pronounced this solemn oath: "Cursed before the Lord is the man who undertakes to rebuild this city, Jericho "At the cost of his firstborn son will he lay its foundations; at the cost of his youngest, will he set up its gates."

So the Lord was with Joshua, and his fame spread throughout the land. (Joshua 6)

Salmon the father of Boaz, whose mother was Rahab, Boaz the father of Obed, whose mother was Ruth. Obed the father of Jesse, and Jesse the father of King David. (Matthew 1:5 – 6)

By faith the prostitute Rahab, because she welcomed the spies, was not killed with those who were disobedient. (Hebrews 11:31

In the same way, was not even Rahab the prostitute considered righteous for what she did when she gave lodging to the spies and sent them off in a different direction. (James 2:25)

Lessons to Learn:

- She was considered righteous
- She is in the genealogy of Jesus Christ
- God loves us the way we are as long as we turn to him
- She saved her family from destruction
- No matter what you and I have done God is always there for us
- All these blessings will come upon you and accompany you if you obey the LORD your God: You will be blessed in the city and blessed in the country
- The fruit of your womb will be blessed, and the crops of your land and the young of your livestock – the calves of your herds and the lambs of your flocks.
- Your basket and your kneading trough will be blessed.
- You will be blessed when you go in and when you go out.

- The LORD will grant that the enemies who rise up against you will be defeated before you. They will come at you from one direction but flee from you in seven.

God is the Umbrella of Women in the Bible!

63. Rebekah – the Wife of Isaac

Who Was This Woman?

- The daughter of Bethuel the Syrian of Padanaram, the son of Milcah, the wife of Abraham's brother Nahor
- The sister of Laban
- She was beautiful and was a virgin
- Abraham sent his servant to look for her when Isaac was 40 years old
- The servant took ten camels and all sorts of good things (Lobola or bride price)
- The Angel of the LORD actually directed Abraham's servant to her
- He said the damsel to whom I shall say, Let down thy pitcher, I pray thee, that I may drink, and she shall say, Drink, and I will give thy camels drink also, let the same be she that thou has appointed for thy servant Isaac, and thereby shall I know thou hast shewed kindness unto my master.

- The servant left for the town of Nahor and camped outside near the well, waiting for the woman to come and draw water toward the evening
- She went down to the well to fetch water
- The servant said please give me a little water from your jar
- She said, 'I will draw water for your camels too'
- She emptied her jar into the trough and she drew enough for all the camels
- Prayer was answered
- She was given a gold nose ring which weighed a beak, two gold bracelets weighing ten shekels
- She was asked by Abraham's servant whether there was room for him to spend a night
- Of course there was room this was already God's plan
- She was unwilling to go with Abraham's servant
- She married Isaac
- She was barren and Isaac prayed to God
- She became pregnant
- She spoke to God about her pregnancy and God told her that two nations shall be separated from her bowels
- She was told that one people shall be stronger than the other people
- That the eldest shall serve the younger

- She gave birth to twins Esau and Jacob
- She told Isaac that she was disgusted with living because of the Hittite women ho had been married by Esau

The Story:

Abraham did not want his son Isaac to marry a Canaanite woman therefore he sent his trusted friend to go and look for a woman from his own country and his own people. The servant went to the town of Nahor. There he found Rebekah the daughter of Laban Rebekah's brother.

She was a beautiful girl, the daughter of Bethuel who was the son of Milcah. Milcah was the wife of Nahor, Abraham's brother. She was very beautiful. When he asked her who she was, he was pleased to know that God had directed his steps. She told him that she was the daughter of Bethuel the son that Milcah bore to Nahor. God had sent him straight to Abraham's relatives.

Rebekah gave water to the stranger and watered his camels just as he had asked God for the right girl to do. He asked her whether there was room at her house for him and his camels. She told him that they had plenty of room for him and the camels.

She went and told her mother's household about this man. His brother ran and welcomed the man to his house, as soon as he had seen the ring and the bracelets on his sister. He invited him to come and stay. And he went to the house and was given food. He refused to eat until he had performed what he came for.

In my culture you cannot eat until you have paid the Lobola or the Bride Price.. Therefore he explained to Laban why he was there. That Sarah had a son Isaac in her old age and Abraham had sent him to look for a wife for him.

He placed a ring on Rebekah's nose and put bracelets on her arms and he bowed down and worshipped the LORD.

The Bible and Rebekah:

Then Rebekah said to Isaac, "I'm disgusted with living because of these Hittite women. If Jacob takes a wife from among the women of this land, from Hittite women like these, my live will not be worth living. (Genesis 27:46)

And Abraham was old, and well stricken in age: and the Lord had blessed Abraham in all things. And Abraham said unto his eldest servant of his house, that ruled over all that he had. Put, I pray thee, thy hand under my thigh: And I will make thee swear by the Lord, the God of heaven, and the God of the earth, that thou shalt not take a wife unto my son of the daughters of the Canaanites, among whom I dwell. But thou shalt go unto my country, and to my kindred, and take a wife unto my son Isaac. And the servant said unto him, Peradventure the woman will not be willing to follow me unto this land: must I needs bring thy son again unto the land from whence thou camest? And Abraham said unto him, Beware thou that thou bring not my son thither again. The Lord God of heaven, which took me from my father's house, and from the land of my kindred, and which spake unto me, saying, Unto thy seed will I give this land, he shall send his angel before thee, and though shalt take a wife unto my son from thence. If the woman will not be willing to follow thee, then thou shalt be clear from this my oath, only bring not my son thither again.

And the servant put his hand under the thigh of Abraham his master, and swore to him concerning the matter.

And the servant took ten camels of the camels of his master, and departed, for all the goods of his master were in his hand; and he arose, and went to Mesopotamia, unto the city of Nahor.

And he made his camels to kneel down without the city by a sell of water at the time of the evening, even the time that women go out to draw water.

And he said, O LORD God of my master Abraham, I pray three, send me good speed this day, and shew kindness, unto my master Abraham.

Behold, I stand here by the well of water, and the daughters of the men of the city come out to draw water.

And let it come to pass, that the damsel to whom I shall say, Let down thy pitcher, I pray thee, that I may drink, and she shall say, Drink, and I will give thy camels drink also, let the same be she that thou has appointed for thy servant Isaac, and thereby shall I know thou hast shewed kindness unto my master.

And it came to pass, before he had done speaking, that, behold, Rebekah came out, who was born to Bethuel, son of Milcah, the wife of Nahor, Abraham's brother, with her pitcher upon her shoulder.

And the damsel was very fair to look upon, a virgin, neither had any man known her, and she went down to the well, and filled her pitcher, and came up.

And the servant ran to meet her, and said, let me, I pray thee, drink a little water of thy pitcher.

And she said, Drink, my lord, and she hasted, and let down her pitcher upon her hand, and gave him drink.

And when she had done giving him drink, she said, I will draw water for thy camels also, until they have done drinking.

And she hasted, and emptied her pitcher into the trough, and ran again unto the well to draw water, and drew for all his camels.

And the man wondering at her held his peace, to wit whether the LORD had made his journey prosperous or not.

And it came to pass, as the camels had done drinking, that the man took a golden earring of half a shekel weight, and two bracelets for her hands of ten shekels weight of gold.

And said whose daughter art though? Tell me, I pray thee is there room in thy father's house for us to lodge in?

And she said unto him, I am the daughter of Bethuel the son of Milcah, which she bare unto Nahor.

She said moreover unto him, we have both straw and provender enough, and room to lodge in.

And the man bowed down his head, and worshipped the LORD,

And he said, blessed, be the LORD God of my master Abraham, who hath not left destitute my master of his mercy and his truth: I being in the way, the LORD led me to the house of my master's brethren.

And the damsel ran, and told them of her mother's house these things.

And Rebekah had a brother, and his name was Laban, and Laban ran out unto the man, unto the well.

And it came to pass, when he saw the earring and bracelets upon his sister's hands, and when he heard the words of Rebekah his sister, saying, Thus spake the man unto me, that be came into the man, and behold he stood by the camels at the well.

And he said, Come in, though blessed of the LORD, wherefore standest though without? For I have prepared the house and room for the camels.

And the man came into the house: and he ungirded his camels, and gave straw and provender for the camels, and water to wash his feet, and the men's feet that were with him.

And there was set meat before him to eat: but he said, I will not eat, until I have told mine errand. And he said, Speak on. And he said, I am Abraham's servant.

And the LORD hath blessed my master greatly, and he is become great and he hath given him flocks, and herds, and silver and gold, and menservants, and maidservants, and camels, and asses.

And Sarah my master's wife bare a son to my master when she was old; and unto him hath he given all that he hath.

And my master made me swear, saying Thou shalt not take a wife to my son of daughters of the Canaanites in whose land I dwell.

But thou shalt go unto my father's house, and to my kindred, and take a wife unto my son.

And I said unto him master; peradventure the woman will not follow me.

And he said unto me, The LORD, before whom I walk, will send his angel with thee, and prosper thy way; and thou shalt take a wife for my son of my kindred, and of my father's house.

Then shalt though be clear from this my oath, when thou comest to my kindred, and if they give not thee one, though shalt be clear from my oath.

And I came this day unto the well, and said, O LORD God of my master Abraham, I now though do prosper my way which I go:

Behold I stand by the well of water; and it shall come to pass, that when the virgin cometh forth to draw water, and I say to her, Give me, I pray three a little water of thy pitcher to drink;

And she say to me, both drink thou, and I will also draw for they camels; let the same be the woman whom the LORD hath appointed out for my master's son.

And before I had done speaking in mine heart, behold, Rebekah came forth with her pitcher on her shoulder and she went down unto the well, and drew water, and I said unto her, Let me drink, I pray thee.

And she made haste, and let down her pitcher from her shoulder and said, Drink, and I will give thy camels drink also so I drank and she made the camels drink also.

And I asked her and said, whose daughter art thou? And she said. The daughter of Bethuel, Nahor's son whom Milcah bare unto him and I put the earring upon her face, and the bracelets upon her hands.

And I bowed down my head and worshipped the LORD and blessed the LORD God of my master Abraham, which had led me into the right way to take my master's brother's daughter unto his son.

And now, if ye will deal kindly and truly with my master, tell me and if not tell me, that I may turn to the right hand or to the left.

Then Laban and Bethuel answered and said, the thing proceedeth from the LORD, we cannot speak unto thee bad or good.

Behold, Rebekah is before thee take her, and go, and let her be thy master's son's wife, as the LORD hath spoken.

And it came to pass, that when Abraham's servant heard their words he worshipped the LORD, bowing himself to the earth.

And the servant brought forth jewels of silver, and jewels of gold, and raiment, and gave them to Rebekah; he gave also to her brother and to her mother precious things.

And they did eat and drink, he and the men that were with him, and tarried all night, and they rose up in the morning and he said, Send me away unto my master.

And her brother and her mother said; Let the damsel abide with us a few days at the least ten, after that she shall go.

And he said unto them, Hinder me not, seeing the LORD hath prospered my way; send me away that I may go to my master.

And they said, we will call the damsel, and ensure at her mouth.

And they called Rebekah, and said unto her, Wilt though go with this man? And she said I will go.

And they sent away Rebekah their sister, and her nurse, and Abraham's servant, and his men.

And they blessed Rebekah and said unto her, Thou art our sister, be though the mother of thousands of millions, and let thy seed possess the gate of those which hate them.

And Rebekah arose, and her damsels, and they rode upon the camels, and followed the man and the servant took Rebekah, and went his way.

And Isaac went out to meditate in the field at the eventide and he lifted up his eyes, and saw, and, behold the camels were coming.

And Rebekah lifted up her eyes, and when she saw, Isaac she lighted off the camel.

For she had said unto the servant, what man is this that walketh in the field, to meet us? And the servant had said, It is my master: therefore she took a veil and covered herself.

And the servant told Isaac all things that he had done.

And Isaac brought her into his mother Sarah's tent, and took Rebekah, and she became his wife, and he loved her and Isaac was comforted after his mother's death. (Genesis 24:1 – 67)

God is the Umbrella of Women in the Bible

And Esau was forty years old when he took to wife Judith the daughter of Beeri the Hittite, and Bashemath the daughter of Elon the Hittite. Which were a grief of mind unto Isaac and to Rebekah. (Genesis 26:34 – 35)

Now Rebekah was listening as Isaac spoke to his son Esau. When Esau left for the open country to hunt game and bring it back, Rebekah said to her son Jacob, "Look, I overhead your father say to your brother Esau, 'Bring me some game and prepare me some tasty food to eat, so that I may give you my blessing in the presence of the LORD before I die.' Now, my son, listen carefully and do what I tell you: Go out to the flock and bring me two choice young goats, so I can prepare some tasty food for your father, just the way he likes it. Then take it to your father to eat, so that he may give you his blessing before he dies."

Jacob said to Rebekah his mother, "But my brother Esau is a hairy man, and I'm a man with smooth skin. What if my father touches me? I would appear to be tricking him and would bring down a curse on myself rather than a blessing."

His mother said to him, "My son let the curse fall on me. Just do what I say; go and get them for me." So he went and got them and brought them to his mother, and she prepared some tasty food, just the way his father liked it. Then Rebekah took the best clothes of Esau her older son, which she had in the house, and put them on her younger son Jacob. She also covered his hands and the smooth part of his neck with the goatskins. Then she handed to her son Jacob the tasty food and the bread she had made. (Genesis 27:5 – 17)

Then Rebekah said to Isaac, "I'm disgusted with living because of these Hittite women. If Jacob takes a wife from among the women of this land, from Hittite women like these, my live will not be worth living. (Genesis 27:46)

So Isaac called for Jacob and blessed him and commanded him: "Do not marry a Canaanite woman. Go at once to Paddan Aram, to the house of your mother's father Bethuel. Take a wife for yourself there, from among the daughters of Laban, your mother's brother. May God Almighty bless you and make you fruitful and increase your numbers until you become a community of peoples. May he give you and your descendants the blessing given to Abraham, so that you may take possession of the land where you now live as an alien, the land God gave to Abraham. Then Isaac sent Jacob on his way and he went to Paddan Aram, to Laban son of Bethuel the Aramean, the brother of Rebekah, who was the mother of Jacob and Esau.

Now Esau learned that Isaac had blessed Jacob and had sent him to Paddan Aram to take a wife from there, and that when he blessed him he commanded him, "Do not marry a Canaanite woman," and that Jacob had obeyed his father and mother and had gone to Paddan Aram. Esau then realized how displeasing the Canaanite women were to his father Isaac; so he went to Ishmael and married Mahalath, the sister of Nebaioth and daughter of Ishmael son of Abraham, in addition to the wives he already had. (Genesis 28:1 – 9)

Then Jacob kissed Rachel and he began to weep aloud. He had told Rachel that he was a relative of her father and a son of Rebekah. So she ran and told her father. As soon as Laban heard the news about Jacob, his sister's son, he hurried to meet him. He embraced him and kissed him and brought him to his home, and there Jacob told him all these things. Then Laban said to him, "You are my flesh and blood." (Genesis 29:11 – 14)

But Deborah, Rebekah's nurse died, and she was buried beneath Bethel under an oak: and the name of it was called Allon-bachuth. (Genesis 35:8)

Jacob came home to his father Isaac in Mamre, near Kiriath Arba (that is Hebron), where Abraham and Isaac had stayed. Isaac lived a hundred and eighty years. Then he breathed his last and died and was gathered to his people, old and full of years. And his sons Esau and Jacob buried him. (Genesis 35:27 – 29)

Lessons to Learn:

- God's plan will always work out
- The mother of Esau and Jacob
- The wife of Isaac
- Mother-in-law's jealousy
- Initiation of tricks
- She is one of the great women in the bible.
- Discuss arranged marriages:

God is the Umbrella of Women in the Bible!

64. Reumah – Nahor's Concubine:

- She was Nahor's concubine
- She was the mother of Tebah, Gaham, Tahash, and Maacah

The Story:

Reumah was Nahor's concubine. Nahor was Abraham's brother.

The Bible and Reumah:

Bethuel became the father of Rebekah. Milcah bore these eight sons to Abraham's brother Nahor. His concubine, whose name was Reumah, also had sons: Tebah, Gaham, Tahash and Maacah. (Genesis 22:20 – 24)

Lessons to Learn:

- She was the mother of Nahor's four children

God is the Umbrella of Women in the Bible!

65. Rizpah – the Daughter of Aiah: (See Aiah)

God is the Umbrella of Women in the Bible!

66. Ruth – the Wife of Boaz:

- She was the wife of Kilion's the son of Elimelech and Naomi
- She was a Moabitess woman
- She had no children with Kilion
- Kilion died
- Naomi left Moab for her country
- Then Naomi said to her two daughters-in-law, "Go back, each of you, to your mother's home. May the Lord show kindness to you, as you have shown to your dead and to me. May the Lord grant that each of you will find rest in the home of another husband.
- Then she kissed them and they wept aloud and said to her, "We will go back with you to your people."
- But Naomi said, "Return home, my daughters. Why would you come with me? Am I going to have any more sons, who could become your husbands? Return home, my daughters. I am too old to have another husband. Even if I thought there was still hope for me – even if I had a husband tonight and then gave birth to sons – would you wait until they grew up?

No, my daughters. It is more bitter for me than for you, because the Lord's hand has gone out against me!" At this they wept again.

- Then Orpah kissed her mother-in-law good-by, but Ruth clung to her.
- Ruth means "friend"
- She is King David's great-grandmother and produced Israel's kings including Solomon and Jesus
- She married Boaz after being encouraged by her mother-in-law Naomi
- Ruth is a demonstration of how God provides for the faithful
- Ruth is a an example of a powerful woman

The Story:

The story of Ruth begins when she meets Kilion a young man who had come with his parents from Bethlehem to Moab. She married Kilion the second son of Elimelech and Naomi. Just like today many young girls marry foreign men who come into their countries.

She lived with Kilion for ten years but they had no children and Kilion died. When Kilion died her mother-in-law Naomi decided to go back to Bethlehem. Naomi said to her and her sister-in-law: "Go back, each of you, to your mother's home. May the LORD show kindness to you, as you have shown to your dead and to me. May the LORD grant that each of you will find rest in the home of another husband."

Then Ruth said: "Don't urge me to leave you or to turn back from you. Where you go I will go, and where you stay I will stay. Your people will be my people and your God my God. Where you die, I will die, and there I will be buried. May the LORD deal with me, be it ever so severely if anything but death separates you and me." This is how Ruth went back with Naomi. When they got to Bethlehem Naomi knew that it was customary for a male close relative to marry a widow of a relative and provide safety and continuity of the family.

Ruth asked her mother-in-law whether she could go and glean behind the harvesters in the barley fields and Naomi agreed. She went to glean in a field that belongs to Boaz who was from the clan of Elimelech.

Ruth was a hard working woman, concentrating on picking up what the harvesters had left behind. She worked so hard that when Boaz came from Bethlehem he saw her and wondered who she was. He actually said: "Whose young woman is that?"

He was told by his foreman, that she was the Moabitess who came back from Moab with Naomi. He was also told that she had requested to glean and gather among the sheaves behind the harvesters. That since she went into the field she had worked steadily from morning till now, except for a short rest in the shelter.

This made Boaz gave her the Green light to go ahead and glean in his field. He said,

"My daughter, listen to me. Don't go and glean in another field and don't go away from here. Stay here with my servant girls. Watch the field where the men are harvesting, and follow along after the girls. I have told the men not to touch you. And whenever you are thirsty, go and get a drink from the water jars the men have filled."

She asked Boaz "Why have I found such favour in your eyes that you notice me a foreigner? Then Boaz told her that he had been told all about what she had done for her mother-in-law since the death of your husband – and how you left you father and mother and your homeland and came to live with a people you did not know before. May the Lord repay you for what you have done? May you be richly rewarded by the LORD, the God of Israel, under whose wings you have come to take refuge." He even gave her bread and wine vinegar, and some roasted grain.

Then Boaz ordered his harvesters that even if she gathered among the sheaves, they should not embarrass her, rather they should pull out some stalks for her from the bundles and leave them for her to pick up and not rebuke her.

Therefore she gleaned in the field until evening, then she went home with what she colleted and the leftovers from what she ate. When she told Naomi about what had happened, Naomi told her that he was a close relative, and she planned how Ruth could be married by Boaz.

One day Naomi her mother-in-law said to her, "My daughter, should I not try to find a home for you, where you will be well provided for?

Is not Boaz, with whose servant girls you have been, a kinsman of ours? Tonight he will be winnowing barley on the threshing-floor.

Wash and perfume yourself, and put on your best clothes. Then go down to the threshing-floor, but don't let him know you are there until he has finished eating and drinking.

When he lies down, note the place where he is lying. Then go and uncover his feet and lie down. He will tell you what to do."

"I will do whatever you say," Ruth answered.

So she went down to the threshing-floor and did everything her mother-in-law told her to do.

When Boaz had finished eating and drinking and was in good spirits, he went over to lie down at the far end of the grain pile. Ruth approached quietly, uncovered his feet and lay down.

In the middle of the night something startled the man, and he turned and discovered a woman lying at his feet.

"Who are you?" he asked; "I am your servant Ruth," she said; "Spread the corner of your garment over me, since you are a kinsman-redeemer."

"The Lord bless you, my daughter," he replied. "This kindness is greater than that which you showed earlier: You have not run after the younger men, whether rich or poor.

And now, my daughter, don't be afraid. I will do for you all you ask. All my fellow townsmen know that you are a woman of noble character.

Although it is true that I am near of kin, there is a kinsman-redeemer nearer than I.

Stay here for the night, and in the morning if he wants to redeem, good; let him redeem. But if he is not willing, as surely as the Lord lives I will do it. Lie here until morning."

So she lay at his feet until morning, but got up before anyone could be recognized; and he said, "Don't let it be known that a woman came to the threshing-floor."

He also said, "Bring me the Shawl you are wearing and hold it out." When she did so, he poured into it six measures of barley and put it on her. Then he went back to town.

When Ruth came to her mother-in-law, Naomi asked, "How did it go, my daughter?" Then she told her everything Boaz had done for her

And added, "He gave me these six measures of barley, saying, 'Don't go back to your mother-in-law empty-handed.' "

Then Naomi said, "Wait, my daughter, until you find out what happens. For the man will not rest until the matter is settled today."

Boaz then worked out how he cold marry Ruth and he did marry her.

The Bible and Ruth:

In the days when the judges ruled, there was a famine in the land and a man from Bethlehem in Judah together with his wife and two sons went to live for a while in the country of Moab.

The man's name was Elimelech's, his wife's name was Naomi, and the names of his two sons were Mahlon and Kilion. They were Ephrathites from Bethlehem, Judah.

Now Elimelech, Naomi's husband, died, and she was left with her two sons.

They married Moabite women, one named Orpah and the other Ruth.

After they had lived there about ten years both Mahlon and Kilion also died and Naomi was left without her two sons and her husband.

When she heard in Moab that the Lord had come to the aid of his people by providing food for them, Naomi and her daughters-in-law prepared to return home from there.

With her two daughters-in-law she left the place where she had been living and set out on the road that would take them back to the land of Judah.

Then Naomi said to her two daughters-in-law, "Go back, each of you, to your mother's home. May the Lord show kindness to you, as you have shown to your dead and to me. May the Lord grant that each of you will find rest in the home of another husband. Then she kissed them and they wept aloud and said to her, "We will go back with you to your people."

But Naomi said, "Return home, my daughters. Why would you come with me? Am I going to have any more sons, who could become your husbands? Return home, my daughters. I am too old to have another husband. Even if I thought there was still hope for me – even if I had a husband tonight and then gave birth to sons – would you wait until they grew up? No, my daughters. It is more bitter for me than for you, because the Lord's hand has gone out against me!"

At this they wept again.

Then Orpah kissed her mother-in-law good-by, but Ruth clung to her.

"Look," said Naomi, your sister-in-law is going back to her people and her gods. Go back with her."

But Ruth replied, "Don't urge me to leave you or to turn back from you. Where you go, and where you stay I will stay. Your people will be my people and your God my God. Where you die I will die, and there I will be buried. May the Lord deal with me, be it ever so severely, if any thing but death separates you and me."

When Naomi realized that Ruth was determined to go with her, she stopped urging her.

So the two women went on until they came to Bethlehem. When they arrived in Bethlehem, the whole town was stirred because of them, and the women exclaimed, "Can this be Naomi?"

"Don't call me Naomi," she told them, "Call me Mara, because the Almighty had made my life very bitter. I went away full, but the Lord had brought me back empty. Why call me Naomi? The Lord had afflicted me; the Almighty has brought misfortune upon me.

So Naomi returned from Moab accompanied by Ruth the Moabitess, her daughter-in-law, arriving in Bethlehem as the barley harvest was beginning.

Ruth Meets Boaz

Now Naomi had a relative on her husband's side, from the clan of Elimelech, a man of standing, whose name was Boaz.

And Ruth the Moabitess said to Naomi, "Let me go to the fields and pick up the leftover grain behind anyone in whose eyes I find favour." Naomi said to her, "Go ahead, my daughter."

So she went out and began to glean in the fields behind the harvesters. As it turned out, she found herself working in a field belonging to Boaz, who was from the clan of Elimelech.

Just then Boaz arrived from Bethlehem and greeted the harvesters, "The Lord be with you!" "The Lord bless you!" they called back.

Boaz asked the foreman of his harvesters, "Whose young woman is that?"

The foreman replied, "She is the Moabitess who came back from Moab with Naomi.

She said, 'Please let me glean and gather among the sheaves behind the harvesters.' She went into the field and has worked steadily from morning till now, except for a short rest in the shelter."

So Boaz said to Ruth, "My daughter, listen to me. Don't go and glean in another field and don't go away from here. Stay here with my servant girls.

Watch the field where the men are harvesting, and follow along after the girls. I have told the men not to touch you. And whenever you are thirsty, go and get a drink from the water jars the men have filled;"

At this, she bowed down with her face to the ground. She exclaimed, "Why have I found such favour in your eyes that you notice me – a foreigner?"

Boaz replied, "I've been told all about what you have done for your mother-in-law since the death of your husband – how you left your father and mother and your homeland and came to live with a people you did not know before.

May the Lord repay you for what you have done. May you be richly rewarded by the Lord, the God of Israel, under whose wings you have come to take refuge."

"May I continue to find favour in your eyes, my lord," she said. "You have given me comfort and have spoken kindly to your servant – though I do not have the standing of one of your servant girls."

At mealtime Boaz said to her, "Come over her. Have some bread and dip it in the wine vinegar." When she sat down with the harvesters, he offered her some roasted grain. She ate all she wanted and had some left over.

As she got up to glean, Boaz gave orders to his men, "Even if she gathers among the sheaves, don't embarrass her.

Rather, pull out some stalks for her from the bundles and leave them for her to pick up, and don't rebuke her."

So Ruth gleaned in the field until evening. Then she threshed the barley she had gathered, and it amounted to about an Ephah.

She carried it back to town, and her mother-in-law saw how much she had gathered. Ruth also brought out and gave her what she had left over after she had eaten enough.

Her mother-in-law asked her, "Where did you glean today? Where did you work? Blessed be the man who took notice of you!" Then Ruth told her mother-in-law about the one at whose place she had been working. "The name of the man I worked with today is Boaz," she said.

"The Lord bless him!" Naomi said to her daughter-in-law. "He has not stopped showing his kindness to the living and the dead." She added, "That man is our close relative; he is one of our kinsman-redeemers."

Then Ruth the Moabitess said, "He even said to me, 'Stay with my workers until they finish harvesting all my grain.' "

Naomi said to Ruth her daughter-in-law, "It will be good for you, my daughter, to go with his girls, because in someone else's field you might be harmed."

So Ruth stayed close to the servant girls of Boaz to glean until the barley and wheat harvests were finished. And she lived with her mother-in-law.

Ruth and Boaz at the Threshing-Floor

One day Naomi her mother-in-law said to her, "My daughter, should I not try to find a home for you, where you will be well provided for?

Is not Boaz, with whose servant girls you have been, a kinsman of ours? Tonight he will be winnowing barley on the threshing-floor.

Wash and perfume yourself, and put on your best clothes. Then go down to the threshing-floor, but don't let him know you are there until he has finished eating 8and drinking.

When he lies down, note the place where he is lying. Then go and uncover his feet and lie down. He will tell you what to do."

"I will do whatever you say," Ruth answered.

So she went down to the threshing-floor and did everything her mother-in-law told her to do.

When Boaz had finished eating and drinking and was in good spirits, he went over to lie down at the far end of the grain pile. Ruth approached quietly, uncovered his feet and lay down.

In the middle of the night something startled the man, and he turned and discovered a woman lying at his feet.

"Who are you?" he asked; "I am your servant Ruth," she said; "Spread the corner of your garment over me, since you are a kinsman-redeemer."

"The Lord bless you, my daughter," he replied. "This kindness is greater than that which you showed earlier: You have not run after the younger men, whether rich or poor.

And now, my daughter, don't be afraid. I will do for you all you ask. All my fellow townsmen know that you are a woman of noble character.

Although it is true that I am near of kin, there is a kinsman-redeemer nearer than I.

Stay here for the night, and in the morning if he wants to redeem, good; let him redeem. But if he is not willing, as surely as the Lord lives I will do it. Lie here until morning."

So she lay at his feet until morning, but got up before anyone could be recognized; and he said, "Don't let it be known that a woman came to the threshing-floor."

He also said, "Bring me the Shawl you are wearing and hold it out." When she did so, he poured into it six measures of barley and put it on her. Then he went back to town.

When Ruth came to her mother-in-law, Naomi asked, "How did it go, my daughter?" Then she told her everything Boaz had done for her

And added, "He gave me these six measures of barley, saying, 'Don't go back to your mother-in-law empty-handed.' "

Then Naomi said, "Wait, my daughter, until you find out what happens. For the man will not rest until the matter is settled today."

Boaz Marries Ruth

Meanwhile Boaz went up to the town gate and sat there. When the kinsman-redeemer he had mentioned came along, Boaz said, "Come over here, my friend, and sit down." So he went over and sat down.

Boaz took ten of the elders of the town and said, "Sit here," and they did so.

Then he said to the kinsman-redeemer, "Naomi, who has come back from Moab, is selling the piece of land that belonged to our brother Elimelech.

I thought I should bring the matter to your attention and suggest that you buy it in the presence of these seated here and in the presence of the elders of my people. If you will redeem it, do so. But if you will not, tell me, so I will know. For no-one has the right to do it except you, and I am next in line." "I will redeem it," he said.

Then Boaz said, "On the day you buy the land from Naomi and from Ruth the Moabitess, you acquire the dead man's widow, in order to maintain the name of the dead with his property."

At this, the kinsman-redeemer said, "Then I cannot redeem it because I might endanger my own estate. You redeem it yourself. I cannot do it."

(Now in earlier times in Israel, for the redemption and transfer of property to become final, one party took off his sandal and gave it to the other. This was the method of legalizing transactions in Israel.)

So the kinsman-redeemer said to Boaz, "Buy it yourself." And he removed his sandal.

Then Boaz announced to the elders and all the people, "Today you are witnesses that I have bought from Naomi all the property of Elimelech, Kilion and Mahlon.

I have also acquired Ruth the Moabitess, Mahlon's widow, as my wife, in order to maintain the name of the dead with his property, so that his name will not disappear from among his family or from the town records. Today you are witnesses!"

Then the elders and all those at the gate said, "We are witnesses. May the Lord make the woman who is coming into your home like Rachel and Leah, who together built up the house of Israel. May you have standing in Ephrathah and become famous in Bethlehem.

Through the offspring the Lord gives you by this young woman, may your family be like that of Perez, whom Tamar bore to Judah."

The Genealogy of David

So Boaz took Ruth and she became his wife. Then he went to her, and the Lord enabled her to conceive, and she gave birth to a son.

The women said to Naomi: "Praise be to the Lord, who this day has not left you without a kinsman-redeemer. May he become famous throughout Israel!

He will renew your life and sustain you in your old age. For your daughter-in-law, who loves you and who is better to you than seven sons, has given him birth."

Then Naomi took the child, laid him in her lap and cared for him.

The women living there said, "Naomi has a son." And they named him Obed. He was the father of Jesse, the father of David.

This, then is the family line of Perez: Perez was the father of Hezron,

Hezron the father of Ram, Ram the father of Amminadab,

Amminadab the father of Nahshon, Nahshon the father of Salmon,

Salmon the father of Boaz, Boaz the father of Obed,

Obed the father of Jesse, and Jesse the father of David. (Ruth)

Lessons to Learn:

- So Boaz took Ruth and she became his wife. Then he went to her, and the Lord enabled her to conceive, and she gave birth to a son.

- The women said to Naomi: "Praise be to the Lord, who this day has not left you without a kinsman-redeemer. May he become famous throughout Israel!

- He will renew your life and sustain you in your old age. For your daughter-in-law, who loves you and who is better to you than seven sons, has given him birth."

- Then Naomi took the child, laid him in her lap and cared for him.

- The women living there said, "Naomi has a son." And they named him Obed. He was the father of Jesse, the father of David.
- This, then is the family line of Perez: Perez was the father of Hezron,
- Hezron the father of Ram, Ram the father of Amminadab,
- Amminadab the father of Nahshon, Nahshon the father of Salmon,
- Salmon the father of Boaz, Boaz the father of Obed,
- Obed the father of Jesse, and Jesse the father of David.

God is the Umbrella of Women in the Bible!

67. Saffira – The Wife of Ananias

Now a man named Ananias, together with his wife Sapphira, also sold a piece of property. With his wife's full knowledge he kept back part of the money himself, but brought the rest and put it at the apostle's feet.

Then Peter said, "Ananias, how is it that Satan has so filled your heart that you have lied to the Holy Spirit and have kept for yourself some of the money you received for the land? What made you think of doing such a thing? You have not lied to men but to God."

When Ananias heard this, he fell down and died. And great fear seized all who heard what had happened. Then the young men came forward, wrapped up his body, and carried him out and buried him.

About three hours later his wife came in not knowing what had happened. Peter asked her, "Tell me, is this the price you and Ananias got for the land?"

"Yes," she said, "that is the price." Peter said to her, "How could you agree to test the Spirit of the Lord? Look! The feet of the men who buried your husband are at the door, and they will carry you out also."

At that moment she fell down at his feet and died. Then the young men came in and, finding her dead, carried her out and buried her beside her husband. Great fear seized the whole church and all who heard about these events. : (Acts 5:1-11)

Lessons to Learn:

Give from the bottom of your hear
- Do not pretend to be a giver when you are not interested in giving
- God does not force you to give him anything
- The whole world and its contents belong to him
- God loves a cheerful giver
- Where God is concerned he knows everything
- The end of the two was death
- What would you have done?

God is the Umbrella of Women in the Bible!

68. Samson's Wife –

- **S**he was seen by Samson in Timnath
- They did not know that it was God's plan that he wanted an occasion with the Philistines
- Samson's father went down to see the her
- She had a seven day wedding festival prepared for her
- Her husband was given thirty companions
- During the seven say festival Samson asked the Philistines to explain a riddle
- She was coaxed by the Philistines to ask Samson for the answer to the riddle or they would kill her and her family
- She threw herself on Samson and cried the whole seven days
- On the seventh day Samson explained the riddle to her
- She in turn explained it to her people
- The Philistines then explained it to Samson
- Her husband knew that they had used her to get the answer

- She was left by Samson because he was angry with her
- She was given to the friend who had attended Samson at the wedding, without him knowing
- Samson later came back for her with a young goat
- He father offered Samson the younger sister and asked him to take her instead.
- Samson refused
- He lit the torches and let the foxes loose in the standing grain of the Philistines
- When the Philistines asked who did this, they were told it was Samson the Timnite's son-in-law because his wife was given to his friend
- The Philistines burned her and her father to death
- Samson then attacked them viciously and slaughtered many of them
- The Philistines went up and camped in Judah spreading out near Lehi
- When asked by the men of Judah why they had come to fight them, they said they had come to take Samson prisoner, to do to him as he had done to us
- Then three thousand men from Judah went down to the cave in the rock of Etam and said to Samson, "Don't you realize that the Philistines are rulers over us? What have you done to us?

- He told them that he was merely doing to them what they had done to him
- They told him that they had come to tie him up and hand him over to the Philistines
- Samson asked them to swear that they would not kill him themselves
- They agreed and said "We will only tie you up and hand you over to them. We will not kill you"
- They bound him up with two new ropes and led him up from the rock
- As he approached Lehi, the Philistines came toward him shouting
- The Spirit of the Lord came upon him in power. The ropes on his arms became like charred flex, and the binding dropped from his hands
- Finding a fresh jaw bone of a donkey, he grabbed it and struck down a thousand man then he said "With a donkey's jawbone, I have made donkeys of them. With a donkey's jawbone, I have killed a thousand men."
- When he finished speaking, he threw away the jawbone; and the place was called Ramath Lehi
- Because he was very thirsty he cried out to the Lord, "You have given your servant this great victory, Must I now die of thirsty and fall into the hands of the uncircumcised?
- Then God opened up the hollow place in Lehi, and water came out of it.

- When Samson drank his strength returned and he revived
- The spring was called En Hakkore, and it is still there in Lehi
- Samson led Israel for twenty years in the days of the Philistines.

The Story:

In our own lives we can learn from the events in this woman, in that God had a plan for Samson to do something with the Philistines. She was used in this event.

The normal thing for Samson to do was to marry from his own brethren. That is from his on father's side of the family. He could also have found a wife from his own mother's side of the family. But instead he went to the Philistines. God wanted to use Samson to deal with the Philistines.

The lion was put there so that Samson could both have a riddle, and could strike down the thirty Philistines to get the reward and then find a way to dump his wife. Though she was threatened by the Philistines she could have told her problem to Samson instead of trying to cheat him in getting the answer. It was all God's plan. She ended up being his friend's wife

The Bible and Samson's Wife:

Samson went down to Timnah and saw there a young philistine woman. When he returned, he said to his father and mother, "I have seen a Philistine woman in Timnah, now get her for me as my wife."

God is the Umbrella of Women in the Bible

His father replied, "Isn't there an acceptable woman among your relatives or among all our people? Must you go to the uncircumcised Philistines to get a wife?"

But Samson said to his father, "Get her for me. She's the right one for me." (His parents did not know that this was from the LORD, who was seeking an occasion to confront the Philistines; for at that time they were ruling over Israel.) Samson went down to Timnah together with his father and mother. As they approached the vineyards of Timnah, suddenly a young lion came roaring toward him. The Spirit of the LORD came upon him in power so that he tore the lion apart with his bare hands as he might have torn a young goat. But he told neither his father nor his mother what he had done. Then he went down and talked with the woman, and he liked her.

Some time later when he went back to marry her, he turned aside to look at the lion's carcass. In it was a swarm of bees and some honey, which he scooped out with his hands and ate as he went along. When he rejoined his parents, he gave them some, and they too ate it. But he did not tell them that he had taken the honey from the lion's carcass.

Now his father went down to see the woman. And Samson made a feast there, as was customary for bride-grooms. When he appeared, he was given thirty companions.

Let me tell you a riddle, "Samson said to them. "If you can give me the answer within the seven days of the feast, I will give you thirty linen garments and thirty sets of clothes. If you can't tell me the answer, you must give me thirty linen garments and thirty sets of clothes."

"Tell us your riddle," they said. "Let's hear it."

He replied, "Out of the eater, something to eat; out of the strong, and something sweet."

For three days they could not give the answer. On the fourth day, they said to Samson's wife, "Coax your husband into explaining the riddle for us, or we will burn you and your father's household to death. Did you invite us here to rob us?"

Then Samson's wife threw herself on him, sobbing. "You hate me! You don't really love me. You've given my people a riddle, but you haven't told me the answer." "I haven't even explained it to my father or mother," he replied, "so why should I explain it to you?" She cried the whole seven days of the feast. So on the seventh day he finally told her, because she continued to press him. She in turn explained the riddle to her people. Before sunset on the seventh day the men of the town said to him, "What is sweeter than honey? What is stronger than a lion?

Samson said to them, "If you had not plowed with my heifer, you would not have solved my riddle."

Then the Spirit of the LORD came upon him in power. He went down to Ashkelon, struck down thirty of their men, stripped them of their belongings and gave their clothes to those who had explained the riddle. Burning with anger, he went up to his father's house. And Samson's wife was given to the friend who had attended him at his wedding. (Judges 14:1 - 20

(Judges 15) (Judges 13:5, 12, 11, 19, 23 – 25)

Lessons to Learn:

- God always has his way
- God uses any one to deal with situations
- Repentance is the only way to get out of the wrong doings

God is the Umbrella of Women in the Bible!

69. Samson's Mother:

- She was the wife of Manoah and she was sterile
- The angel of the LORD appeared to her first
- She spoke with the angel of the LORD
- She conceived and gave birth to a son
- She named him Samson

The Story:

The angel of the Lord appeared to her and told her that she was sterile and childless, but that she was going to conceive and have a son. The angel gave her instructions that she should not drink no wine or other fermented drink and that she should not eat anything unclean, because she was going to conceive and give birth to a son. He told her that no razor may be used on his head, because the boy was going to be a Nazirite, set apart to God from birth, and he will begin the deliverance of Israel from the hands of the Philistines.

Then she went to her husband and told him that a man of God had come to her. He looked like an angel of God, very awesome. She had not asked where he came from, and he didn't tell me his name. But he said to me, I will conceive and give birth to a son. She told her husband everything the angel of the LORD had told her.

Manoah prayed to the Lord and begged him to let the man of he had sent to come again to teach them how to bring up the boy who was to be born

God heard Manoah, and the angel of God came again to her while she was out in the field; but her husband Manoah was not with her. The she hurried to tell her husband, and told him that the man who had appeared to her the other day was there.

Manoah got up and followed here. When he came to the man, he asked him whether he was the man who talked to my wife. The angel of the LORD said yes he was.

So Manoah asked him that when his words were fulfilled, what was to be the rule for the boy's life and work.

The angel of the Lord again told him that his wife was do all that he had told her. She was not eat anything that comes from the grapevine, nor drink any wine or other fermented drink nor eat anything unclean. She was to do everything I have commanded he.

Manoah then offered the angel of the Lord food but the angel of the Lord told him that even though he would detain him, he would not eat any of their food. But they could prepare a burnt offering and offer it to the LORD. Manoah did not realize it was the angel of the Lord and asked for his name. The angel of the LORD told him that it is beyond understanding.

Then Manoah took a young got, together with the grain offering, and sacrificed it on a rock to the Lord. And the Lord did an amazing thing while Manoah and his wife watched. As he flame blazed up from the altar toward heaven, the angel of the Lord ascended in the flame. Seeing this, Manoah and his wife fell with their faced to the ground. When the angel of the Lord did not show himself to Manoah and his wife, Manoah realized that it was the angel of the Lord.

"We are doomed to die" he said to his wife. "We have seen God."

But his wife answered, "If the Lord had meant to kill us, he would not have accepted a burnt offering and grain offering from our hands, nor shown us all these things or told us this."

She gave birth to a boy and named him Samson. He grew and the Lord blessed him and the Spirit of the Lord began to stir him while he was in Mahaneh Dan, between Zorah and Eshtaol.

The Bible and Samson's Mother:

Again the Israelites did evil in the eyes of the Lord, so the Lord delivered them into the hands of the Philistines for forty years.

A certain man of Zorah, named Manoah, from the clan of the Danites, had a wife who was sterile and remained childless. The angel of the Lord appeared to her and said, "You are sterile and childless, but you are going to conceive and have a son. Now see to it that you drink no wine or other fermented drink and that you do not eat anything unclean, because you will conceive and give birth to a son. No razor may be used on his head, because the boy is to be a Nazirite, set apart to God from birth, and he will begin the deliverance of Israel from the hands of the Philistines."

Then the woman went to her husband and told him. "A man of God came to me. He looked like an angel of God, very awesome. I didn't ask him where he came from, and he didn't tell me his name. But he said to me, "You will conceive and give birth to a son. Now then, drink no wine or other fermented drink and do not eat anything unclean, because the boy will be a Nazirite of God from birth until the day of his death.'"

Then Manoah prayed to the Lord. "O Lord, I beg you, let the man of God you sent to us come again to teach us how to bring up the boy who is to be born."

God heard Manoah, and the angel of God came again to the woman while she was out in the field; but her husband Manoah was not with her. The woman hurried to tell her husband, "He is here! The man who appeared to me the other day."

Manoah got up and followed his wife. When he came to the man, he said, "Are you the one who talked to my wife?" "I am," he said. So Manoah asked him, "When your words are fulfilled, what is to be the rule for the boy's life and work?"

The angel of the Lord answered, "Your wife must do all that I have told her. She must not eat anything that comes from the grapevine, nor drink any wine or other fermented drink nor eat anything unclean. She must do everything I have commanded her."

Manoah said to the angel of the Lord, "We would like you to stay until we prepare a young got for you."

The angel of the Lord replied, "Even though you detain me, I will not eat any of your food. But if you prepare a burnt offering, offer it to the Lord." (Manoah did not realize it was the angel of the Lord.)

Then Manoah inquired of the angel of the Lord, "What is your name, so that we may honour you when your word comes true?"

He replied, "Why do you ask my name? It is beyond understanding."

Then Manoah took a young got, together with the grain offering, and sacrificed it on a rock to the Lord. And the Lord did an amazing thing while Manoah and his wife watched. As he flame blazed up from the altar toward heaven, the angel of the Lord ascended in the flame. Seeing this, Manoah and his wife fell with their faced to the ground. When the angel of the Lord did not show himself to Manoah and his wife, Manoah realized that it was the angel of the Lord.

"We are doomed to die" he said to his wife. "We have seen God."

But his wife answered, "If the Lord had meant to kill us, he would not have accepted a burnt offering and grain offering from our hands, nor shown us all these things or told us this."

The woman gave birth to a boy and named him Samson. He grew and the Lord blessed him and the Spirit of the Lord began to stir him while he was in Mahaneh Dan, between Zorah and Eshtaol. (Judges 13:1 – 15)

Lessons to Learn:

- You are sterile and childless, but you are going to conceive and have a son
- Are there things that you think might be leading you to this situation?
- You have to change the way you have been doing things
- Do not drink wine or other fermented drink
- Do not eat anything unclean – say anything that upsets your normal routine
- You will conceive and give birth to a son
- Your son will be a Nazirite, set apart to God from birth

God is the Umbrella of Women in the Bible!

70. Sarai – Sarah – Mother of all Nations

Who Was This Woman?

- Abram's half sister
- Abram's wife
- Barren
- Beautiful
- A good Hostess
- She was admired by king Abimelech
- Liar
- Too Forward
- Obedient
- Considerate
- Mistreated
- She was rejuvenated at 90 years of age
- Her youth was renewed
- She gave birth to Isaac
- She nursed Isaac till he was weaned
- She lived to be 127 years

- She died at Kiriath Arba (that is Hebron) in the land of Canaan
- Abraham went to mourn her and weep over her
- Abraham bought burial land from Ephron son of Zohar
- He paid 400 shekels of silver for Ephron's field at Machpelah near Mamre
- Abraham buried Sarah his wife in the cave of Machpelah
- It was deeded to Abraham as a burial site (Genesis 23:1 - 2

The Story:

The name of Abram's wife was Sarai; she was the daughter of Terah by a different wife from Abram's mother. She was his half sister. Sarai was a beautiful woman. Sarai was barren.

At one point there was a famine in their land, and Abram decided to take Sarai to Egypt to live there while the famine was severe. As they entered Egypt, he feared for his life because Sarai was a beautiful woman. He actually asked Sarai to tell a lie. He told her that when the Egyptians asked who she was, she was to say that she was his sister.

He thought they would kill him and let Sarai live. But if she said she was his sister they would be treated well and his life will be spared because of her.

When they came to Egypt, the Egyptians saw that Sarai was a very beautiful woman. She told them she was Abram's sister, and Pharaoh's officials praised her to Pharaoh, She was taken into his palace. He treated Abram well for her sake, and Abram acquired sheep and cattle, male and female donkeys, menservants and maidservants, and camels.

But the LORD inflicted serious diseases on Pharaoh and his household. So Pharaoh summoned Abram and gave him his wife. Then Pharaoh gave orders about Abram to his men, and they sent him on his way, with his wife and everything he had.

Sarai gave instructions to Abram to sleep with her maidservant Hagar so that she could build a family through her. However, when Hagar was pregnant she started to despise Sarai. Then Sarai went back again to Abram and complained about what Hagar was doing; and surely Abram laid the blame on her. She is the one who had put her in that position and she could do whatever she wanted. After all she was her maidservant. Then she mistreated Hagar who then ran away. Hagar later met the Angel of the LORD and was told to go back to her mistress. She gave birth to a son and Abram named him Ishmael.

God changed both their names Abram to Abraham, and Sarai to Sarah. He blessed her, and said she will have a son and that she would become the mother of nations; and kings of people would come from her.

God told them the he would establish his covenant with Isaac, whom Sarah was going to bear unto Abraham. Abraham was ninety-nine and Sarah was ninety years old. She could not believe what she was hearing and she laughed. And God told her that nothing was impossible for God. Sarah gave became pregnant and gave birth to Isaac at an old age.

The Bible and Sarai/Sarah:

This is the account of Terah: Terah became the father of Abram, Nahor and Haran. And Haran the father of Lot.

God is the Umbrella of Women in the Bible

While his father Terah was still alive, Haran died in Ur of the Chaldeans. In the land of his birth. Abram and Nahor both married. The name of Abram's wife was Sarai, and the name of Nahor's wife was Milcah; she was the daughter of Haran, the father of both Milcah and Iscah. Now Sarai was barren; she had no children.

Terah took his son Abram, his grandson Lot son of Haran, and his daughter-in-law Sarai; the wife of his son Abram, and together with set out from Ur or the Chaldeans to go to Canaan. But they came to Haran and settled there. Terah lived 205 years and he died. (Genesis 11:27 - 32)

He took his wife Sarai, his nephew Lot, all the possessions they had accumulated and the people they had acquired in Haran, and they set out for the land of Canaan and they arrived there. (Genesis 12:5)

Now there was a famine in the land, and Abram went down to Egypt to live there for a while because the famine was severe. As he was about to enter Egypt, he said to his wife Sarai, "I know what a beautiful woman you are. When the Egyptians see you, they will say, 'This is his wife.' Then they will kill me but will let you lie. Say you are my sister, so that I will be treated well for your sake and my life will be spared because of you."

When Abram came to Egypt, the Egyptians saw that she was a very beautiful woman. And when Pharaoh's officials saw her, they praised her to Pharaoh, and she was taken into his palace. He treated Abram well for her sake, and Abram acquired sheep and cattle, male and female donkeys, menservants and maidservants, and camels.

But the LORD inflicted serious diseases on Pharaoh and his household because of Abram's wife Sarai. So Pharaoh summoned Abram. "What have you done to me?" He said. "Why didn't you tell me she was your wife? "Why did you say, 'She is my sister,' so that I took here to be my wife? "Now then here is your wife. Take her and go!" Then Pharaoh gave orders about Abram to his men, and they sent him on his way, with his wife and everything they had. (Genesis 12::10 – 20)

God also said to Abraham, "As for Sarai thy wife, thou shalt not call her Sarai, but Sarah shall her name be. And I will bless her, and give thee a son also of her: yea, I will bless her, and she shall be a *mother* of nations; kings of people will come from her "

Will Sarah, bear a child at the age of ninety? (Genesis17:15 - 17)

Sarah thy wife shall bear thee a son indeed; and thou shall call his name Isaac; and I will establish my covenant with him for an everlasting covenant and with his seed after him.

"Will a son be born to a man a hundred years old? Will Sarah bear a child at the age of ninety?

(Genesis 17:19)

"But my covenant will I establish with Isaac, which Sarah shall bear unto thee at the set times in the next year. Abraham was ninety-nine and Sarah was ninety years old.

(Genesis 17:21

Sarai gave instructions to Abram to sleep with her maidservant Hagar so that she could build a family through her. However, when Hagar was pregnant she started to despise Sarai. Then Sarai went back again to Abram and complained about what Hagar was doing; and surely Abram laid the blame on her. She is the one who had put her in that position and she could do whatever she wanted. After all she was her maidservant. Then she mistreated Hagar who then ran away.

So Abraham hurried into the tent to Sarah. "Quick," he said, "get three seahs of fine flour and knead it and bake some bread."

"Where is your wife Sarah?" they asked him.

"There in the tent," he said.

"Then the LORD said, "I will surely return to you about this time next year, and Sarah your wife will have a son."

Now Sarah was listening at the entrance to the tent which was behind him. Abraham and Sarah were already old and well advanced in years, and Sarah was past the age of childbearing. So Sarah laughed to herself as she thought. "After I am worn out and my master is old, will I now have this pleasure?

Then the Lord said to Abraham, "Why did Sarah laugh and say, 'Will I really have a child, now that I am old? Is anything too hard for the LORD? I will return to you at the appointed time next year and Sarah will have a son."

Sarah was afraid, so she lied and said, "I did not laugh."

But he said, "Yes you did laugh."(Genesis 18:6 – 15)

Lessons to Learn:

- The birth of Ishmael by Hagar
- Gave birth at old age
- Rushed decisions are not always correct

God is the Umbrella of Women in the Bible!

71. Serah – The daughter of Asher the son of Zilpah:

Who Was This Woman?

- She was the daughter of Asher
- She was the great-granddaughter of Isaac and Rebekah
- She was the granddaughter of Jacob and Zilpah, the maidservant of Leah. Jacobs wife
- She was the sister of Imnah, Ishvah, Ishvi, and Beriah
- She was the cousin of Zephon, Haggi, Shuni, Ezbon, Arodi and Areli

The Story:

Abraham and Sarah gave birth to Isaac at the late ages of ninety-nine and ninety respectively. Then Isaac married Rebekah, the daughter of Bethuel son of Milcah, who was the wife of Abraham's brother Nahor. Abraham actually organized for his servant to go and look for a wife for his son from his own people in Haran. Isaac and Rebekah gave birth to twin boys Esau and Jacob.

Isaac and Rebekah also sent Jacob to Paddan Aram to the house of Bethuel Rebekah's father to get a wife. Jacob then married two sisters Leah and Rachel the daughters of Laban. Laban gave her daughters maidservants. Leah's maidservant was Zilpah and Rachel's maidservant was Bilhah.

The two sisters at some time both gave their maidservants to their husband Jacob to sleep with in order to have children.

Zilpah's sons were Gad and Asher and Asher was the father of Serah. Altogether, Zilpah's children and their children were sixteen in number.

The Bible and Serah:

The sons of Gad: Zephon, Haggi, Shuni, Ezbon, Arodi and Areli.

The sons of Asher: Imnah, Ishvah, Ishvi, and Beriah.

Their sister was Serah.

The sons of Beriah: Berber and Malkiel.

These were the children born to Jacob by Zilpah, whom Laban had given to his daughter Lear – sixteen in all. (Genesis 46:16 – 18)

Lessons to Learn:

- Her name is written in the Bible and it means something.

God is the Umbrella of Women in the Bible!

72. Shelomith – the Daughter of Zerubbabel:

The sons of Pedaiah: Zerubbabel and Shimei. The sons of Zerubbabel: Meshullum and Hananiah. Shelomith was their sister.

God is the Umbrella of Women in the Bible!

73. Shiprah – The Hebrew Midwife

Who Was This Woman?

- She was one of the Hebrew midwives to whom the king of Egypt had given orders to kill the boys and save the girls
- She feared God and let the boys live
- She told the king that Hebrew women are not Egyptian women, they are vigorous and they gave birth before the midwifes arrived
- God was kind to her
- Pharaoh then ordered that every boy that was born was to be thrown into the Ni

The Story:

When Joseph and all his brothers and all their generation had died, the Israelites had become fruitful and multiplied greatly and had become exceedingly numerous in Egypt, a new king came to power. He did not know anything about Joseph.

He then pondered a way of reducing the numbers of the Israelites. Firstly he oppressed them and worked them ruthlessly. He made their lives bitter by giving them hard labour in brick and mortar and with all kinds of work in the fields. When all this was not working he decided to go further and kill the Israelite new babies.

The Bible and Shiprah:

The king of Egypt said to the Hebrew midwives, whose names were Shiprah and Puah, "When you help the Hebrew women in childbirth and observe them on the delivery stool, if it is a boy, kill him, but if it is a girl let her live."

The midwives, however, feared God and did not do what the king of Egypt had told them to do; they let the boys live. Then the king of Egypt summoned the midwives and asked them, "Why have you done this? Why have you let the boys live?

The midwives answered Pharaoh, "Hebrew women are not like Egyptian women; they are vigorous and give birth before the midwives arrive.

So God was kind to the midwives and the people increased and became even more numerous. And because the midwives feared God, he gave them families of their own.

Then Pharaoh gave this order to all his people; "Every boy that is born you must throw into the Nile but let e very girl live." (Exodus 1:15 – 22)

Lessons to Learn:

- God was kind to the midwives

- The people increased and became even more numerous
- Because the midwives feared God, he gave them families of their own.
- Then Pharaoh gave this order to all his people; "Every boy that is born you must throw into the Nile but let e very girl live."
- That is the reason why Jochebed was afraid to keep her son Moses and placed him in the basket in the river Nile

God is the Umbrella of Women in the Bible!

74. Shua's Daughter – the Wife of Judah:

Who Was This Woman?

- She was the daughter of Shua
- She married Judah
- She was the mother of Er
- She was the mother of Onan
- She was the mother of Shelah

The Story:

She was married by Judah. Judah had left his brothers, and went down to stay with a man at Adullam named Hirah. It was at Hirah's house that Judah met her. She was the daughter of a Canaanite man named Shua.

After she was married she had three sons namely Er, Onan and Shelah. After a long time she died. Therefore her story is that she married Judah and had three sons with him, and died after a long time. Later her son Er married Tamar and was wicked to her. The LORD put him to death. Then Judah asked Onan her second son to fulfill his duties as a brother-in-law to Tamar and produce children for his brother Er. Er also was wicked to Tamar and spilled his semen on the ground as he did not want to have children for his brother. Then the LORD put him to death also.

Judah became scared to give Tamar Shelah the third son. He then asked Tamar to go to her parents and wait for Shelah to grow up. But when Shelah had grown up Judah had not kept his promise and Tamar the daughter-in-law of Shua's daughter tricked Judah and slept with him while he thought she was a prostitute. Then she gave birth to Perez and Zerah.

Judah had three sons with Shua's daughter. The sons were Er the first born, Onan the second born and Shelah the third born. Not much is written about this woman although she is important in the life story of Judah and his sons.

The Bible and Shua's Daughter:

"At that time Judah left his brothers, and went down to stay with a man at Adullam named Hirah. There Judah met the daughter of a Canaanite man named Shua. He married her, and lay with her; she became pregnant and gave birth to a son, who was named Er. She conceived again and gave birth to a son and named him Onan. She gave birth to still another son and named him Shelah. It was at Kezib that she gave birth to him.

Judah got a wife for Er, his firstborn, and her name was Tamar. But Er, Judah's firstborn, was wicked in the LORD's sight; so the LORD put him to death.

Then Judah said to Onan, "Lie with your brother's wife and fulfill your duty to her as a brother-in-law to produce offspring for your brother." But Onan knew that the offspring would not be his, so whenever he lay with his brother's wife, he spilled his semen on the ground to keep from producing offspring for his brother. What he did was wicked in the LORD's sight; so he put him to death also.

After a long time Judah's wife, the daughter of Shua, died. When Judah had recovered from his grief, he went up to Timnah, to the men who were shearing his sheep, and his friend Hirah the Adullamite went with him. (Genesis 38:1 – 14)

Lessons to Learn:

- When she died two of her sons also died
- Judah after the time of mourning slept with a woman whom he thought was a prostitute; in reality she was Tamar Er's wife
- Tamar gave birth to Perez and Zerah, Judah's sons
- Shua's daughter became the grandmother of her husband's two children from her daughter-in-law

God is the Umbrella of Women in the Bible!

75. Sisera's Mother:

The mother of Sisera looked out at a window, and cried through the lattice, why is his chariot so long in coming? Why tarry the wheels of his chariots? Her wise ladies answered her, yea, she returned answer to herself. Have they not sped? Have they not divided the prey; to every man a damsel or two; to Sisera a prey of divers colours of needlework, on both sides, meet for the necks of them that take the spoil. (Judges 5:28 – 30)

Lessons to Learn:

- She had always waited for her son to bring spoils back from his encounters
- Would you say she had any feelings for other people her son was killing?
- She felt for the chariots more than people
- Have you ever had an encounter with people who cared less for other human beings?
- She looked forward to her son and his compatriots bringing back young women whom they will have captured.

- Can you visualize Sisera's Mother dressed as a Queen waiting for her son, looking out through the window and shouting to the maids?

God is the Umbrella of Women in the Bible!

76. Solomon's wives – Pharaoh's Daughter, Moabites, Ammonites, Edomites, Sodomans and Hittites

King Solomon, however, loved many foreign women besides Pharaoh's daughter – Moabites, Ammonites, Edomites, Sidonians and Hittites. They were from nations about which the LORD had told the Israelites, "You must not intermarry with them, because they will surely turn your hearts after their gods."

Nevertheless, Solomon held fast to them in love. He had seven hundred wives of royal birth and three hundred concubines, and his wives led him astray. As Solomon grew old, his wives turned his hart after other gods, and his heart was not fully devoted to the LORD his God, as the heart of David his father had been.

(1 Kings 11:1 – 4)

Lessons to Learn:

- There were eight hundred women in all.
- Discuss how these women were seen by Solomon in their marital status.

77. Susanna and Other Women:

And it came to pass afterward, that he went throughout every city and village, preaching and showing the glad tidings of the kingdom of God; and the twelve were with him, and certain women, who had been healed of evil spirits and infirmities, Mary called Magdalene, out of who went seven devils.

And Joanna the wife of Cuza, Herod's steward, and Susanna, and many others, who ministered unto him of their substance. And when much people were gathered together, and were come to him out of every city, he spake by a parable.

(Luke 8:3)

Lessons to Learn:

- What do you do after you have been healed —Susanna followed Jesus!
- These women had a lot of faith
- They ministered to those present with their own substance
- It gives you satisfaction to minister to others or to be able to minister to others!
- With God nothing is impossible

God is the Umbrella of Women in the Bible!

78. Tabitha or Dorcas:

Who Was This Woman?

- She was a disciple. A follower of Jesus Christ
- She lived in Joppa
- She was a well known kind person
- She always helped the poor
- She did good deeds in her community
- She made robes and other clothing for the poor and widows
- She became sick and she died

The Story:

Her story is a story of just doing well for other people, especially the poor and the widows. I am sure she catered for a variety of people in her community. The widows came when they heard that she had died.

They all knew that she was a believer. She must have converted some of them too. They knew that if they could get hold of the Apostle Peter, he could come and assist them.

The believers sent for Peter as they heard he was nearby in Lydda.

Peter wasted no time, came and prayed for her and she was raised from the dead.

The Bible and Tabitha or Dorcas:

As Peter traveled about the country, he went to visit the saints in Lydda. There he found a man named Aeneas, a paralytic who had been bedridden for eight years. "Aeneas," Peter said to him, "Jesus Christ heals you. Get up and take care of your mat." Immediately Aeneas got up. All those who lived in Lydda and Sharon saw him and turned t the LORD.

In Joppa there was a disciple named Tabitha (which, when translated, is Dorcas), who was always doing good and helping the poor. About that time she became sick and died, and her body was washed and placed in an upstairs room. Lydda was near Joppa; so when the disciples heard that Peter was in Lydda, they sent two men to him and urged him, "Please come at once!"

Peter went with them, and when he arrived he was taken upstairs to the room. All the widows stood around him, crying and showing him the robes and other clothing that Dorcas had made while she was still with them.

Peter sent them all out of the room; then he got down on his knees and prayed. Turing toward the dead woman, he said, "Tabitha, get up." She opened her eyes, and seeing Peter she sat up. He took her by the hand and helped her to her feet. Then he called the believers and the widows and presented her to them alive. This became known all over Joppa, and many people believed in the LORD. Peter stayed in Joppa for some time with a tanner named Simon. (Acts 9:32 – 43)

Lessons to Learn:

- When she died, the poor and the widows did not take it lying down
- They brought things that Tabitha had made for them, they wanted her back
- Peter was sent for, came and prayed for her.
- She was raised from the dead.
- The story of Tabitha or Dorcas is a very striking one!
- It encourages us to do what is right in life.
- She was a very prominent woman in that community, by just being there for the widows, orphans and the poor.

God is the Umbrella of Women in the Bible!

79. Tamar – The Sister of Absalom:

- The daughter of David
- She was beautiful
- She was young
- She was Absalom's sister
- She was Jonadab's cousin
- She was lured by Ammon into his bedroom
- She was raped by Ammon her half brother
- She was chased off by Ammon after the rape

The Story

Tamar was a beautiful young woman. She was a virgin. She was the daughter of King David. As king David had many wives she was also the half sister of Ammon, who was the oldest son of the king.

Like all young people she must have dreamt of one day marrying, may be a young prince or someone of good standing. May be she had other dreams about her own future.

Ammon was her brother and he had feelings of love for her. These were not good feelings. If he had good feelings being a half brother, he could have asked his own father for permission to marry Tamar. Instead his feelings made him sick as they frustrated him. He was frustrated because his intentions were not good.

Ammon had a best friend who was also his uncle's son. His name was Jonadab. Jonadab also was not a good person because he failed to give his friend Ammon good advice. The two of them should have looked after the interests of their sister or cousin Tamar but they did not.

Ignorant of the plan her brother Ammon had Tamar went to her brother's house.

Took some dough, kneaded it, made bread in his sight and baked it. Then she took the pan and served him the bread, but he refused to eat.

The Bible and Tamar

Jonadab was a shrewd person which you can deduce from his words. He asked Ammon "Why do you, the king's son, look so haggard morning after morning?"

(2 Samuel 13:4)

What he meant was there was no reason for a king's son to be in that state or to feel that way. Why? Because he was a king's son he could do whatever he wanted to do. He wanted Ammon to feel that he was haggard. This means that he looked lean, hollow eyed and gaunt, from weariness or from hunger. He also wanted him to know that morning after morning he was looking haggard.

Ammon then told him that he was in love with his sister Tamar, Absalom's sister. Jonadab already had a plan for him. He said "Go to bed and pretend to be ill," "When your father comes to see you then say to him 'I would like my sister Tamar to come and give me something to eat. Let her prepare the food in my sight so that I may watch her and eat it from her had.

That was what happened, when King David heard that his son Ammon was in bed he went to see him and Ammon said to him 'I would like my sister Tamar to come and make some special bread in my sight, so that I may eat from her hand."

The king obviously responded by sending word to Tamar "Go to the house of your brother Ammon and prepare some food for him." (2 Samuel 13:7)

So Tamar went to the house of her brother Ammon, who was lying down. She took some dough, kneaded it, made the bread in his sight and baked it. Then she took the pan and served him the bread, but he refused to eat. "Send everyone out of here," Ammon said. So everyone left him. Then Ammon said to Tamar, "Bring the bread here into my bedroom so I may eat from your hand." And Tamar took the bread she had prepared and brought it to her brother Ammon in his bedroom. But when she took it to him to eat, he grabbed her and said "Come to bed with me my sister"

"Don't my brother!" she said to him. "Don't force me. Such a thing should not be done in Israel! Don't do this wicked thing. What about me? Where could I get rid of my disgrace? And what about you? You would be like one of the wicked fools in Israel. Please speak to the king; he will not keep me from being married to you."

But he refused to listen to her, and since he was stronger than she was, he raped her.

Then Ammon hated her with intense hared. In fact, he hated her more than he had loved her. Ammon said to her, "Get up and get out!"

"No!" she said to him, "Sending me away would be a greater wrong than what you have already done to me."

But he refused to listen to her. He called his personal servant and said, "Get this woman out of here and bold the door after her." So his servant put her out and bolted the door after her. She was wearing a richly ornamented robe, for this was the kind of garment the virgin daughters of the king wore. Tamar put ashes on her head and tore the ornamented robe she was wearing. She put her hand on her head and went away, weeping aloud as she went.

Her brother Absalom said to her, "Has that Ammon your brother been with you? Be quiet now, my sister; he is your brother. Don't take this thing to heart." And Tamar lived in her brother Absalom's house, a desolate woman.

When King David heard all this, he was furious. Absalom never said a word to Ammon, either good or bad; he hated Ammon because he had disgraced his sister Tamar. (2 Samuel 13:8 – 22)

But Jonadab son of Shimeah, David's brother, said, "My lord should not think that they killed all the princes; only Ammon is dead. This has been Absalom's expressed intention ever since the day Ammon raped his sister Tamar. My lord the king should not be concerned about the report that all the king's sons are dead. Only Ammon is dead. (2 Samuel 13:32- 33)

Lessons to Learn:

- Tamar's life was ruined forever
- Absalom two years later killed his brother Ammon
- King David was furious at this rape of his daughter by Ammon.
- Lust destroys people's lives

- Where there is love such things do not happen.
- Have you heard of rape incidences?
- Can you relate them to this situation?
- Fathers raping their daughters
- Discuss this problem and learn from it!

God is the Umbrella of Women in the Bible!

80. Tamar – the Wife of Er:

- Wife of Er son of Judah
- Her Husband Er passed away and she became a widow
- She then became the wife of Onan, the brother of Er, the second son of Judah
- Onan passed away and she was a widow a second time
- Judah promised to give her to his third son Shelah when he grew up
- She was sent back to her parents to wait for Shelah
- Pregnant by Judah after she had disguised herself as a Prostitute
- Mother of the twins Perez and Zerah sons of Judah

The Story:

Tamar was the wife Judah got for his son Er. His son was wicked in the sight of the Lord and the Lord put him to death.

It was customary in those days, as it is in some of our own nations today, that when a husband dies the family allows one of the brothers to take over and maintain the name of the dead. In this case Judah asked his second son to take the widow of his brother so that he could have children with her. However, Onan was not keen on having children with his brother's widow.

Onan knew that the offspring that would have with Tamar would not be his; so whenever he lay with his brother's wife, he spilled his semen on the ground. That was also wicked and the Lord also him o death.

This meant that Tamar had no child either from her own husband Er or from the inheritor Onan. She must have lived a life full of worries and loneliness. Mothers always expect to have children though sometimes it is not possible. Still Judah was supposed to settle this problem for her.

Then Judah told her to go and live with her family and wait until Shelah had grown up. However, it seems Judah was afraid that Shelah would also die. He therefore never followed his promise with his daughter-in-law.

Tamar then heard the news that her father-in-law was going about his business and was visiting Timnah where his sheep were being sheared. She had already noticed that although Shelah was grown up, Judah had not given him to her as he had promised.

She then took off her mourning clothes and disguised herself as a prostitute. She actually was laying a trap for Judah. The bible says she covered herself with a veil and then sat down at the entrance to Enaim, which is on the road to Timnah. As she expected, when Judah saw her he thought she was a prostitute. He went over to her and asked her to come and sleep with him. Of course he did not realize that this was his daughter-in-law Tamar the wife of Ur.

Tamar asked Judah what he will give her after she slept with her and he told her that he was going to send her a young goat from his flock.

She wanted to be sure that she would be able to identify Judah at a later date, therefore she asked him to give her something as a pledge until she got the goat. Judah who had lost his wife fell for this and asked Tamar what she would like him to give her. She then told him, to give her his seal and its cord, and his staff which was in his hand. He gave them to her and slept with her and she became pregnant.

Later Judah sent the goat with his friend but the prostitute was nowhere to be found.

Three months later Judah was told that his daughter-in-law Tamar is guilty of prostitution, and as a result she is now pregnant. He told them to bring her out and have her burned to death. As she was being brought out, she sent a message to him and said, "I am pregnant by the man who owns these," and she added, "See if you recognize whose seal and cord and staff these are."

Judah recognized them and said she was more righteous than him

She had twin boys in her womb. As she was giving birth, one of them put out his hand; and the midwife took a scarlet thread and tied it on his wrist and said, "This one came out first." But when he drew back his hand, his brother came out, and she said, "So this is how you have broken out!" And he was named Perez which means breaking out. Then his brother, who had the scarlet thread on his wrist, came out and he was given the name Zerah which means scarlet or brightness.

Thus Tamar had two children with Judah her father-in-law.

The Bible and Tamar the Wife of Er:

"At that time Judah left his brothers, and went down to stay with a man at Adullam named Hirah. There Judah met the daughter of a Canaanite man named Shua. He married her." (Genesis 38:1 – 3)

Judah had three sons with her. The sons were Er the first born, Onan the second born and Shelah the third born.

"Judah got a wife for Er, his firstborn, and her name was Tamar. But Er, Judah's firstborn, was wicked in the Lord's sight, so the Lord put him to death." (Genesis 38:6)

"Then Judah said to Onan, "Lie with your brother's wife and fulfill your duty to her as a brother-in-law to produce offspring." "But Onan knew that the offspring would not be his; so whenever he lay with his brother's wife, he spilled his semen on the ground to keep from producing offspring for his brother. What he did was wicked in the Lord's sight; so he put him to death also." Genesis 38:8 – 10)

"Judah then said to his daughter-in-law Tamar, "Live as a widow in your father's house until my son Shelah grows up." For he thought, "He may die too, just like his brothers." So Tamar went to live in her father's house."

After some time Judah's wife the daughter of Shua, died and when he had recovered from his grief he went to Timnah to the men who were shearing his sheep. He was accompanied by his friend Hirah the Adullamite.

Before this Judah had promised his daughter-in-law his third son. "Judah then said to his daughter-in-law Tamar, "Live as a widow in your father's house until my son, Shelah grows up." For he thought, "He may die too, just like his brothers." So Tamar went to live in her father's house. (Genesis 38:11)

Tamar then heard the news that her father-in-law was going about his business and was visiting Timnah where his sheep were being sheared. She had already noticed that although Shelah was grown up, Judah had not given him to her as he had promised.

She then took off her mourning clothes and disguised herself as a prostitute. She actually was laying a trap for Judah. The bible says she covered herself with a veil and then sat down at the entrance to Enaim, which is on the road to Timnah. As she expected, when Judah saw her he thought she was a prostitute. He went over to her and asked her to come and sleep with him. Of course he did not realize that this was his daughter-in-law Tamar the wife of Ur.

She asked him "And what will you give me to sleep with you?" He told her that he was going to send her a young goat from his flock.

She wanted to be sure that she would be able to identify Judah at a later date, therefore she asked him to give her something as a pledge until she got the goat. Judah who had lost his wife fell for this and asked Tamar what she would like him to give her. She then told him, "Your seal and its cord, and the staff in your hand," so he gave them to her and slept with her and she became pregnant (Genesis 38:18)

Later Judah sent the goat with his friend but the prostitute was nowhere to be found.

Three months later Judah was told, "Your daughter-in-law Tamar is guilty of prostitution, and as a result she is now pregnant." Judah said, "Bring her out and have her burned to death!" As she was being brought out, she sent a message to her father-in-law. "I am pregnant by the man who owns these," she said. And she added, "See if you recognize whose seal and cord and staff these are."

Judah recognized them and said, "She is more righteous than I, since I wouldn't give her to my son Shelah." And he did not sleep with her again.

When the time came for her to give birth, there were twin boys in her womb. As she was giving birth, one of them put out his hand; so that the midwife took a scarlet thread and tied it on his wrist and said, "This one came out first." But when he drew back his hand, his brother came out, and she said, "So this is how you have broken out!" And he was named Perez which means breaking out. Then his brother, who had the scarlet thread on his wrist, came out and he was given the name Zerah which means scarlet or brightness. (Genesis 38:28 – 39)

Lessons to Learn:

- Two of Judah's sons died
- Judah had two sons with her unknowingly
- It is important to keep your word.
- Would you be frightened to give your son to a widow of your other son?
- What would you think if the second son also dies?
- Do you think Judah should have consulted God about this type of inheritance?
- Was it in God's plan for this to happen to Judah and his sons?

- Have you ever heard of a story where a father-in-law has sex with his daughter-in-law; knowing or unknowingly?
- What lessons do we learn from these people?

God is the Umbrella of Women in the Bible!

81. The Canaanite Woman and her Daughter:

Who Was This Woman?

- She was a Canaanite woman
- She had a daughter who was suffering from demon possession
- She cried out "Lord have mercy on me"
- Her daughter was suffering terribly from demon possession
- She kept on crying out loud
- Jesus said I was send only to the lost sheep of Israel
- She knelt before him and said, "Lord help me"
- He replied "It is not right to take the children's bread and toss it to their dogs"
- "Yes Lord" she replied "but even the dogs eat the crumbs, that fall from their masters table"
- Then Jesus answered, woman you have great faith. Your request is granted
- Her daughter was healed from that hour

Florence Mutambanengwe

The Story

This woman lived in the region of Tyre and Sidon. She had a daughter who was suffering terribly from demon possession. She must have been looking for treatment from various angles.

She heard about the Jesus of Nazareth and who know how long she had been waiting for him to come to that area. When he did she ceased the opportunity. She already knew in her heart the Jesus would heal her daughter.

So she came to Jesus and of course he was surrounded by his disciples and other people and she knew what to do. She cried out "Lord have mercy on me" Her daughter was suffering terribly from demon possession.

Jesus took his time and did not even answer her. Then the disciples told him to send her away as they thought she was making noise by keeping on shouting. May be Jesus wanted them to learn something from this woman's problems. He told them that he was not only sent to the lost sheep of Israel. Meaning he also came for this woman's sake.

She kept on crying out loud saying Lord help me. Then Jesus answered her and said, "I was not sent only to the lost sheep of Israel." This made her even more persistent and she came and knelt before him, and continued asking: Lord, help me. Still Jesus replied, "It is not right to take the children's bread and feed it to their dogs." She knew and said, "Yes, Lord, but even the dogs eat the crumbs that fall from their masters' table." Then He said, "Woman, you have great faith! Your request is granted. And her daughter was healed from that very day.

The Bible and the Canaanite Woman:

Leaving that place, Jesus withdrew to the region of Tyre and Sidon. A Canaanite woman from that vicinity came to him, crying out, "Lord Son of David have mercy on me! My daughter is suffering terribly from demon possession."

Jesus did not answer a word. So his disciples came to him and urged him "Send her away for she keeps crying out after us."

He answered, "I was not sent only to the lost sheep of Israel."

The woman came and knelt before him, "Lord, help me!" she said.

He replied, "It is not right to take the children's bread and feed it to their dogs."

"Yes, Lord," she said, "but even the dogs eat the crumbs that fall from their masters' table."

Then Jesus answered, "Woman, you have great faith! Your request is granted.

And her daughter was healed from that very day. (Matthew 15:21 – 28)

Lessons to Learn:

- She found what she was looking for
- She was taught something about the gospel of Jesus Christ
- Her daughter was healed of demon possession
- The power of a praying mother demonstrated
- Seek and you will find.

- She persevered in her request for the healing of her daughter
- She was not afraid to ask Jesus for what she wanted,
- Have you ever attended a huge conference and felt intimidated to ask for prayers?
- Do you think people are open to go forth when they are asked to come forward?
- Do you feel that believers are doing enough in the area of praying for the sick?
- What else can we do in this direction?

God is the Umbrella of Women in the Bible!

82. The Daughter of Jesse - Abigail:

Jesse was the father of Eliab his first born; the second son was Abinadab, the third Shimea, the fourth Nethanel, the fifth Raddai, the sixth Ozem and the seventh David. Their sisters were Zeruiah and Abigail. Zeruiah's three sons were Abishai, Joab and Asahel. Abigail was the mother of Amasa whose father was Jether the Ishmaelite.
(1 Chronicles 2:13 – 17)

God is the Umbrella of Women in the Bible!

83. The Daughter of Jesse - Zeruiah:

Jesse was the father of Eliab his first born; the second son was Abinadab, the third Shimea, the fourth Nethanel, the fifth Raddai, the sixth Ozem and the seventh David. Their sisters were Zeruiah and Abigail. Zeruiah's three sons were Abishai, Joab and Asahel. Abigail was the mother of Amasa whose father was Jether the Ishmaelite.
(1 Chronicles 2:13 – 17)

God is the Umbrella of Women in the Bible!

84. The Elect Lady:

Who Was This Woman?

- She was a chosen lady
- She had children
- John loved her for what she was doing
- She was loved by those who knew the truth
- John wrote to her
- Many remembered her for her work

The Story:

There are people who are gifted in mentoring others. They do things for others. They do not want to see people suffering when they can be helped by the word of God which is the truth. The truth will set them free.

John saw this in this lady and decided to tell her through this letter to her. He prayed that grace, mercy and peace from God the Father and from Jesus Christ, the Father's son, will be with her and others in truth and love.

He therefore decided to encourage her in what she was doing which was not knew but was present right from the beginning. He actually saw how she was handling the young people and others and wanted her to continue to walk in love as commanded by the Lord Jesus Christ.

She was a powerful woman, and John promised to visit her as there were still many more things to discuss which could not be put on the paper.

The Bible and the Elect Lady:

The Elder: To the chosen lady and her children, whom I love in the truth – and not I only, but also all who know the truth – because of the truth, which lives in us and will be with us forever.

Grace, mercy and peace from God the Father and from Jesus Christ, the Father's son, will be with us in truth and love.

It has given me great joy to find some of your children walking in the truth, just as the Father commanded us. And now, dear lady, I am not writing you a new command, but one, we have had from the beginning. I ask that we love one another. And this is love: that we walk in obedience to his commands. As you have heard from the beginning, his command is that you walk in love.

Many deceivers, who do not acknowledge Jesus Christ as coming in the flesh, have gone out into the world. Any such person is the deceiver and the anti-Christ. Watch out that you do not lose what you have worked for, but that you may be rewarded fully. Anyone who runs ahead and does not continue in the teaching of Christ does not have God; whoever continues in the teaching has both the Father and the Son. If anyone come to you and does not bring this teaching, do not take him into your house or welcome him. Anyone who welcomes him shares in his wicked work.

I have much to write to you, but I do not want to use paper and ink. Instead, I hope to visit you and talk with you face to face, so that our joy may be complete.

The children of your chosen sister send their greetings. (2 John)

Lessons to Learn:

- We are commanded to walk in love: However, read the following and think about it?
- If anyone comes to you and does not bring the teaching of Jesus Christ, do not take him into your house or welcome him. Anyone who welcomes him shares in his wicked work.
- This is a warning about people who speak against Christ.
- Nowadays people speak openly about their beliefs, but we as Christians who believe in Jesus Christ are warned not to associate with these people.

God is the Umbrella of Women in the Bible!

85. The Ruler's Daughter

Who Was This Woman?

- She was dead
- Her father believed that she would live if Jesus came and put his hand on her
- Jesus got up and went with her father
- The disciples also went with him
- Flute players and a noisy crowd was around
- Jesus said the girl was not dead but asleep
- The crowds laughed at Jesus
- Jesus went in and took the girl by the hand and said "Talitha khoum!"
- She got up
- News of her spread through the whole region
- (Matthew 9:18)

The Story:

When Jesus had again crossed over by boat to the other side of the lake, a large crowd gathered around him while he was by the lake. Then one of the synagogue rulers, named Jairus, came there. Seeing Jesus, he fell at his feet, and pleaded earnestly with him. "My little daughter is dying. Please come and put your hands on her so that she will be healed and live." So Jesus went with him.

The Bible and a Ruler's Daughter

When Jesus had again crossed over by boat to the other side of the lake, a large crowd gathered around him while he was by the lake. Then one of the synagogue rulers, named Jairus, came there. Seeing Jesus, he fell at his feet, and pleaded earnestly with him. "My little daughter is dying. Please come and put your hands on her so that she will be healed and live." So Jesus went with him.

A large crowd followed and pressed around him. And a woman was there who had been subject to bleeding for twelve years. She had suffered a great deal under the care of many doctors and had spent all she had, yet instead of getting better she grew worse. When she heard about Jesus, she came up behind him in the crowd and touched his cloak, because she thought, "If I just touch his clothes, I will be healed." Immediately her bleeding stopped and she felt in her body that she was freed from her suffering.

At once Jesus realized that power had gone out from him. He turned around in the crowd and asked, "Who touched my clothes?"

"You see the people crowding against you," his disciples answered, "and yet you can ask, 'Who touched me?' "

But Jesus kept looking around to see who had done it. Then the woman knowing what had happened to her came and fell at his feet and, trembling with fear, told him the whole truth. He said to her, "Daughter, your faith has healed you. Go in peace and be freed from your suffering."

While Jesus was still speaking, some men came from the house of Jairus, the synagogue ruler. "Your daughter is dead," they said "Why bother the teacher any more?"

Ignoring what they said, Jesus told the synagogue ruler, "Don't be afraid; just believe."

He did not let anyone follow him except Peter, James and John the brother of James. When they came to the home of the synagogue ruler Jesus saw a commotion, with the people crying and wailing loudly. He went in and said to them, "Why all this commotion and wailing? The child is not dead but asleep." But they laughed at him.

After he put them all out, he took the child's father and mother and the disciples who were with him, and went in where the child was. He took her by the hand and said to her, "Talitha koum!"(Which means, "Little girl, I say to you, get up!"). Immediately the girl stood up and walked around (she was twelve years old). At this they were completely astonished. He gave strict orders not to let anyone know about this, and told them to give her something to eat. (Mark 5:21 - 43)

Lessons to Learn:

- She was raised from the dead by Jesus
- Her father had the faith in Jesus
- His prayer was answered
- We have a right to pray for our children to have good, healthy, and long lives.
- Have you been in a situation where you prayed for your own child?

- Share your experiences if any or those of others that you have heard.

God is the Umbrella of Women in the Bible!

86. The Daughters of Zelophehad: Mahlah, Noah, Hoglah, Milcah and Tirzah:

Who Were These Women?

- Their father died in the wilderness during the forty years
- The land was then apportioned to the number of male names that were counted
- They were missed out as they were women
- They complained to Moses, Eleazar the priest and the leaders of the community for their inheritance
- They wanted to preserve their fathers name
- Moses consulted God on this issue
- They were given their portions of the land
- They had to marry within the clan of their father's tribe which they did

The Bible and the Daughters of Zelophehad:

Zelophehad son of Hepher had no sons; he had only daughters whose names were:

Mahlah, Noah, Hoglah, Milcah and Tirzah. (Numbers 26:33)

The Daughters of Zelophehad son of Hepher, the son of Gilead, the son of Makir, the son of Manasseh, belonged to the clans of Manasseh son of Joseph. The names of the daughters were Mahlah, Noah, Hoglah, Milcah and Tirzah. They approached the entrance to the Tent of Meeting and stood before Moses, Eleazar the priest, the leaders and the whole assembly, and said, "Our father died in the desert. He was not among Korah's followers, who banded together against the LORD, but he died for his own sin and left no sons. Why should our father's name disappear from his clan because he had no son? Give us property among our father's relatives."

So Moses brought their case before the LORD and the LORD said to him, "What Zelophehad's daughters are saying is right. You must certainly give them property as an inheritance among their father's relatives and turn their father's inheritance over to them.

Say to the Israelites, 'If a man dies and leaves no son, turn his inheritance over to his daughter. If he has no daughter, give his inheritance to his brothers. If he has no brothers, give his inheritance to his father's brothers. If his father had no brothers, give his inheritance to the nearest relative in his clan, that he may possess it. This is to be a legal requirement for the Israelites, as the LORD commanded Moses. (Numbers 27:1 – 11)

This is the thing which the LORD doth command concerning the daughters of Zelophehad, saying, Let them marry to whom they think best; only the family of the tribe of their father shall they marry. So shall not the inheritance of the children of Israel remove from tribe to tribe; for every7 one of the children of Israel shall keep himself to the inheritance of the tribe of his fathers. And every daughter, that possesseth an inheritance in any tribe of the children of Israel, shall be wife unto one of the family of the tribe of her father, that the children of Israel may enjoy every man the inheritance of his fathers. Neither shall the inheritance remove from one tribe to another tribe; but every one of the tribes of the children of Israel shall keep himself to his own inheritance. Even as the Lord commanded Moses, so did the daughters of Zelophehad: For Mahlah, Tirzah, and Hoglah, and Milcah, and Noah, the daughters of Zelophehad, were married unto their father's brothers' sons: And they were marred into the families of the sons of Manasseh the son of Joseph, and their inheritance remained in the tribe of the family of their father. (Numbers36:6 – 12)

Lessons to Learn:

- Daughters can be given their father's property to inherit
- They stood up for themselves and asked for the property
- God ruled in their favour
- They were asked to marry from the clan of their father's tribe
- Do you think Women should ask for what they feel is due to them?

- Can you relate to these women?
- Give some examples of situations that you have heard or come across.

God is the Umbrella of Women in the Bible!

87. The Widow of Zarephath:

Who Was This Woman?

- God knew her
- God send Elijah to her
- She had reached the end of her road
- She was waiting to die
- She had a handful of flour in a jar and a little oil in a jug,

The Story:

When I was growing up I was told stories of how Africans prayed for rain and God would give it to them. Hard to understand but if you read the story of Elijah you will see how God provides for his people.

God actually sent the Prophet Elijah to go to Zarephath where he was to find a widow who would supply him with food.

When Elijah got there he saw a widow gathering sticks. Have you ever met someone like her in your life? They may be messengers of God to your life. Elijah called to her and asked "Would you bring me a little water in a jar so I may have a drink?" "And bring me, please, a piece of bread."

Then she replied to him and told him that as surely as the Lord his God lived she did not have any bread – only a handful of flour in a jar and a little oil in a jug, She told him that she was gathering a few sticks to take home and make a meal for herself and her son, that they may eat and die.

Have you ever been in this type of situation? Though you may not be thinking of dying, you will be thinking of what will happen next.

When I was at home in Zimbabwe, I had reached a stage where I was very comfortable. There was no growth for me in my house, in my work and of course at church. I was contended and was actually thinking that this was it until I die. But God has other plans for us. In my house I had all the furniture, utensils and clothes I wanted. Of course I could change things here and there. All my daughters were married and had children. I thought to myself, "What a blessing." I had just retired at my work, though it was early retirement, still I thought with my pension I would manage and I was contended.

At my church I was an Elder. I remember Bishop Sande telling me "Florence you are going to be an Elder. I do not want to be an Elder; I am quite fine as a Deacon in the church. No! He said, "God wants you to be an Elder." It was hopeless for me to refuse. Then I was ordained as an Elder. What else I thought now that's all God wants me to be and to do. It was fine with me. But God had his own plans and now here I am writing books for God. Some of the things God does look foolish in normal people's eyes. I am still on a journey, just like the Widow of Zarephath. This is the fourth book I have written so far and am still on my way for God.

Elijah told her to go home and do as she had said. He told her to make a small cake for him and bring it to him then to go and make for herself and her son. He told her that God had said the jar of flour will not be used up and the jug of oil will not run dry until the day He gave them rain on the land. Wow what a provision that was for her son, and Elijah.

Later her son died and she asked Elijah whether he had come to remind her of her sin and kill her son. However Elijah took the boy to the upper room and placed him on his bed. He cried to the Lord and the boy's life returned to him.

The Bible and the Widow at Zarephath:

Now Elijah the Tishbite, from Tishbe in Gilead, said to Ahab, "As the |LORD, the God of Israel, lives, whom I serve, there will be neither dew nor rain in the next few years except at my word."

Then the word of the LORD came to Elijah: "Leave here, turn eastward and hide in the Kerith Ravine, east of the Jordan. You will drink from the brook, and I have ordered the ravens to feed you there."

So he did what the LORD had told him. He went to Kerith Ravine, east of the Jordan, and stayed there. The ravens brought him bread and meat in the morning and bread and meat in the evening, and he drank from the brook.

Some time later the brook dried up because there had been no rain in the land. Then the word of the LORD came to him: "Go at once to Zarephath of Sidon and stay there. I have commanded a widow in that place to supply you with food." So he went to Zarephath. When he came to the town gate, a widow was there gathering sticks. He called her and asked her, "Would you bring me a little water in a jar so I may have a drink?" As she was going to get it, he called "And bring me, please, a piece of bread."

As surely as the LORD your God lives," she replied, "I don't have any bread — only a handful of flour in a jar and a little oil in a jug. I am gathering a few sticks to take home and made a meal for myself and my son that we may eat — and die."

Elijah said to her, "Don't be afraid. Go home and do as you have said. But first make a small cake of bread for me from what you have and bring it to me, and then make something for yourself and your son. For this is what the LORD, the God of Israel, says: "The jar of flour will not be used up and the jug of oil will not run dry until the day the LORD gives rain on the land."

She went away and did as Elijah had told her. So there was food everyday for Elijah and for the woman and her family. For the jar of flour was not used up and the jug of oil did not run dry, in keeping with the word of the LORD spoken by Elijah..

Some time later the son of the woman who owned the house became ill. He grew worse and worse and finally stopped breathing. She said to Elijah, "What do you have against me, man of God? Did you come to remind me of my sin and kill my son?"

"Give me your son," Elijah replied. He took him from her arms, carried him to the upper room where he was staying, and laid him on his bed. Then he cried out to the Lord, "O LORD my God, have you brought tragedy also upon this widow, I am staying with, by causing her son to die?" Then he stretched himself out on the boy three times and cried to the LORD, "O LORD my God, let this boy's life return to him!"

The LORD heard Elijah's cry, and the boy's life returned to him, and he lived. Elijah picked up the child and carried him down from the room into the house. He gave him to his mother and said, "Look, your son is alive!"

Then the woman said to Elijah, "Now I know that you are a man of God and that the word of the LORD from your mouth is the truth." (1 Kings 17:1 - 24)

Lessons to Learn:

- She went on a journey of faith
- The flour and oil never finished until God brought rain on the land
- Elijah was fed for as long as the LORD wanted him to be there
- Her son died and was raised from the dead
- She believed that Elijah was a man of God
- Have you had an experience where your oil never ran out, share it!
- Have you ever asked any man of God to pray for your child?

God is the Umbrella of Women in the Bible!

88. The Widow and Oil:

Who Was This Woman?

- She was a widow
- Her husband was a prophet
- She was in debt
- She wanted to pay the debt and be free
- She was a woman of great faith
- She was obedient
- She loved her family

The Story:

This woman's story is peculiar to many women in the body of Christ today married to the men of God. This applies to them whether the men are alive or dead.. They have financial problems.

Her husband, a servant of Elisha, a man who revered the LORD had died. Then his

Creditors came to her and were after their monies. They wanted to take her sons to go and work for them as slaves to pay for their father's debt.

She considered herself to have nothing at all. This is something that we must get away from. It is important to know that we have something in our possession that may be lying there and it is a stepping stone to solving our problems. If you were to be asked today, what is it that you would say straight away that you have; that can take you out of your situation. Think. You might have a friend, a brother or a sister, a colleague from your church, your work or your neighbourhood. Use what you have.

In this case she had The Prophet Elisha; she went to him and put her case to him. She said to him, "Your servant my husband is dead, and you know that he revered the Lord. But now his creditor is coming to take my two boys as his slaves."

Elisha then asked her what she though he should do. He knew there was something she could do and he asked her what she had in her house; something that she could use to get out of this situation.

She told him that she had nothing there at all, except a little oil." That is it

Elisha said to her, then go around and ask all your neighbours for empty jars. Don't ask for just a few. Then go inside and shut the door behind you and your sons. Pour oil into all the jars, and as each is filled, put it to one side."

She left him and afterward shut the door behind her and her sons. They brought the jars to her and she kept pouring. When all the jars were full, she said to her son, bring me another one but her son said there was not a jar left. Then the oil stopped flowing.

She went and told Elisha what had happened and he told her to go and sell the oil and pay the debts and then she could live on what was left with her sons.

The Bible and the Widow's Oil:

The wife of a man from the company of the prophets cried out to Elisha, "Your servant my husband is dead, and you know that he revered the Lord. But now his creditor is coming to take my two boys as his slaves."

Elisha replied to her, "How can I help you? Tell me what do you have in your house?"

"Your servant has nothing there at all," she said, "except a little oil."

Elisha said "Go around and ask all your neighbours for empty jars. Don't ask for just a few. Then go inside and shut the door behind you and your sons. Pour oil into all the jars, and as each is filled, put it to one side."

She left him and afterward shut the door behind her and her sons. They brought the jars to her and she kept pouring. When all the jars were full, she said to her son, bring me another one."

But he replied. "There is not a jar left" Then the oil stopped flowing

She went and told the man of God, and he said, "Go sell the oil and pay your debts. You and your sons can live on what is left." (2Kings 4:1 -7)

Lessons to Learn:

- The word of God says "You will lend to many nations but will borrow from non
- God will always take care of his own prophets
- Fellowship with the men of God always
- She believed in God

- She trusted God that is why she carried out the instructions
- She had faith in God
- She used what she had a little oil
- Creditors were paid in full and her sons were free from slavery
- Listen to the man of God
- Identify what your problems are
- Something that you have might be the key to the solution of your problems
- Identify your pot of oil and give it to God and see what will happen to it.

God is the Umbrella of Women in the Bible!

89. The Wives of Ashur the father of Tekoa:

Ashur the father of Tekoa had two wives, Helah and Naarah.

Naarah:

Naarah bore him Ahuzzam, Hepher, Temeni, and Haahashtari. These were the descendants of Naarah.

God is the Umbrella of Women in the Bible!

Helah:

The sons of Helah: Zereth, Zohar, Ethan, and Koz, who was the father of Anub and Hazzobebah and of the clans of Aharhel son of Harum. (1 Chronicles 4 5 – 8)

God is the Umbrella of Women in the Bible!

90. The Wife of Haman – Zeresh:

Haman went out that day happy and in high spirits; But when he saw Mordecai at the king's gate and observed that he neither rose nor showed fear in his presence, he was filled with rage against Mordecai. Nevertheless, Haman restrained himself and went home.

Calling together his friends and Zeresh, his wife, Haman boasted to them about his vast wealth, his many sons, and all the ways the king had honoured him and how he had elevated him above the other nobles and officials. "And that's not all," Haman added. "I'm the only person Queen Esther invited to accompany the king to the banquet she gave. And she has invited me along with the king tomorrow. But all this gives me no satisfaction as long as I see that Jew Mordecai sitting at the king's gate."

His wife Zeresh and all his friends said to him, "Have a gallows built, seventy-five feet high, and ask the king in the morning to have Mordecai hanged on it. Then go with the king to the dinner and be happy." This suggestion delighted Haman, and he had the gallows built. (Esther 5:9 – 14)

Afterward Mordecai returned to the king's gate. But Haman rushed home, with his head covered in grief, and told Zeresh his wife and all his friends everything that had happened to him.

His advisers and his wife Zeresh said to him, "Since Mordecai, before whom your downfall has started, is of Jewish origin, you cannot stand against him – you will surely come to ruin!" While they were still talking with him, the king's eunuchs arrived and hurried Haman away to the banquet Esther had prepared.
(Esther 6:12 – 14)

God is the Umbrella of Women in the Bible!

91. The Witch of Endor:

Who Was This Woman?

- She was a Witch who lived in Endor
- Saul asked whether there was a woman who was a medium
- She was well known as they said there was one in Endor
- Saul disguised himself and took two men to go to consult this woman
- Saul asked her to consult the spit for him
- She knew that Saul had cut off mediums and spiritists from the land
- Saul swore to her by the LORD, and said that she would not be punished for this.
- She asked who to bring and she brought up Samuel
- She cried when she saw Samuel
- She knew that Saul and had deceived her
- She offered Saul food which he refused but ate later after being persuaded by his men

The Bible and the Witch of Endor:

In those days the Philistines gathered their forces to fight against Israel. Achish said to David, "You must understand that you and your men will accompany me in the army. David said, "Then you will see for yourself what your servant can do. Achish replied, "Very well, I will make you my bodyguard for life.

Now Samuel was dead, and all Israel had mourned for him and buried him in his own town of Ramah, Saul had expelled the mediums and spiritists from the land.

The Philistines assembled and came and set up camp at Shunem, while Saul gathered all the Israelites and set up camp at Gilboa. When Saul saw the Philistine army, he was afraid, terror filled his heart. He inquired of the LORD, but the LORD did not answer him by dreams or Urim or prophets. Saul then said to his attendants, "Find me a woman who is a medium, so I may go and inquire of her." "There is one in Endor" they said.

So Saul disguised himself, putting on other clothes and at night he and two men went to the woman. "Consult a spirit for me," he said, "and bring up for me the one I name."

But the woman said to him, "Surely you know what Saul has done. He has cut off the mediums and spiritists from the land. Why have you set a trap for my life to bring about my death?"

Saul swore to her by the LORD, "As surely ad the LORD lives, you will not be punished for this." Then the woman asked, "Whom shall I bring up for you?"

"Bring up Samuel," he said. When the woman saw Saul, She cried out at the top of her voice and said to Saul; "Why have you deceived me? You are Saul!" The king said to her, "Don't be afraid. What do you see?" The woman said, "I see a spirit coming up out of the ground." "What does he look like?" he said, "An old man wearing a robe is coming up," she said. Then Saul knew it was Samuel, and he bowed down and prostrated himself with his face to the ground. Samuel said to Saul, "Why have you disturbed me by bringing me up?"

"I am in great distress," Saul said, "The Philistines are fighting against me, and God has turned away from me. He no longer answers me, either by prophets or but dreams. So I have called on you to tell me what to do.

Samuel said, "Why do you consult me, now that the LORD has turned away from you and become your enemy? The LORD has done what he predicted through me. The LORD has torn the kingdom out of your hands and given it to one of your neighbours - to David. Because you did not obey the LORD or carry out the fierce wrath against the Amalekites, the LORD has done this to you today. The LORD will hand over both Israel and you to the Philistines, and tomorrow you and your sons will be with me. The LORD will also hand over the army of Israel to the Philistines.

Immediately Saul fell full length on the ground filled with fear because of Samuel's words. His strength was gone, for he had eaten nothing all that day and night.

When the woman came to Saul and saw that he was greatly shaken, she said, "Look, your maidservant has obeyed you. I took my life in my hands and did what you told me to do. Now please listen to your servant and let me give you some food so you may eat and have the strength to go on your way. He refused and said, "I will not eat."

But his men joined the woman in urging him, and he listened to them. He got up from the ground and sat on the couch. The woman had a fattened calf at the house which she butchered at once. She took some flour kneaded it and baked bread without yeast. That same night they got up and left. (1 Chronicles 28:1 – 25)

92. The Wives for the Benjaminites (Judges 21:1 - 25)

God is the Umbrella of Women in the Bible!

The Wives of Caleb: - Azubah and Ephrath:

Caleb son of Hezron had children by his wife Azubah (and by Jerioth). These were her sons; Jesher, Shobab and Ardon. When Azubah died Caleb married Ephrath, who bore him Hur. Hur was the father of Uri, and Uri the father of Bezalel.
(1 Chronicles 2:18 – 20)

God is the Umbrella of Women in the Bible!

93. The Concubine of Caleb –Ephah:

She was the mother of Haran, Moza and Gazez. Haran was the father of Gazez.
(1 Chronicles 2:46)

God is the Umbrella of Women in the Bible!

The Concubine of Caleb – Maacah:

She was the mother of Sheber and Tirhanah. She also gave birth to Shaaph the father of Madmannah and to Sheva the father of Macbenah and Gibea. Caleb's daughter was Acsah.
(1 Chronicles 2:48 – 49)

God is the Umbrella of Women in the Bible!

94. The Daughter of Caleb – Acsah:

Caleb's daughter was Acsah. (1 Chronicles 2:49)

God is the Umbrella of Women in the Bible!

95. The Woman from Tekoa:

Joab son of Zeruiah knew that the king's heart longed for Absalom. So Joab sent someone to Tekoa and had a wise woman brought from there. He said to her, "Pretend you are in mourning. Dress in mourning clothes, and do not use any cosmetic lotions. Act like a woman who has spent many days grieving for the dead. Then go to the king and speak these words to him," And Joab put the words in her mouth.

When the woman from Tekoa went to the king she fell with her face to the ground to pay him honour, and said, "Help me O king!" The king asked her, "What is troubling you?"

She said, "I am indeed a widow; my husband is dead; I your servant had two sons. They got into a fight with each other in the field, and no one was there to separate them. One struck the other and killed him. Now the whole clan has risen up against your servant; they say, 'Hand over the one who struck his brother down, so that we may put him to death for the life of his brother whom he killed; then we will get rid of the heir as well;' They would put out the only burning coal I have left, leaving my husband neither name nor descendant on the face of the earth."

The king said to the woman, "Go home, and I will issue an order in your behalf." But the woman from Tekoa said to him, "My lord the king, let the blame rest on me and on my father's family, and let the king and his throne be without guilt." The king replied, "If anyone says anything to you, bring him to me, and he will not bother you again." She said, "Then let the king invoke the LORD his God to prevent the avenger of blood from adding to the destruction, so that my son will not be destroyed." "As surely as the LORD lives," he said, "not one hair of your son's head will fall to the ground."

Then the woman said, "Let your servant speak a word to my lot the king."

"Speak," he replied. The woman said, "Why then have you devised a thing like this against the people of God? When the king says this, does he not convict himself, for the king has not brought back his banished son? Like water spilled on the ground, which cannot be recovered, so we must die. But God does not take away life; instead, he devices ways so that a banished person may not remain estranged from him.

And now I have come to say this to my lord the king because the people have made me afraid. Your servant thought, 'I will speak to the king perhaps he will do what his servant asks. Perhaps the king will agree to deliver his servant from the hand of the man who is trying to cut off both me and my son from the inheritance God gave us.'

And now your servant says, 'May the word of my lord the king bring me rest, for my lord the king is like an angel of God in discerning good and evil. May the LORD your God be with you.'"

Then the king said to the woman, "Do not keep from me the answer to what I am going to ask you." "Let my lord speak" the woman said.

The king asked, "Isn't the hand of Joab with you in all this?

The woman answered, "As surely as you live, my lord the king, no one can turn to the right or to the left from anything my lord the king says. Yes it was your servant Joab who instructed me to do this and who put all these words into the mouth of your servant. Your servant Joab did this to change the present situation. My lord has wisdom like that of an angel of God – he knows everything that happens in the land."

The king said to Joab, "Very well, I will do it. Go bring back the young man Absalom." (2 Samuel 14:1 – 21)

God is the Umbrella of Women in the Bible!

96. The Woman With The Issue of Bleeding:

Who Was This Woman?

- She had suffered with the issue of blood for twelve years
- She had spent a lot of money trying to get treatments from all over
- She was unclean for those twelve years
- She was despised for her condition
- She was a frustrated woman
- She heard of the many miracles that Jesus was doing
- She was waiting for her chance to see Jesus and be healed
- She had made up her mind that if only she could touch the hem of his garment she would be healed
- She was a determined woman
- When she heard that Jesus was in the area she grabbed the chance

- She said to herself: If only I touch his cloak, I will be healed.
- She forced her way through the crowd to get closer to Jesus
- She came up behind Jesus and touched the edge of his garment
- Jesus turned around and saw her
- He said, "Take heart daughter your faith had healed you
- She was healed at that moment

The Story:

This woman had suffered with the issue of blood for twelve years. In those days women were considered unclean when they were having their monthly periods. Therefore imagine being unclean for twelve years.

She tried all sorts of treatments that were available and they all failed. Year after year she was frustrated with this problem. I personally suffered with migraine headaches for twenty-one years and suffered greatly. Looking back I do not even know how I coped. I tried all sorts of medicines. I remember my husband even brought some type of grass which grows near the river banks. It grows very tall and is fluffy at the top. Somebody told him that if I burn the fluffy bits and cover myself in the smoke of this grass I would be healed. I tried and I nearly died from suffocation. My husband then gave up on me and the headache continued. Twenty-one years on, and the LORD healed me.

This woman must have gone through a lot of pain and suffering. People thought she was unclean and therefore would not like to be associated with her. I am sure she could not find anyone to marry her, who could take a wife who is forever bleeding. She never lost hope. Then her time came she heard the following stories:

A man with leprosy had fallen in front of Jesus with his face to the ground and begged him to make him clean, and he was made clean.

Some men had brought a paralyzed man on a mat, and because they could not take him in through the door to Jesus; they went up the roof, took some tiles off and lowered him down to Jesus and his sins were forgiven.

A man with a shriveled hand had been healed by Jesus in front of many people on a Sabbath day.

A Centurion's servant was healed without even Jesus going into the house to see him, because of his master's faith.

A Widow's son who was dead and in the coffin was raised just by Jesus touching the coffin.

Now Jesus was on his way to heal Jairus's only daughter who was twelve years old and was dying.

She must have said to herself, this is my turn; she pressed through the crowd and touched the hem of his garment. You know what, she was healed immediately.

The Bible and the Woman with the Issue of Blood:

When Jesus had again crossed over by boat to the other side of the lake, a large crowd gathered around him while he was by the lake. Then one of the synagogue rulers, named Jairus, came there. Seeing Jesus, he fell at his feet, and pleaded earnestly with him. "My little daughter is dying. Please come and put your hands on her so that she will be healed and live." So Jesus went with him.

A large crowd followed and pressed around him. And a woman was there who had been subject to bleeding for twelve years. She had suffered a great deal under the care of many doctors and had spent all she had, yet instead of getting better she grew worse. When she heard about Jesus, she came up behind him in the crowd and touched his cloak, because she thought, "If I just touch his clothes, |I will be healed." Immediately her bleeding stopped and she felt in her body that she was freed from her suffering.

At once Jesus realized that power had gone out from him. He turned around in the crowd and asked, "Who touched my clothes?"

"You see the people crowding against you," his disciples answered, "and yet you can ask, 'Who touched me?' "

But Jesus kept looking around to see who had done it. Then the woman knowing what had happened to her came and fell at his feet and, trembling with fear, told him the whole truth. He said to her, "Daughter, your faith has healed you. Go in peace and be freed from your suffering."

While Jesus was still speaking, some men came from the house of Jairus, the synagogue ruler. "Your daughter is dead," they said "Why bother the teacher any more?"

Ignoring what they said, Jesus told the synagogue ruler, "Don't be afraid; just believe."

He did not let anyone follow him except Peter, James and John the brother of James. When they came to the home of the synagogue ruler Jesus saw a commotion, with the people crying and wailing loudly. He went in and said to them, "Why all this commotion and wailing? The child is not dead but asleep." But they laughed at him.

After he put them all out, he took the child's father and mother and the disciples who were with him, and went in where the child was. He took her by the hand and said to her, "Talitha koum!"(Which means, "Little girl, I say to you, get up!"). Immediately the girl stood up and walked around (she was twelve years old). At this they were completely astonished. He gave strict orders not to let anyone know about this, and told them to give her something to eat. (Mark 5:21 - 43)

A man with leprosy had fallen in front of Jesus with his face to the ground and begged him to make him clean, and he was made clean. (Luke 5:13)

Some men had brought a paralyzed man on a mat, and because they could not take him in through the door to Jesus; they went up the roof, took some tiles off and lowered him down to Jesus and his sins were forgiven. (Luke 7:9)

A man with a shriveled hand had been healed by Jesus in front of many people on a Sabbath day. (Luke 6:10)

A Centurion's servant was healed without even Jesus going into the house to see him, because of his master's faith.

A Widow's son who was dead and in the coffin was raised just by Jesus touching the coffin. (Luke 7:16)

Lessons to Learn:

- She had a good life after this
- Jesus Heals, he is the same yesterday, today and forever
- Just believe and you will be healed

God is the Umbrella of Women in the Bible!

97. Zebidah – The Mother of Jehoiakim:

Jehoiakim was twenty-five years old when he became king and he reigned in Jerusalem eleven years. His mother's name was Zebidah daughter of Pedaiah; she was from Rumah. (2 Kings 23:36)

God is the Umbrella of Women in the Bible!

98. Zeruah – Jeroboam's Mother:

Also Jeroboam son of Nebat rebelled against the king. He was one of Solomon's officials, an Ephramite from Zeredah, and his mother was a widow named Zeruah.
(1 Kings 11:26)

God is the Umbrella of Women in the Bible!

99. Zillah – Lamech's wife

Who Was This Woman?

- She was Lamech's wife
- She was the mother of Tubal-Cain who forged all kinds of tools out of bronze and iron
- She was also the mother of a daughter Naamah
- Her husband told her that he had killed a man for wounding him, a young man for injuring him
- If Cain is avenged seven times, then Lamech seventy-seven times."

The Story

Cain lay with his wife, and she gave birth to Enoch. Cain was building a city, and he named it Enoch. To Enoch was born Irad and Irad was the father of Mehujael, and Mehujael was the father of Methushael, and Methushael was the father of Lamech. Lamech married Adah and Zillah. At 182 years he had a son. He named him Noah saying, "He will comfort us in the labour and painful toil of our hands caused by the ground the LORD has cursed." After Noah, Lamech lived 595 years, and had sons and daughters. Lamech lived 777 years.

The Bible and Zillah:

Lamech married two women, one named Adah and the other Zillah. Adah gave birth to Jabal; he was the father of those who live in the tents and raise livestock. His brother's name was Jubal; he was the father of all who play the harp and flute. Zillah also had a son, Tubal-Cain, who forged all kinds of tools out of bronze and iron. Tubal-Cain's sister was Naamah.

Lamech said to his wives,

"Adah and Zillah listen to me, wives of Lamech, hear my words. I have killed a man for wounding me, a young man for injuring me. If Cain is avenged seven times, then Lamech seventy-seven times." (Genesis 4::19 – 24)

Lessons to Learn:

- Zillah's son Tubal-Cain, forged (shaped metal by heating and hammering) all kinds of tools out of bronze and iron.
- This makes me wonder whether my Grandfather did not get his skills from Tubal Cain as he forged all kinds of tools from iron.
- She was also the mother of Naamah
- She was one of the two wives of Lamech

God is the Umbrella of Women in the Bible!

100. Zilpah – Leah's Maid

Who Was This Woman?

- Laban, Leah's father gave Zilpah to Leah as a maidservant when she became Jacob's wife
- Leah gave Zilpah to her husband to her husband after she had four sons and had stopped having children
- Gad – Was her first son whom she birthed for Leah
- Asher – Was her second son whom she birthed for Leah

The Story:

She started off as a servant for Leah's father Laban. Then she was given to Leah as a servant. Then she was given to Jacob by Leah to produce more children for her. Zilpah ended up have two sons for Leah and Jacob whose names were Gad and Asher.

Florence Mutambanengwe

The Bible and Zilpah:

When Rachel saw that she was not bearing Jacob any children, she became jealous of her sister. So she said to Jacob, "Give me children, or I'll die!"

Jacob became angry with her and said, "Am I in the place of God, who has kept you from having children?" Then she said, here is Bilhah, my maidservant. Sleep with her so that she can bear children for me and that through her I too can build a family."

So she gave him her servant Bilhah as a wife, Jacob slept with her, and she became pregnant and bore him a son. Then Rachel said, "God has vindicated me; he has listened to my plea and given me a son." Because of this she named him Dan.

Rachel's servant Bilhah conceived again and bore Jacob a second son. Then Rachel said, "I have had a great struggle with my sister and I have won." So she named him Naphtali.

When Leah saw that she had stopped having children, she took her maidservant Zilpah and gave her to Jacob as a wife. Leah's servant Zilpah bore Jacob a son. Then Leah said, "What good fortune!" So she named him Gad.

Leah's servant Zilpah bore Jacob a second son. Then Leah said, "How happy I am!" The women will call me happy." So she named him Asher.

During wheat harvest, Reuben went out into the fields and found some mandrake plants, which he brought to his mother Leah. Rachel said to Leah, "Please give me some of your son's mandrakes."

But she said to her, "Wasn't it enough that you took away my husband? Will you take my son's mandrakes too?"

"Very well," Rachel said, "he can sleep with you tonight in return for your son's mandrakes." So when Jacob came in from the fields that evening, Leah went out to meet him. "You must sleep with me," she said, "I have hired you with my son's mandrakes." So he slept with her that night.

God listened to Leah, and she became pregnant and bore Jacob a fifth son. Then Leah said, "God has rewarded me for giving my maidservant to my husband." So she named him Issacher.

Some time later she gave birth to a daughter and named her Dinah.

Then God remembered Rachel; he listened to her and opened her womb. She became pregnant and gave birth to a son and said, "God has taken away my disgrace." She named him Joseph, and said "May the Lord add to me another son." (Genesis 30:1 – 24)

Lessons to Learn:

- She had two sons with Jacob for Leah
- Her sons were Gad and Asher
- Is it still important for women to have children to the extent of asking someone to bear them for you?
- Are there any such cased today?

God is the Umbrella of Women in the Bible!

101. Zipporah – Moses wife

Who Was This Woman?

- She was the daughter of Jethro
- She was Moses' wife
- Her father was a priest of Midian who had seven daughters
- They came to draw water and fill the troughs to water their father's flock.
- Some shepherds came along and drove them away, but Moses got up and came to their rescue and watered their flock.
- Jethro was surprised when the girls returned to Reuel their father
- He asked them, Why they had returned so early that day
- They told him that an Egyptian rescued them from the shepherds and he even drew water for us and watered the flock.
- And where is he?" he asked his daughters. "Why did you leave him? Invite him to have something to eat."

- Moses agreed to stay with the man, who gave his daughter Zipporah to him in marriage
- Zipporah gave birth to a son, and Moses named him Gershom, saying, "I have become an alien in a foreign land."
- She saved Moses from death by circumcising her son.

The Story:

What impresses me about Women in the Bible is the fact that there is always a long story behind any woman's name in the bible. This whole story is in order to bring us to Zipporah and how Moses found her.

The Egyptian had to beat the Hebrew man for Moses to intervene and kill him.

Then if it had been left at that Moses could not have left. However, this time her name is also mentioned in the bible. When his own people were fighting, he intervened again and they then told him that they had seen what he had done the previous day.

Those made him run away from Egypt to Midian where he met the seven daughters of Reuel at the well. What God has planned for you no one can take away from you.

All the other shepherds were not interested in Zipporah. She was just waiting for Moses to come from Egypt.

It is interesting how Moses intervenes again and helps the girls to draw water and water their flocks.

The girls must have thanked him and went away but the mission was not complete as their father was surprised to see them so early.

On hearing the whole story he sent them back to collect this kind man whom he later gave his daughter Zipporah to marry.

Moses had to do something in Egypt in order to run away from Egypt and to go to Median.

The Bible and Zipporah – Moses' wife:

One day, after Moses had grown up, he went out to where his own people were and watched them at their hard labour. He saw an Egyptian beating a Hebrew, one of his own people. Glancing, this way and that and seeing no one, he killed the Egyptian and hid him in the sand. The next day he went out and saw two Hebrews fighting. He asked the one in the wrong, "Why are you hitting your fellow Hebrew?

The man said, "Who made you ruler and judge over us? Are you thinking of killing me as you killed the Egyptian? Then Moses was afraid and thought, "What I did must have become known." When Pharaoh heard of this he tried to kill Moses, but Moses fled from Pharaoh and went to live in Midian, where he sat down by a well.

Now a priest of Midian had seven daughters, and they came to draw water and fill the troughs to water their father's flock. Some shepherds came along and drove them away, but Moses got up and came to their rescue and watered their flock.

When the girls returned to Reuel their father, he asked them, "Why have you returned so early today?" They answered, "An Egyptian rescued us from the shepherds. He even drew water for us and watered the flock.

"And where is he?" he asked his daughters. "Why did you leave him? Invite him to have something to eat."

Moses agreed to stay with the man, who gave his daughter Zipporah to Moses in marriage. Zipporah gave birth to a son, and Moses named him Gershom, saying, "I have become an alien in a foreign land."

During that long period, the king of Egypt died. The Israelites groaned in their slavery and cried out, and their cry for help because of their slavery went up to God. God heard their groaning and he remembered his covenant with Abraham, with Isaac and with Jacob. So God looked on the Israelites and was concerned about them.
(Exodus 2:11 – 25)

At a lodging place on the way, the LORD met Moses and was about to kill him. But Zipporah took a flint knife, cut off her son's foreskin and touched Moses' feet with it. "Surely you are a bridegroom of blood to me." So the LORD let him alone. (At that time she said "bridegroom of blood," referring to circumcision.) (Exodus 4:24 – 26)

After Moses had sent away his wife Zipporah, his father-in-law Jethro received her and her two sons. One son was named Gershom, for Moses said, "I have become an alien in a foreign land"; and the other was named Eliezer, for he said, "My father's God was my helper; he saved me from the sword of Pharaoh."

Jethro, Moses' father-in-law, together with Moses sons and wife, came to him in the desert, where he was camped near the mountain of God. Jethro had sent word to him, "I, your father-in-law Jethro, am coming to you with your wife and her two sons."

So Moses went to meet his father-in-law and bowed down and kissed him. They greeted each other and then went into the tent. Moses told his father-in-law about everything the LORD had done to Pharaoh and the Egyptians for Israel's sake and about all the hardships they had met along the way and how the LORD had saved them.

Jethro was delighted to hear about all the good things the LORD had done for Israel in rescuing them from the hand of the Egyptians. He said, "Praise be to the LORD who rescued you from the hand of the Egyptians and of Pharaoh, and who rescued the people from the hand of the Egyptians. Now I know that the LORD is greater than all other gods, for he did this to those who had treated Israel arrogantly." Then Jethro, Moses' father-in-law, brought a burnt offering and other sacrifices to God, and Aaron came with all the elders of Israel to eat bread with Moses' father-in-law in the presence of God. (Exodus 18:2 – 12)

Lessons to Learn:

- She was the mother of Gershom and Eliezer
- She saved Moses by circumcising her son
- She is one of the great women in the bible

God is the Umbrella of Women in the Bible!

Appendix 1

A LIST OF THE WOMEN AND BIBLE VERSES:

1. A Crippled Woman Healed on the Sabbath (Luke 13:10 – 17)
2. A Levite Concubine (Judges 20 & 21)
3. A Wise Woman – In Abel Beth Maacah
4. Abigail – Nabal's Wife (2 Samuel 2:2) (1 Samuel 27:3)
5. Abihail – The Wife of Abishur – (1 Chronicles 2:29)
6. Abijah – The wife of Hezron (1 Chronicles 2:21 – 24)
7. Abishag- 1 Kings 1:15 – 27 (and Bathsheba)
8. Adah – Lamech's Wife (Genesis 4:19 – 26)
9. Adah – The Wife of Esau (Genesis 27:34) (Genesis 27:46)
10. Aiah – The Mother of Rizpah (2 Samuel 21:1 - 14) (2 Samuel 3:7)
11. Anna – The Prophetess (Luke 2:36 – 38)
12. Asenath – Joseph's Wife (Genesis 41:41 – 45) (Genesis 41:50 – 52) (Genesis 46:19 – 27)
13. Atarah the Wife of Jerahmeel the son of Hezron:
14. Athaliah – 2 Chronicles 22 and(2 Kings 11:1-21) (2 Kings :25 – 27)

15. Basemath - Esau's second wife (Genesis 26:34, 46)
16. Bathsheba – the Mother of King Solomon (2 Samuel 11)(2 Samuel 12:1)
17. Bilhah – the Mother of Dan and Naphtali
18. Candace – the Queen of the Ethiopians (Acts 8:26 -32)
19. Deborah – The Prophetess- The Judge – Judges 4 and 5
20. Dinah – Leah's Daughter – (Genesis 46:13)
21. Elizabeth – The Mother of John The Baptist – (Luke 1:5 – 25, 36) 1:39) (4:15)
22. Eve – the Mother of Cain and Abel – (Genesis 1:21 – 25)
23. Hagar – the Mother of Ishmael – (Genesis 16:1 – 15) (Genesis21:8 – 20) (Genesis 25:12 -18) (1 Chronicles1:29 - 30)
24. Hamutal – the Daughter of Jeremiah2 Kings 23:31 – 36)
25. Hannah – the Mother of Samuel (1 Samuel 1)
26. Hazzelelponi – The Daughter of Etam
27. Herodias – The Wife of Philip the Brother of Herod (Matthew 14:1 – 12)
28. Huldah – The Prophetess
29. Jael – the Killer of Sisera – Judges 5:24 – 27
30. Jochebed - the Wife of Amram (Exodus 2:1 – 10) (Exodus 6:20) (Numbers 26:58 – 61)
31. Jehosheba - the Wife of Jehoiada the Priest(2 Chronicles 22;110
32. Jezebel –the Wife of Ahab (1 Kings 21) (1 Kings 16:29 – 34) (2 Kings 9:22, 3 -37) (2 Kings 10:12-13)
33. Ketura – Abraham's Wife After Sarah's Death (Genesis 25:1 – 11)
34. Leah – the Wife of Jacob (Genesis 31 and 32)

35. Loice and Eunice – Timothy's Grandmother and Mother – (2 Timothy 1:3 - 7)
36. Lot's Wife (Genesis 12:1 – 2) (Genesis 14:16)(Genesis 19:24 – 37) (Numbers 21:15)
37. Lydia – the First Convert of the Apostle Paul (Acts 16:11 – 15)
38. Mahalath – the Daughter of Ishmael (Genesis 25:23; 26:9; 26:34; 27:46)
39. Martha – the Sister of Lazarus (Luke 10:38 – 42)
40. Mary – the Sister of Lazarus (John 11:17) (John 12:1 – 11)
41. Mary – the Mother of Jesus (Luke 2:21 – 30, 52) (John 2:15) Like 1:26) (Luke 2:13 – 15) (Luke 2:11 – 12) (Matthew 1:18 – 24)
42. Mary Magdalene – the First Person to See Jesus after Resurrection (John 20:1 – 18)
43. Matred – the Mother of Mehetabel
44. Mehetabel – the Wife of Hadad
45. Merab – the Daughter of Saul (2 Samuel 21)
46. Michal – the Wife of David (1 Samuel 18:17 – 29) (1 Samuel 19:11-17) (1 Samuel 30:4) (2 Samuel 3:13 – 21)
47. Milcah – the Wife of Nahor (Genesis 22:20 – 24)
48. Miriam – the Older Sister of Aaron and Moses (Exodus 2:1 – 10) (Exodus 15:20- 21) Numbers 12:1 – 16) (Numbers 26:58 – 61)
49. Naomi – the wife of Elimelech
50. Noah's Wife (Genesis 5:32; 6:18; 7:7; 7:13; 8:18)
51. Orpah – the Wife of Mahlon (Ruth 1)
52. Peninnah – the Second Wife of Elkanah (1 Samuel 1)
53. Peter's Mother-in-law (Matthew 8:14)
54. Phoebe – and Other Women (Roman's 16:1 – 3)

55. Priscilla - the wife of Aquila (Romans 16:3) (Romans 16:12)
56. Puah - The Hebrew Midwife (Exodus 1:1 - 22)
57. Queen Esther – the Wife of King Xerxes
58. Queen Macaah – the Wife of Rehoboam (1 Kings 15:9 – 13) (2 Chronicles 13:1)
59. Queen Sheba – Monarch of the ancient kingdom of Sheba (1 Kings 3:7-9, 24 - 25) (1 Kings 4:32) (1 Kings 10:6 – 7)
60. Queen Vashti – The Wife of King Xerxes (Esther 1)
61. Rachel– the Wife of Jacob (Genesis 29:30 – 35; 30:1 – 24; 35:16 – 26)
62. Rahab The Prostitute - The Mother of Boaz –Joshua 2: 6:17, 25
63. Rebekah – the Wife of Isaac (Genesis 24, 28:1 – 9) (Genesis 2:48)
64. Reumah – Nahor's Concubine (Genesis 22:20 – 24)
65. Rizpah – the Daughter of Aiah (2 Samuel 21)
66. Ruth – the Wife of Kilion (Ruth1; 2; 3; 4)
67. Saffira – The Wife of Ananias (Acts 5:1 – 11)
68. Samson's Wife (Judges 13:512, 11, 19, 23 – 25)
69. Samson's Mother – the Wife of Manoah – (Judges 13:5,12,19,23,- 25)
70. Sarai/Sarah - the Mother of All Nations (Genesis 12:5 - 7) Genesis 17 and 18 and (21:1 – 7) (Genesis 23:1 : 20)
71. Serah – the daughter of Asher the son of Zilpah (Genesis 46:17) (Genesis 29:24)
72. Shelomith – the Daughter of Zerubbabel (1 Chronicles 3:19)
73. Shiprah – the Hebrew Midwife (Exodus 1:1 - 22)
74. Shua's Daughter – the wife of Judah (Genesis 38:1 – 2, 12)
75. Sisera's Mother Judges (5:28 – 31)

76. Solomon's wives – Pharaoh's Daughter, Moabites, Ammonites, Edomites, Sodomans and Hittites – (1 Kings 11:1 – 13)
77. Susanna and Other Women – (John 20:1 – 18)
78. Tabitha/Dorcas (Act:32 – 43)
79. Tamar - Sister of Absalom (2 Samuel 13)
80. Tamar – The Widow of Ur and Wife of Judah (Genesis 38:6 – 30)
81. The Canaanite Woman and her Daughter (Matthew 15:21 – 28)
82. The Daughter of Jesse – Abigail (1 Chronicles2:13 – 17)
83. The Daughter of Jesse – Zeniah (1 Chronicles2:13 – 17)
84. The Elect Lady – (2 John)
85. The Ruler's Daughter (Matthew 9:18)
86. The Daughters of Zelophehad Mahlah, Noah, Hoglah, Milcah and Tirzah (Numbers 27, 36,) (Deuteronomy 8, 11)
87. The Widow of Zarephath (1 Kings 1:7)
88. The Widow and Oil (2 Kings 4:1 – 7) (1 Kings 17
89. The Wives of Ashur the Father of Tekoa
90. The wife of Haman – Zeresh (Esther 5:9 – 14) (Esther 6:12 – 14)
91. The Witch of Endor – (1 Samuel 28)
92. The Wives for the Benjaminites (Judges 21:1 - 25)
93. The Wives of Caleb – Azubah, Jerioth, and Ephrath (1 Chronicles 2:18 – 20)
94. The daughter of Caleb – Acsah(1 Chronicles 2:49)
95. The Woman from Tekoa (2 Samuel 14)
96. The Woman with the Issue of Bleeding (Mark 5:21 – 43) (Luke 5:13; 6:10; 7:9; 7:16)
97. Zebidah –the Mother of Jehoiakim (2 Kings 23:36)
98. Zeruah – Jeroboam's Mother (1 Kings 11:26)

99. Zillah – Lamech's Wife (Genesis 4:19 – 26)
100. Zilpah – Leah's Maid (Genesis 30:1 – 24)
101. Zipporah the Wife of Moses (Exodus 2:11 – 25; 4:24 – 26; 18:2 – 12)

Appendix 2

God is the Umbrella of Women in the Bible!

Are you a woman who thinks that you are in a worse situations than anyone else? Does your situation look like it is beyond reprieve? May be you think you have reached the end of the road and wonder why? Why is this happening to me of all people? No one else has ever gone through what you are going through then read what these women went through and ponder.

God would like you to know that he has been there; he is there and will always be there for you always, now, check the following situations:

Success	Defeat	Confrontation	Separation
Possibilities	Long suffering	Sudden change	Forced Marriage
Lies	Pretence	Cover-ups	Demons
Pain	Happiness	Mother-in-laws	Polygamy
Conversion	Politics	Loneliness	Power
Death	Rape	Abuse	Prophecy
Miracles	Motivation	Loss	Leadership
Captivity	Cruelty	Love	Prostitution
Deceit	Murder	Force	Fools
Sickness	Disease	Deformity	Health
Fear	Birth	Birth	Power
Abandonment	Poverty	Wealth	Travel

Have you been affected by any one of the above then this book will be an eye opener to some of the things that happened to other women and it will be of assistance to you too. God is the Umbrella of Women everywhere. You are also under his Umbrella. Just find your way into his shelter.

The bible says that: The LORD watches over you – the LORD is your shade at your right hand; the sun will not harm you by day nor the moon by night. (Psalm 121:5 – 5)

The knowledge and understanding that comes with knowing what these women went through will bring you to a level in your life that God wants you to get to. It will help you to associate and solve various situations that will even surprise you, because God's Umbrella will cover all the situations.

God is the Umbrella of Women in the Bible and the World
A Protection against the Rain and the Sun

10